FROM HOMEMAKERS TO
BREADWINNERS TO
COMMUNITY LEADERS

FROM HOMEMAKERS TO BREADWINNERS TO COMMUNITY LEADERS

Migrating Women, Class, and Color

NORMA FUENTES-MAYORGA

RUTGERS UNIVERSITY PRESS
New Brunswick, Camden, and Newark, New Jersey
London and Oxford

Rutgers University Press is a department of Rutgers, The State University of New Jersey, one of the leading public research universities in the nation. By publishing worldwide, it furthers the University's mission of dedication to excellence in teaching, scholarship, research, and clinical care.

Library of Congress Cataloging-in-Publication Data
Name: Fuentes-Mayorga, Norma, author.
Title: From homemakers to breadwinners to community leaders: migrating women, class, and color / Norma Fuentes-Mayorga.
Description: New Brunswick: Rutgers University Press, [2023] | Includes bibliographical references and index.
Identifiers: LCCN 2021032977 | ISBN 9781978822122 (paperback) | ISBN 9781978822139 (hardback) | ISBN 9781978822146 (epub) | ISBN 9781978822153 (mobi) | ISBN 9781978822160 (pdf)
Subjects: LCSH: Dominican American women—New York (State)—New York—Social conditions | Mexican American women—New York (State)—New York—Social conditions | Dominican American women—New York (State)—New York—Cultural assimilation. | Mexican American women—New York (State)—New York—Cultural assimilation. | Hispanic Americans—New York (State)—New York—Race identity. | Hispanic Americans—New York (State)—New York—Ethnic identity. | Women immigrants—New York (State)—New York—Social conditions. | Working class women—New York (State)—New York—Social conditions. | Dominican Republic—Emigration and immigration—Case studies. | Mexico—Emigration and immigration—Case studies.
Classification: LCC E184.D6 F84 2022 | DDC 362.83/98120747—dc23
LC record available at https://lccn.loc.gov/2021032977

A British Cataloging-in-Publication record for this book is available from the British Library.

References to internet websites (URLs) were accurate at the time of writing. Neither the author nor Rutgers University Press is responsible for URLs that may have expired or changed since the manuscript was prepared.

♾ The paper used in this publication meets the requirements of the American National Standard for Information Sciences—Permanence of Paper for Printed Library Materials, ANSI Z39.48-1992.

rutgersuniversitypress.org

In memory of my grandmother, Justina

This book is for my mother, my grandmother, my daughters, and all the Latina women whose immigrant journeys I am privileged to document.

CONTENTS

CONTENTS

FROM HOMEMAKER TO
BREADWINNERS TO
COMMUNITY LEADERS

PROLOGUE

In the absence of smartphones or the internet, my childhood memories of my mother were only fed by the handwritten notes she sent inside the registered letters my grandmother received every month with remittances. The tone of her voice, even the feel of her embrace, was stored as part of the secret yearnings of early adolescence. Upon seeing her face at the airport amid a crowd of strangers, something long asleep inside my soul stirred back to life. Her foreign looks, the scent of her clothes, and even the contents of her luggage had a distinct new, cool smell, alluding to a place where things were plentiful, even magical.

In 1968 my mother arrived in New York City from the Dominican Republic, carrying my two-year-old sister in her arms. That year the implementation of the Immigration and Nationality Act of 1965 had prioritized the reunification of U.S. immigrant families. As the mother of a child born in Puerto Rico, my mother qualified within a few years for legal permanent residency. In addition to the significance of the Act, the availability of industrial work increased my mother's chances of finding gainful work and qualifying for a loan from her factory's credit union to cover the fees to regulate her immigrant status. In December 1972, and after nearly five years of absence, my mother came back for me.

During her short stay at my grandmother's house, family members, and even a few visitors from my grandmother's church, with their humble gestures and bodily stances, conferred respect for my mother, even though she was unaccompanied by a man, divorced, and a single mother of two girls. In retrospect, I have surmised they were also attracted to her youth, her white skin (or "racial capital," as I conceptualize it in this book). Her different looks, and her sexual freedom and economic independence, made my mother an exception among family women in the early 1970s. Her older brother—my uncle and proxy father, Mario, who was a police sergeant—seemed encouraged by my mother's immigrant stories. Invariably, when my uncle visited us (most often for lunch), my mother would sit not far from the uniformed men that escorted him. Their laughter and loud voices were new to me; this sort of communion had never been allowed by my grandmother, the widow of a poor, evangelical, rural minister. My uniformed uncle would hold my small hands inside his, bowing his head to kiss them while we listened to my mother's New York stories, or while he helped me with my math homework or showed me how to draw a rose in bloom, with perfect-sized petals. Listening to my mother's immigrant stories, my uncle would also share the trials and tribulations of a poor youth; he and my mother had become orphaned at ages ten and nine, respectively, after their father died of typhoid fever. My uncle Mario would speak of the miracle of his work ascendancy: first as a poor, young rural cadet, then as a naive sergeant, who soon, and before his fortieth birthday, had become an admired professor in the police academy within the Dominican Republic's Operaciones Especiales. At times he would offer my mother a glass of beer—a concession my grandmother would only grant to "save him face" in front of his men. But, really, she conceded because, for most of her widowed life, my mother, and to some extent my uncle, had been the main breadwinner in our family.

Aside from U.S. dollars and gifts, my mother brought with her a new outfit for me to wear, though she kept it folded, inside her luggage, until the day of our flight back to the United States. It comprised an olive-green suit made of soft corduroy, with a semipleated skirt and a long-sleeved, cropped, and collared jacket with front rows of small green buttons; white knee socks with pom-poms; and black patent leather Mary Jane shoes. When we boarded a midmorning Pan Am flight a few days after Christmas, the miracle of its ascent in the midst of thick Caribbean clouds, along with the serenity of the blue-eyed flight attendant's face, led me to rest my head on my mother's shoulder and dream of New York City, my mother's newfound world of freedom. I held my mother's hand, never letting go, until we landed.

MY MOTHER'S RURAL-TO-URBAN MIGRATION

Almost a decade earlier my mother had embarked on her first domestic migration. Fatherless at age nine, and then a mother at seventeen, she was forced to leave me behind with my grandmother six months after my birth. She left Catalina Alta, the small, mountaintop village of her, her mother's, and my own birth to find work as a helper in a small town's restaurant/kitchenette, about an hour away by horse or a half hour by public bus. She had to go, "to send money for your milk and for us to eat," as my grandmother always explained my mother's intermittent and long absences from my life. My oldest uncle and proxy father had been the first to migrate from their small rural village when he joined the military as a cadet; this was—and remains—the only pathway out of poverty for poor young men of good conduct and rural origins.

Just around the time my uncle joined the military, when I was about three, my mother married a man twice her age, prompting her second domestic migration. This time, she moved from the semirural town—where as a kitchen helper she toiled from dawn to dusk—to Santo Domingo, the nation's capital. She arrived as the new wife of a middle-class professional who towered close to six feet in height, something that is quite unusual for the average Dominican man of the time. My mother was attracted to his rare Asian-Latino phenotype as the progeny of a Chinese mother and Dominican father, his cinnamon-brown skin, and his intelligence and gentle demeanor. My mother would always joke, when looking at the photo albums she had saved and brought with her to New York, that they were proof of the most beautiful years of courtship and romance she had known. By the time they met, my stepfather had already been married and fathered two sons, the youngest of whom was very close in age to my mother. He was, according to my grandmother, "a self-made man, living proof that the poor can move up in the world." His first job was as a clerk, and his second as a civil engineer; later he served in an executive capacity for a British multinational mining company with subsidiaries in the Caribbean and other parts of Latin America. Throughout the seven years he was married to my mother, my stepfather helped three of her younger siblings find clerical work through his company. Until she died, my grandmother thanked God and then my stepfather for two things: for offering to adopt me on the same day of his very private wedding to my mother (with the help of the same justice of the peace), and for insisting that my grandmother and her four youngest children, ages nine to twenty, come to live with him and my mother.

On a hot and humid day my uncle Mario moved all of us in the back of a dusty police truck from the mountain village of our births to Santo Domingo. In the back of the truck, my second-oldest uncle, Manaces (the only one really "white" among my mother's siblings, as he had inherited my grandfather's looks, as well as his evangelical heart and gentle demeanor); my two youngest uncles, Rafael and Freddy (the ones with the darkest shade of brown among the five, were still in elementary school); and my two aunts, Doris and Felicia (in their early teenage years, with honeyed and brown skin), all watched as their ancestral village of Catalina Alta faded in the distance, the place where my grandfather's body remained, in humble burial grounds, along with those of his and my grandmother's long line of ancestors. Thanks to her daughter's marriage to a man with an education and a "heart of gold," and owing "to the grace of God," my grandmother would jest, we were saved from abject poverty and transplanted from a rural town to a rented, attached cinder block house in the struggling urban sprawl of Santo Domingo.

A FIRST ENCOUNTER WITH INEQUALITY: THE INTERSECTION OF CLASS, GENDER, AND RACE

Our rented home, and those of a few other tenants on our block, was built on a shared lot, in the back of a street alley, or *callejon*, facing the back of a small, privately run, medical clinic. The clinic's head doctor, a Haitian man in his early forties, spoke Spanish with a strong French Creole accent. Dr. Mitchelle delivered the first baby of my auntie Doris (a "close call," he said) on Noche Buena (Christmas Eve), which required the doctor to stay overnight at the clinic and enjoy an impromptu holiday dinner at our house. Over time he became almost a family member. On Saturdays and weekend evenings, when patients were at the clinic making progress on their labor contractions or recuperating from the traumatic pains of birthing, he often played a hand of dominoes while sampling *uno or dos palitos*, as my stepfather called his shots of rum. Dr. Mitchelle's inflected Spanish sounded even funnier to me after he accepted the rum, especially when he tried to mock the way I spoke Spanish at age four or the way I tried to divine his quizzes regarding my pre-K school's *abecedario* (alphabet book).

This was a neighborhood still on the margins of the city, with no clear boundaries separating the permanent from the temporary poor. Generations of darkskinned and Black families, including Haitians, and light-skinned campesinos from the distant hinterland, like my family, traditionally found refuge in marginalized areas, at the periphery of the national district or its main capital. About two years after we moved to this neighborhood, my stepfather moved us into a home he purchased in a nearby *municipio*, one that mixed struggling poor families with the aspiring middle class—that is, those with some schooling and good connections. My ally in this new neighborhood was a small six-year-old Dominican Haitian girl nicknamed Cocoreca. Her extended family lived across the street, just a block away, on a plot of land where immigrants and the poor converged in temporary makeshift houses of zinc plank rooftops amid scattered rows of *platano* (plantain), *guandule* (pigeon pea), and *yuca* (yucca) trees. Across the street, in the block where we lived, cheap versions of cinder block Swiss chalet structures housed intergenerational families. Many of them derived their secured lots in life from jobs in the lower ranks of governmental bureaucracies or the military, thanks to the benevolence or clientelism of very powerful connections with *Balagueristas*, the ardent supporters of the then reelected president, Joaquin Balaguer—as my stepfather and Dr. Mitchelle would complain after a few *palitos*.

A struggling *colmado*, or large vegetable and food staples store, was the neighborhood's only attraction. On most days groups of men gathered inside the store by its winding countertop, either standing or seated on wooden stools, to savor hot *pastelitos* (pastries), *quipes* (meat patties), fried *batatas* (sweet potatoes), *tostones* (fried plantains), or *longanizas* (sausages) along with a few cold beers. The men who gathered there worked at the bottom rung of the local military, or were temporarily off duty, back home from their interned posts as marine or air force cadets. On the thirtieth of every month, a payday, especially if the day coincided with a weekend or holiday, my grandmother would warn my uncles and my aunties away from crossing the street, or even standing in front of our house, to avoid the sight of these rowdy men, the *hombres del mundo* (men of the world). Her main complaint was that they would drink, play dominoes while blasting the jukebox, and attune their gaze to the contours of young women's bosoms or derrieres as they entered or left the *colmado* with groceries.

My stepfather and my grandmother both fussed at my insistence on having my only friend in the neighborhood, Cocoreca, over for meals or for sleepovers. My grandmother felt Cocoreca needed to take a bath and comb her bulging, untamed mane, especially during the midday heat, before we would sit at the table. My stepfather was more laid back, inviting us to sit and offering us a special treat of a *refresco rojo* (soda) if we finished the rice and beans on our plates, though he secretly hoped that I soon would find new friends at the start of the private school year. But I loved to play with Cocoreca, for she knew how to build make-believe playhouses up in the top of almond trees or in the shadows of her communal backyard yucca trees or the prickly rose bushes in our home's small garden. Her mother would allow us to play during *la hora recia*—the hottest time of the day—when most kids were forced to take siestas. Cocoreca had the sweetest dimples and smiles, and she told me that when I got to be her age, I would get mine too. To me she was the big sister I longed for in a house filled with adults. Besides, she knew how to eat *gofio*, sweetened corn powder, without either choking or getting it in her eyes. She showed me how to climb trees without scraping the skin off my belly, and how to open almond pits with just the bang of a rock and without banging my fingers. And, even more, Cocoreca was not afraid of the dark when we played hide-and-seek, or of street boys, or of the mean girls from the Swiss chalet houses who called her names for keeping her thick hair loose or for wearing baggy clothes or no shoes or for hanging out with a kid much younger than her.

THE MIRAGE OF MARRIAGE AND A MIDDLE-CLASS LIFE

In the 1960s in the Dominican Republic, my mother's new social status, her middle-class home, her daily subsistence, and that of her family, which included my own private schooling, depended on her husband's occupation, his white-collar income, and his conjugal love. My happiness also greatly depended on having for the first time a real father, someone who was smart, gentle, and loving. My grandmother used to say that my biological father, whom I had not yet met, was handsome, distinguished, and a brilliant and esteemed doctor of the poor, but, unlike my stepfather, who was dignified in her eyes, my biological father was a *sinverguenza* (shameful man) for fathering too many children out of wedlock and for taking advantage of innocent, vulnerable, and poor young women—while married to another woman. Unlike the tainted father I had not met, my stepfather drove me to school each morning on his way to work. He sat me in the back of his big, fancy car—first a white Chevrolet Impala and later an equally white

Mercedes with leather seats. As he drove me to school, I played the part of a *peluche*, or doll, in my blue-and-white private school uniform. But to a five-year-old child, these things had no special meaning. What did leave an indelible mark was having a tall, handsome, and distinguished man walk me into my first day of kindergarten, holding my small hand and carrying the small chair he had built for me. He would often take my mother to the beach or the mountains for short escapes on weekends or holidays. One day he took me to the zoo and then to a bakery to get a cake. This was the first and only birthday cake I had ever had as a child, for both my grandmother's orthodox religious upbringing and her literal interpretation of the Old Testament dictated that this was an unnecessary frivolity. As a civil engineer in some executive capacity for an international company, my stepfather introduced my mother and her humble family to aspire to a middle-class life of discipline and work but also of intermittent leisure and joy, even if for a short time. Often, during business trips to mining sites in the Caribbean and Latin America, but mostly to Puerto Rico, my stepfather would take my mother along. During my mother's frequent absences, my grandmother and Cocoreca would remain as the cradle of my childhood world—that is, until the day my mother came back from Puerto Rico with my newborn sister in her arms.

Dependent as she was on her husband for financial security, my mother's situation was vulnerable, as were those of most middle-class women in the nation at the time. Her rural origins and lack of formal education made things worse. Despite her beauty, racial capital, and innate intelligence, as well as her feisty temperament, my mother's demeanor, and especially her accent, hinted of her poor rural birth and upbringing in El Cibao, in the northwest of the Dominican Republic. The region's ecology is mainly framed by two large cordilleras, at the west and the east, isolating this region's lush habitable valleys and protecting the richest agricultural and cattle economy in the nation. El Cibao's local accent is distinguished by a linguistic roll/trill that exchanges the *i*'s for the *r*'s, as in the Spanish verb *comer* (to eat), which is pronounced by the locals as *comei*. My mother tells me her rural accent was an icebreaker often used by her husband as a term of endearment, to exalt her attractiveness or make her blush. Despite the pride most Cibaeños derive from their regional distinctions, which often conflate both a regional accent and White racial capital, my mother's limited third-year elementary school education and rural demeanor drew symbolic boundaries and connoted an inferior status within her husband's middle-class circles.

On the eve of my sister's second birthday, my mother's marriage collapsed—and with it her new and short-lived middle-class life—when her husband's promise of fidelity became a mirage. With only three years of rural schooling, my mother's work-life chances in Santo Domingo in the mid-1960s were limited to domestic work. Yet her own hardships (losing her father at age nine, and facing motherhood alone at seventeen) must have imbued early on the strength to weigh love and fidelity above material security. With the consent of both her mother and her older brother, one early morning, after her estranged husband drove to work in his luxury sedan, my mother took an airplane to New York, taking only my little sister with her, the only one with a blue passport. I remained behind—again.

At the time of my mother's international migration, she and my grandmother arranged for me to live with my biological father and his religious wife. From the age of ten until I was fourteen, I lived in an affluent neighborhood within the colonial center of Santo Domingo. For the most part, this meant living with my stepmother, whom I grew to love as a proxy mother, as my father's occupation as a rural doctor brought him home only one or two weekends per month, mostly to deliver his paychecks. For these four years my mother's factory wages paid for my trips to New York City every summer and winter break. During my visits to New York, while my mother took one bus and two subway trains from Yonkers to work at a garment factory in Midtown Manhattan, I attended a public school where I studied English as a second language in a program for immigrant youth. Until 1974, when I came to live permanently with my mother, my family (my mother, grandmother, older uncle, and biological father) had all agreed that it was best to leave me in the Dominican Republic until I had completed the ninth grade in a very good private school, which was paid for solely by my biological father.

Five years before I came to live in New York, my mother had married and quickly divorced another Cibaeño man who, unlike her first husband, was of short stature and, with a high school diploma, had airs of self-importance. His arrogance was emboldened by his white skin, green eyes, and mixed Dominican Iberian and mulatto heritage, as well as by one of his brothers' strong links to influential people within the Dominican General Consulate in New York City. After the birth of my brother, his and my mother's only child, he often made jokes or sardonically complained about my baby brother being too dark to be his progeny. He boasted that his son had inherited his good looks but that the dark skin must have come from my mother's side or from who knows where. My mother soon began to resent these deprecating jokes and veiled insults. One day, when she "got up from the wrong side of the bed," as my grandmother would say, she asked her self-consumed husband to leave her home; he was no longer welcome or regarded as a member of her family. Four months later, my mother decided to bring me to New York City to be reunited with her.

MIGRATION TO OLD AND NEW DESTINATIONS

By the time I came to permanently live in New York City in 1974, my mother's two younger sisters had already joined her. A few years later, the youngest, Felicia, moved to the then thriving industrial suburb of Yonkers, following her husband's employment gig in a construction company owned and staffed by Italians and Portuguese men, also of peasant stock. My middle auntie, Doris, stayed in Manhattan, on the West 90s, where her husband worked as a handyman for a Puerto Rican man who was the superintendent of a building near Central Park. There they lived with their two sons in a windowless one-bedroom basement apartment. By the time I arrived, my auntie Felicia had already filed a petition to claim her mother (my grandmother) and her two youngest siblings as part of a family reunification process. Felicia had arrived in New York with five years' experience as an office clerk for an international mining company. Before that she had managed to get a job as a secretary for the Fiat car company in the Dominican Republic; her second-oldest brother, Manaces, also worked for Fiat, as a bookkeeper. My second-oldest auntie, Doris, similarly attractive and scarily intelligent, was the first to arrive, on a tourist visa. Like my mother, she had also imported high racial capital, with light honeyed skin and a generally Western European phenotype (physical appearance). Though she had ten years of skilled work as a keypunch operator, upon her arrival in the United States she found work in a pocketbook factory. A few years later, my grandmother and my two youngest uncles (now in their late teens) also came to live in Yonkers, a new immigrant destination for Latinos in the 1970s.

A decade later my three uncles married and moved out to Brooklyn and Queens. The second-oldest uncle, Manaces, became a part-time Evangelical pastor while also going to night school and working in a government office. My second-youngest uncle, Rafael, the darkest of all the siblings, worked factory and maintenance jobs and joined the U.S. Army Reserve, where he benefited from tuition credits to pay for an associate's degree. Thanks to his good grades, Freddy, my youngest uncle, only seven years my senior, received a scholarship and attended Pratt Institute in Brooklyn, majoring in electrical engineering. He later moved up in the ranks of General Electric, and then Lockheed Martin and Boeing, becoming a successful aeronautic electrical engineer. He was the only member of the family to marry out of his ethnic group—to a White Protestant woman from the South. They met while he worked for General Electric in Maryland.

Before migrating to New York, my grandmother and my two younger uncles and I attended weekly services at an Evangelical Protestant church run by a U.S. southern missionary. This experience, I believe, shaped my soul as well as my inclinations to engage in reflection about my commitment to serve the less fortunate. My religious upbringing and my two youngest uncles always took care of me, as we attended the same school. Only nine and seven years my senior, they interpreted things from the Bible and tutored me in arithmetic and language. I owe to them my achieving a high school diploma with honors, despite trials and tribulations in bilingual classrooms in Yonkers.

Before the 1990s, Yonkers was a new destination for Dominicans and most other Latinos. Since then it has undergone dramatic and economic transformations, becoming an industrial hub and the fourth-largest city in New York State.

The arrival of new waves of immigrants from Asia, the Eastern bloc countries, Ireland, and Latin America has changed the city's demographic tapestry. Native-born Puerto Ricans from Chicago, Philadelphia, and the southeastern coastal regions of Florida paved the way for other Latino immigrants to Yonkers, but the largest share has come from the Bronx. Many were first-generation immigrants, straight from semirural areas in Puerto Rico, like my longtime friend from my teen years, Elizabeth—nicknamed "Cookie"—and her five siblings. Cookie's family members were all blue- and green-eyed White Puerto Ricans, except for her older sister and youngest brother, who had brown eyes and brown sugar-colored skin. Their eastern European phenotypes, however, made people confuse them with Middle Easterners or North Indians.

In the early 1980s my girlfriend Cookie and her family moved from Chicago's public housing projects to Yonkers into another public housing structure, two blocks away from where my family lived. Our home was a third-floor apartment in an old and decaying attached three-story house with six apartment units, three on each side. My grandmother lived in an apartment on the first floor; my youngest auntie, on the third floor, next door to ours. My mother headed our family as a single mother of three children, with me as the oldest yet the only one not born in the United States. My youngest auntie, Felicia, was the first to arrive to Yonkers and to procure a lease in this small building, after her husband got a construction job in the city. We were the only tenants or non-family members living in the building, as the owner and his adult, married children all occupied the other apartments. They were all Christians from Amman, Jordan, and they all had white skin and blueish-gray eyes. The owner's wife was the exception. She had skin with an olive tone, dark black hair, and eyes like the color of sand dunes at dusk. Although she was younger than her husband by ten or fifteen years, she looked prematurely aged. Most afternoons, while the men napped or watched TV, the landlord's wife would sit outside in front of our building's small entry-way, surrounded by her older daughter and two daughters-in-law. She always wore a dark head scarf and a long dark skirt; she often ate dried sunflower seeds and drank lots of hot tea. Upon noticing me entering the building, she would often wave her hands to summon that I come sit by her. When I did, she would hold my face with both of her large, motherly hands and speak the same phrases in Arabic (telling her daughters that I looked like one of them). Then she would kiss or pinch my cheeks, exclaiming, "Ah! Helwa!" (How beautiful!) and always give me her blessing: "Alhamdulillah!" (Thank God!).

Yonkers had been transformed by the arrival of Arabs—mostly Christians from Jordan, Lebanon, and Syria—and then by the first and second waves of Latin Americans, including Cuban refugees. These Cubans were mostly White or of light skin, and most brought with them entrepreneurial illusions and financial connections to Florida's banks. Later, Dominicans—largely "Cibaeños," most of light skin—importing entrepreneurial skills or land-holding credits in

Dominican banks followed in search of small business ventures, such as in taxicabs and bodegas, but mostly factory jobs in the Clairol, General Electric, General Motors, and Otis Elevator Company factories.

THE NETWORKS OF BREADWINNER MOTHERS

Starting in the mid-1970s, my mother commuted by bus and subway from Yonkers to do piecework as a machine operator in Midtown Manhattan. She eventually moved up, first as a floor seamstress in a coat factory and then as a pattern maker for fine leathers and luxury furs. As a single mother and the main breadwinner for three children, and with an incredible drive for work, she managed to gain the trust of the factory owners, an Argentine Jewish family. Fifteen years later, following the diagnosis of epileptic seizures, she was promptly terminated from work. In the mid1980s, a few years after my high school graduation, my mother was determined to be disabled and unable to work, though she refused to accept the medical diagnosis or to live in poverty. The ties established with a large and diverse group of Latinos within her Baptist church in northern Manhattan, and the more diverse and far-flung links of her younger and educated immigrant sister in Yonkers, helped my mother to find other informal sewing work at home. She did garment reparations or special orders until late at night, until her epilepsy evolved into grand mal seizures. One evening in December, while preparing a large pot of arroz con pollo for her church's New Year's Eve dinner, my mother suffered a powerful seizure, resulting in third-degree burns to her right hand. The accident required the amputation of most of her right hand's fingers, reconstructive surgery, and long-term hospitalization, incapacitating her physically and mentally for life and forcing me to assume the role of care provider and mediator with doctors and our local (and not very nice) public aid bureaucracies.

While migration allowed my uncles and aunts to obtain a higher education, to find economic security (mostly through public-sector jobs), and to purchase homes, my mother's declining health prevented her from achieving the "immigrant dream" of economic security. Yet her three children's higher education has given her a great sense of accomplishment and made America even greater, according to my now deceased grandmother. When I was a teenager transitioning to young adulthood, my mother's falling into poverty gave me a different understanding of the many variants of migration. Since then I have become aware of the realities that Black, Brown, and White Latinos—and especially single mothers and the undocumented—face.

My mother's immigration to New York in the late 1960s as a single mother with some vestiges of a middle-class culture was unusual; most Dominican women arrived in the company of spouses or came to the United States to be reunited with them.[1] These earlier cohorts included a good share of landed elites from El Cibao, as well as displaced politicians and top-ranked public officials from urban centers. Yet the average Dominican immigrant from rural areas imported little human capital—including those whose domestic migration to urban centers allowed them to gain some form of an education or office skills, like my aunties and uncles. Without the availability of gainful work at a factory or in the Army Reserve, and without financial aid, these educated first-generation immigrants probably would face permanent downward mobility or poverty. While earlier gender and migration scholarship documents the experiences of Latinas in manufacturing, agricultural, or domestic sectors, this book's comparative analysis casts new light on experiences of women in service sector jobs. Equally important, it illustrates the personal and contextual factors that push an increasing number of vulnerable light-skinned but increasingly Afro-Caribbean and Indigenous Mesoamerican minorities to migrate from Latin America despite their college education or professional skills. My family story as told herein helps to illustrate how women-led migration contributes to the higher education and social mobility of other women left behind—especially daughters.

The red dirt road that leads to the village where my grandmother, mother, and I were born is framed by lavish *piñones*—thin, white-spotted trees with dark green needles of varying widths that move quickly with the wind. These trees fill the empty spaces between rows of parceled land and small but colorful wooden houses. The melodic and sorrowful sounds of the *bachata*, as well as *perico ripiao*—a more traditional merengue played with a *güira* (grater), *gancho* (scraper), double-headed *tambora* drums, and an accordion—announce the way to our home village of Catalina Alta, as do the stray dogs that sleep beside doorsteps and on curbsides. Blue skies and fast-moving clouds foretell the coming of the rains of May and the blooming of Flamboyan[2] trees, whose crimson flowers in late spring portend the passion (and elopements) of young lovers. The chatter of wild birds and the aroma of boiling milk and *café de pilon* signal dawn, while redolent *moro de guandules* (smoky pigeon peas cooked with rice) simmering that of the midday, making the happiest of lunch hours in the humblest of homes. Such memories have nursed the longings of migrant families from this region for their homeland; they have helped my mother keep her body and soul together on freezing, windy, or lonely days in her small apartment in downtown Yonkers, near the Hudson River, for nearly fifty years.

1 · INTRODUCTION

Female migrants outnumber male migrants in all regions except Africa and Asia.[1] Latin America and the Caribbean rank second to Europe in the migration of women. Unbeknownst to most migration and gender scholars, these streams of women migrants are mostly destined for the United States. Equally significant, Latin American nations with the largest Afro-descendant populations send the greatest number of migrant women, as is the case in Brazil, Colombia, the Dominican Republic, and Panama. Only a handful of nations' migrants are predominantly male, mainly from Indigenous populations, as is the case with Bolivia, Guatemala, and Mexico. Since the 1990s, sustained economic growth and government efforts guaranteeing civil rights protections, including the access to higher education, have increased the middle-class mobility of some ethnoracial minorities in Latin America. Despite government efforts, and as the findings will reveal, migrant remittances have played a key role in the access to higher education and social mobility among historically excluded Black and Indigenous women in the Dominican Republic and Mexico. Despite these developments, a legacy of systemic inequality and social exclusion has relegated most ethnoracial minorities in Latin America to the margins of society, pushing many to migrate, paradoxically, after joining the middle class.

Once in the United States, women arriving from the Dominican Republic and Mexico tend to concentrate in traditional immigrant destination cities like Los Angeles or New York. By 2016, in states like California and Texas, for example, the share of foreign-born Mexican women had already reached parity with that of men.[2] During the same year, in New York City the aggregate share of Dominican and Mexican foreign-born women had surpassed that of men by 60 percent. While New York is a relatively new destination for Mexicans, it has been the traditional destination for Dominicans, and women have led this migration for nearly a half century, since the early 1970s.[3] Yet in recent decades the increasing immigration of Dominican and Mexican women has been paralleled by restrictive, anti-immigration policies that, since the 9/11 crisis, have largely targeted the apprehension and repatriation of Latinos and Muslims—and mostly men.[4] In fact, since the 2008 economic crisis, the number of Mexicans arriving and leaving the United States (or the net migration for the group for a given year) has dropped,[5] reaching zero in 2010. Yet as the net migration rate for Mexican men has declined or stagnated, it has continued to rise for women. These demographic shifts represent the reversing of a century-old gendered migration pattern, especially for Mexican men (who, until recently, had led and dominated Mexican-U.S. immigration). These demographic shifts suggest that a new pattern of gendered migration and of racialization characterizes the immigration and integration experiences of Dominican and Mexican groups in New York City.

Beyond documenting a reversing pattern of gendered immigration, this book brings evidence on how race (skin color and physiognomy) and class (education and immigrant status) intersect to differently affect the integration and sorting of immigrant women workers in different service work sectors in New York City. A number of studies document the concentration of African American women and Latina women in the low-wage service sectors, especially in historical destination cities like Los Angeles and New York.[6] This book further documents the stratification of dark- and light-skinned Latinas in service sectors and how gentrification complicates this process. One key finding is that gentrification is driven by the arrival of either White or non-White residents at old and new immigrant destinations. When the gentrification process is driven by non-White residents, light skin, middle-class education, or even demeanors will be more valued and commodified by service employers. When the process is driven by White residents in historically Black and Latino neighborhoods, dark skin or non-White identity is also commodified as a form of *racial capitalism*, a process through which White employers benefit from the presence of non-White workers to attract local clients to the businesses and, at the same time, justify the presence of White businesses in historically Black or Brown residential areas.

This book—focused on the divergent migration and subsequent fates of Afro-Caribbean and Indigenous women in New York City—is timely and compelling, for it takes place at a time when women, not men, increasingly lead the international migration. It also takes place in the midst of a world pandemic that has laid bare the ravages that structural and implicit racism have on the life chances and mortality rates of Black and Latino populations. Drawing on the case of Dominicans and Mexicans as the fastest-growing Latin American immigrant groups in New York City, this book explores the structural and individual inequalities that affect the migration and adjustment of middle-class women at both old and new immigrant destinations. The findings contribute to situating the centrality of a Latina feminist, intersectional approach in the study of international migration and race.[7] I argue that the inequalities that push Black and Indigenous women to migrate are different from those experienced by other Latin Americans.

In 2009–10, during the second field data collection phase for this book, I observed that within traditional areas of settlement in New York City, Dominicans and Mexicans continued to work in low-wage service sectors, but in different work niches and for different employers.[8] For example, in Harlem, a traditional African American and Puerto Rican community, Mexicans increasingly worked for ethnic White employers in restaurants or at green groceries, while Dominicans faced different forms of class and racial isolation in small businesses that were mostly owned or operated by co-ethnics or racialized minorities. As chapter 3 illustrates, these contrasting employment and spatial integration patterns become the most distinct in neighborhoods undergoing fast gentrification.

In 2004, and after landing my first position as an assistant professor at Fordham University, I began to gather longitudinal ethnographic insights about the overlapping yet distinctive work experiences of Dominican and Mexican immigrants in the Bronx and Manhattan, the boroughs where the two groups, and particularly Dominicans, have concentrated since the early 2000s. I conducted intermittent participant observations in the nearby ethnic community of Little Italy, in the Bronx, where Mexicans occupy visible front-stage positions with Albanian and Italian employers while Dominicans experience social and economic exclusion.

While conducting informal observations in an affluent and touristic neighborhood in Midtown Manhattan, I was challenged with distinguishing the identity of a Mexican sushi chef from that of Asian chefs working behind the counter of a Japanese restaurant's sushi bar. The Mexican chef's simulation of an Asian demeanor while performing his work deepened my curiosity. The lack of visible Black or dark-skinned Latinos, in this and other establishments of the city, led me to further explore the role of race and ethnicity in the securing of jobs in informal service sectors.

In 2014, after finding a new position at the City College of New York in Harlem, I continued to observe that Dominicans and Mexicans worked for different service employers and occupied different functions in both back- and front-stage settings. I observed the same pattern in both affluent and working-class neighborhoods, in both East and West Harlem. One thing these historically minority-majority neighborhoods had in common was the rapid transformation of their spatial ecology and of the racial and class composition of residents—one that was driven by gentrification.[9] Since then I have documented the service sectors in which immigrants work and the functions that employers assign them, as well as the material and ideological resources that employers associate with the hiring of Black and non-Black immigrants.[10] I have also documented how gentrification complicates the way employers select and sort Latino immigrant workers at old and new immigrant destinations.

Finally, while conducting interviews and ethnographic observations in East and West Harlem, I was struck by the heightened vulnerability of undocumented women, especially those who act as the main breadwinners or heads of households for their families. Drawing on sociologist Mathew Desmond's findings of the long-term consequences of eviction on poor Black families in Milwaukee, Wisconsin,[11] I began to document the long-term impacts of gentrification and eviction on immigrant mothers and their children. Desmond's study shows that the stigma of losing a home leads poor Black mothers to suffer long-term depression and can even lead to suicide. The findings in this book reveal that for immigrant mothers the loss of homes causes long-lasting trauma, as it represents a different and profound sense of material loss and psychological dislocation after they have already borne the loss of their first homes in their countries of origin. This is especially true for the undocumented, for whom a home represents a sanctuary, the only place where vulnerable immigrants can reproduce a material and symbolic sense of security and belonging.

Based on longitudinal insights, including interviews and ethnography, *From Homemakers to Breadwinners to Community Leaders* explores how intersectional forms of inequality push Latina women to migrate and settle in New York City. Specifically, it examines how gender, racial, and class inequality may explain the growing immigration of Afro-Caribbean and Indigenous women, respectively, from the Dominican Republic and Mexico and the subsequent contributions these women make to the sending and receiving communities.

THE IMMIGRATION OF AFRO-DESCENDANT AND INDIGENOUS LATINAS

The increasing immigration of Dominican and Mexican women to New York City takes place at a time when a virulent anti-immigrant backlash challenges the status and future life chances of the larger Latino ethnoracial group in the United States. In recent years, the city's adoption of Sanctuary Laws to support immigrants has paralleled a nativist, anti-immigration rhetoric, one mainly targeting Mexicans and Central Americans.[12] While I was writing this book, the Department of Homeland Security's enactment of the Declaration of Self-Sufficiency,[13] or proof that immigrants seeking to regulate their status will not pose a "public charge," reflects the rise of a conservative backlash or the revival of long-term ideologies about the racialization of non-European immigrants as "illegal aliens" or unassimilable.[14] To complicate matters, the COVID-19 pandemic has opened two new Pandora's boxes. On the one hand, it has revealed that Latino (and mostly vulnerable undocumented) immigrants perform what are considered essential services— services without which many of us could not eat, go to work, or even provide care for our children or elderly family members. On the other, the pandemic has made it clear that Blacks and Latinos in general experience the worst forms of health inequalities, comorbidities, and fatalities. The decimation of the Black and Latino population during the pandemic attests to legacies of systemic structural and social inequalities affecting racialized minorities in the United States.

While the White population in the United States continues to decline, immigrants from Asia and Latin America offset the loss of employable native-born people. In fact, by 2003, Latinos had surpassed African Americans as the largest minority group,[15] and by 2020 the population had grown to 62.1 million, with Mexicans as the largest subgroup among Latinos. New York is one of nine states where the largest shares of Latinos concentrate.[16] Most significantly, the United States faces a precipitous decline in the number of families with children. Since 2010, the share of the dependent population (those younger than 18 and older than 65) has outpaced the share of the working-age population.[17] The decline of the White population, especially among the baby boomers, contributes to the blurring of racial and class boundaries in the labor market, or to what scholars claim is an opening of skilled, white-collar work opportunities for legendarily excluded ethnoracial minorities such as African Americans and Latinos.[18] It is amid stark demographic and economic shifts that a new and virulent anti-immigrant backlash resurges in the United States and in many other advanced nations in Europe and Latin America. Without replenishing its population, however, the United States cannot compete in a globalized and technologically inter-connected global economy.[19]

Traditionally, contrasting patterns of gendered immigration and geographic concentration have characterized the integration experiences of Dominicans and Mexicans in the United States. Until the mid-1960s, for example, the immigration of Mexicans was mostly seasonal, led by male laborers contracted for temporary work in agricultural sectors, mostly in isolated and marginalized areas of California and the Southwest. Most of these migrants were expected to return when the agricultural season was over.[20] Since the mid-1980s, economic upheavals, changes in federal immigration laws, and the increased policing of the Mexican-U.S. border have altered this circular pattern of male-led immigration into a more permanent, family-led pattern of immigration and settlement.[21] Unprecedented numbers of women and children, including unaccompanied minors, have sought to migrate as increasingly restrictive immigration laws in the United States threaten to permanently separate them from their families.

The immigration of Mexican women to New York City began in earnest in the 1980s. A displaced entrepreneurial and middle-class sector joined this migratory stream in the mid-1990s, following the enactment of the North American Free Trade Agreement (NAFTA) in 1994 between Canada, Mexico, and the United States. These larger shifts have contributed to the growing and more permanent settlement of Mexican families in New York City,[22] with women taking a leading role—until now unrecognized—in the securing of resources and establishment and leadership of ethnic institutions, as chapter 5 illustrates.

Unlike for Mexicans, U.S. immigration for Dominicans has been historically led by women; as this book documents, this has been the case for women in nations in Latin America and the Caribbean with the largest concentration of Black populations. Since the 1960s, Dominican migrants have concentrated in the U.S. Northeast, attracted to jobs in manufacturing. Yet, unlike Mexicans, the immigration of Dominicans has been mediated by family reunification since the passing of the Immigration and Nationality Act of 1965.[23] Since the beginning of the twenty-first century, however, the enactment of anti-immigration laws has also altered the group's geographical distribution within old and new migrant destinations.[24] My qualitative and quantitative insights suggest that Dominican and Mexican women are increasingly leading both the domestic and international migration to New York, as chapter 2 shows. These feminized migration patterns contrast with those experienced by women among earlier cohorts, who followed or accompanied spouses as part of the family reunification process.[25]

Finally, a new pattern of women-led immigration also reveals differences in the geography of origin between older and newer cohorts. For example, unlike the more rural origins of earlier immigrant cohorts, women in this study come from urban sprawl areas along the periphery of a national district or capital. Unlike earlier cohorts with origins in the northeastern and western parts of the El Cibao region, most of today's Dominican women migrants come from developing areas in the southern and eastern regions of the island—the areas of historical African slave settlement and where the descendants of those slaves, as well as immigrants from Haiti and the West Indies, reside.[26] These new insights contribute to the scholarship on gendered migration, development, human and social mobility, and the different forms of inequality experienced by ethnoracial middle-class women in Latin America and the Caribbean.

Most significantly, the increasing immigration of Black and Indigenous women from Latin America contributes to changes in the racial and class composition and stratification of the Latino population of New York City. For example, unlike the light-skinned middle class that arrived in earlier cohorts, today's Dominican immigration includes larger shares of Black middle-class populations. Similarly, despite the large share of Indigenous minorities that have arrived since the 1980s—mostly from the Mixteca Baja, the poorest regions of southern and western Mexico[27]—contemporary cohorts are more heterogeneous. They include a more stratified segment of immigrants from rural and also from urban areas along the periphery of Mexico City, as well as adjoining towns and states experiencing economic development. These new cohorts include Ladino and Mestizo populations, bringing with them higher levels of education or skilled work experience, as well as racial capital. Analysis of U.S. Census data and emerging research confirm my qualitative insights,[28] as over one-third of Dominican women and about one-sixth of Mexican women import at least one year of college education. These findings expand on an emerging scholarship that has argued that more highly educated women are increasingly joining the international migration.[29] They also support an existing literature documenting the growing heterogeneity of Latin American immigration, which in contemporary waves has included a bifurcated class from the manual labor and professional sectors.[30]

ABOUT THIS BOOK

Antecedents to This Study

The idea for this book began to evolve in the late 1990s, when I was invited by the Carnegie Endowment for International Peace to participate in a research project focused on poverty and immigration policies taking place in the cities of Los Angeles and New York. The study explored how the passing of the Personal Responsibility and Work Opportunity Reconciliation Act of 1996 impacted poor Dominican and Mexican immigrant families' abilities to make ends meet in both cities. Major stipulations of the act were the restriction of welfare benefits to U.S. citizens and the imposition of statewide limitations on public assistance for dependent children. I was invited to oversee New York City's field research component and to contribute to the design of culturally sensitive measures for the study's interview protocol. Participation in this longitudinal and comparative study facilitated the gathering of preliminary insights informing the writing of my PhD research proposal, still in embryonic form and focused on the immigration and integration experiences of Dominican and Mexican families in New York City. An overarching question driving this earlier research was why Dominicans, a group with a much longer tenure in New York City and a viable, economic ethnic enclave, experienced the most poverty among all Latino groups, paralleling those of historically racialized African Americans?

The onset of this earlier research phase took place in the aftermath of the 9/11 crisis amid a heightened suspicion of anyone who is Black or Brown or looks Muslim or foreign born—like me. In 2001 the USA PATRIOT Act—designed to prevent nationwide terrorism—accelerated the apprehension, incarceration, and deportation rates of Dominicans and Mexicans as the two fastest-growing foreign-born Black and Brown Latino groups in the city. Since then, attitudes toward immigrants in Europe, the United States, and most of the western hemisphere have toughened, leading to what migration policy scholars now argue is a new gendered and racialized pattern of immigrant immigration and exclusion.[31]

My earlier works have documented that Dominican and Mexican New Yorkers work in different sectors and for varied ethnic and racial employers. This work pattern has mediated the two groups' distinct spatial integration in the city, with women facing the highest racial and class isolation.[32] Yet even now little knowledge exists about the mobility life chances of these and other Latina groups in New York. Apart from the concentration of Dominicans in informal sectors (such as hair salons) or small businesses owned mostly by coethnics,[33] or the fates of Mexican women in factories (mostly owned by Asian employers),[34] not much is known about their experiences in low-wage service sectors, where Mexican men have been preferred laborers since the early 1990s.[35] Earlier scholarship mostly centered on the experiences of Central American and Mexican women in California and the Southwest details these immigrant women's experiences in domestic work, or behind closed doors, where the "chasm of social differences plays out in physical proximity" between Brown workers and affluent White employers, as observed by sociologist Pierrette Hondagneu-Sotelo,[36] and later by historian Vicky Ruiz.[37] In New York City, however, class and racial divides extend beyond native-born White employers and their Black or Brown immigrant workers to those between older and newer cohorts of non-White immigrants, as the case of the Mexican sushi chef mentioned earlier in this chapter suggests and as chapter 6 documents.

Beyond documenting the work integration and stratification of the two groups in New York City service sector jobs, this book documents the ideologies that drive employers to prefer one Latino group over the other and how gender, race, class, and gentrification complicate this process. During the first stages of my field research, the narrative of a thirty-nine-year-old owner of a small restaurant in New York City's Lower East Side, on the border of a gentrifying Puerto Rican and nearby Chinese working-class community, alerted me to some of the ideologies that lead employers to prefer Mexicans over other racialized Latinos like Dominicans or Puerto Ricans: "In the Southwest, Mexicans are as noticeable as the elephant in the living room! Within the [New York] restaurant industry, Asians, like the Chinese, and even Mexicans are preferred—like the Polish workers. These groups are perceived as motivated. Dominicans and Puerto Ricans have been here for generations; this makes it more complicated. It seems that these groups have an edge with the main culture, one which has also been fueled by the media."

This employer's narrative echoes scholarship documenting the preference for Mexican labor in New York City.[38] Yet as chapters 5 and 6 reveal, co-ethnic women have been left out of this scholarship, as most immigrant work in the low-wage sectors in New York has been associated with men—and mostly Mexican men. This book offers a new perspective on the role of gender, class, and race (skin color and phenotype) in the stratification of Dominican and Mexican women workers in informal service sectors at old and new immigrant destinations undergoing gentrification.

The interdisciplinary frameworks informing my analysis of findings benefit from the academic mentorship I received at the Center for Migration and Development (CMD) at Princeton University while a visiting research fellow during the 2012–14 academic years. At the CMD, I collaborated as a co-instructor in a yearlong seminar on race and ethnicity conducted by Edward Telles, the CMD's director at the time. This collaboration deepened my understanding of the significance of skin color and phenotype in the different forms of inequality and social mobility that Afro-descendant and Indigenous minorities experience in Latin America.[39] I hypothesized that a legacy of exclusion based on skin color and phenotype, complicated by gender, partially explains the increasing domestic and international migration of Afro-descendants and Indigenous women, paradoxically, after joining the middle class in the Dominican Republic.

Similarly, my participation in a handful of seminars on the sociology of emotions and the transfer of money that were organized by distinguished professor Viviane Zelizer also informs my analysis of the role of feminized remittances (money sent by migrant women to families left behind) on the educational mobility of Black and Indigenous women in communities of origin.[40] Finally, coauthoring a paper with migration and race scholar Marta Tienda that focused on the paradoxes emerging from the increasing spatial distribution and parallel segregation of U.S.-born Latinos deepened my analysis on the new geographies of origin for Dominican and Mexican immigrant women destined to New York City.[41] Most significantly, my analysis of the mechanisms explaining the international migration of women from Latin America benefits from the foundational work established by legendary Princeton University professor Douglas Massey and his collaborations with gender and migration scholars.

The Migration of Black and Indigenous Latinas and Contributions to the Migration, Gender, and Racialization Literature

While the main focus of *From Homemakers to Breadwinners to Community Leaders* is on women, spouses and conjugal partners play a key role in the emergence of a reversing pattern of gendered migration, social mobility, and racialization that today characterizes the experiences of Dominican and Mexican women in New York. This book also borrows from the development and gendered migration literature, with a new focus on the resilience of women who assume roles as heads of households in Latin America and the United States.[42] It renders new insights on the mobility and career strategies of Afro-descendant and Indigenous minorities who join the middle class in Latin America and then are forced to migrate due to legacies of patriarchal oppression and institutional exclusion.[43] A final contribution of this book is the documentation of the contributions that highly educated yet racialized immigrant women make to the host community, as volunteers or leaders in migrant organizations and institutions and through increasing social cohesion and civic engagement, which often include the protection of their racialized and impoverished immigrant communities.[44]

New Themes

Several themes in this book draw and expand on new knowledge in interdisciplinary studies focused on gendered migration, immigrant integration, boundary crossing, racialization, and feminist intersectional approaches. A key new theme in this book is the growing immigration of Afro-Caribbean and Indigenous women from Latin America and the concentration of Dominican and Mexican women within old and new destinations both inside and outside New York City. To begin, this book documents how the geographic and demographic characteristics of Dominican and Mexican groups in New York contrast markedly with those of earlier cohorts. For example, between the 1960s and the 1970s most

Dominicans arriving in New York came largely from the El Cibao region of the Dominican Republic. Many of these earlier immigrants settled in Massachusetts, New Jersey, and New York.[45] This early immigration also included a good share of landed elites, displaced politicians, diplomatic corps members, and entrepreneurs.[46] Another share of light-skinned Dominicans from the middle strata arrived prior to the 1990s, as portrayed on the cover of what is by now a classic book, *Between Two Islands*.[47] A large segment of this migration settled in the northeastern and southeastern regions of the United States—mostly in Florida, New York, and Washington, DC.[48]

Similarly, as early as the 1940s and up to the 1980s, the first waves of Mexicans to arrive in New York City included political dissidents, diplomats, and a commercial class, mostly from urban sectors, including refugees and asylum seekers who were displaced by the Partido Revolucionario Institucional, the conservative political party that ruled Mexico for nearly seventy-five years.[49] Since the enactment of NAFTA in 1994, members of the middle class and gradually the upper professional class have also joined migrant flows to the United States.[50] My qualitative insights, as well as census data,[51] suggest a growing share of highly educated women, including professionals and working-class minorities of Mestizo and Indigenous descent, have arrived in New York City since the late 1990s, a number of whom are included in this study.

A second theme in this book is the mobility pathways of Black and Indigenous Latinas in the sending and receiving communities. Chapter 2 provides a typology of migration by class, family structure, skin color, and phenotype, illustrating factors that distinguish this increasingly feminized migration for women who lead their families' migration compared with those who follow spouses or conjugal partners and the role of geography, gender, education, and skin color in the migration of women. A relevant theme is how service jobs impact the social mobility of Dominican and Mexican women, spouses and conjugal partners, upon arrival to New York City. A number of studies reveal that most Latinos concentrate in low-wage sectors, especially in historical destination gateway cities like Los Angeles and New York.[52] *From Homemakers to Breadwinners to Community Leaders* expands on earlier insights by distinguishing the experiences of Black and Brown immigrants in New York City's lower-skilled sectors of the care industry (e.g., working as domestics, nannies) from those in more highly skilled positions (e.g., working in community organizations, hospitality, or airlines).

A third theme explored in this book is the relevance of skin color and phenotype in the integration of non-White immigrant workers in the service sector. Insights suggest that lighter-skinned Latinos occupy positions with more visibility among the clienteles and the public. The more affluent the worksite, the more skin color and phenotype organize both the work and the mobility prospects of Dominicans and Mexicans in New York City. The findings herein expand on the literature documenting the role of skin color and phenotype, as well as education, in explaining inequality and mobility prospects for mixed-race groups in Latin America,[53] with a focus on the United States. The findings also expand on an existing literature that focuses on the role of skin color among successful Latinos, viewed as exceptional minorities or "proxy" Whites,[54] with the use of a Latino feminist intersectional approach now focused on the intersectional hierarchies of skin color, phenotype, education, and immigrant status on the sorting of Latino immigrant workers in service sector jobs, as chapters 5 and 6 document.

The fourth and final theme in this book is how gendered immigration affects new patterns of spatial and housing integration and segregation among Latino immigrants within new and old destinations.[55] Extending earlier studies focused on the spatial distribution of Latinos in the United States, including those who are foreign born, this book compares the spatial integration of Dominican and Mexican families in gentrifying neighborhoods in New York City—with a special focus on the housing and living arrangements of the undocumented and mothers who head homes alone. The findings have consequences for the design of future policies on immigration, labor markets, and housing, with an emphasis on the protection of vulnerable populations, including poor, frail families and undocumented immigrants. It also contributes new insights on the economic and cultural contributions that Latinos, including the undocumented, make to the revitalization of inner-city neighborhoods.

Analytical Frameworks and Concepts

This book's analytical frameworks borrow from an interdisciplinary body of work focused on gendered migration, immigrant integration, boundary crossing, the sociology of emotions, racialization theory, and intersectionality theory. The findings make a special contribution to an emerging Latina feminist intersectionality literature that addresses the multiple forms of inequalities, oppression, and resilience that women of color experience in the United States.[56] The book contributes to this literature with new comparative insights on the multiple forms of inequality and social mobility that both push and pull Afro-Caribbean and Mesoamerican Indigenous women in Latin America toward migrating to the United States.

This book also contributes to established scholarship on gendered migration,[57] including emerging knowledge on the heterogeneity of Latin American immigrants and the role of race, ethnicity, family structure, and class in the migration and integration experience.[58] Drawing on in-depth interviews, ethnographies, and census data, chapter 2 brings a new and nuanced understanding of the premigration experiences of an emerging yet fragile Black and Indigenous Latin American middle class,[59] one that now increasingly joins the undocumented and the poor in New York. Finally, the findings extend earlier works on development and stratification in Latin America that have documented the exclusion and inequality that ethnoracial minorities have experienced since colonial times. This book brings new insights on the intersectional forms of inequalities that push Afro-descendant and Indigenous minorities to migrate after joining the middle class.[60] The findings also contribute to the development literature with new insights on how feminized remittance contributes to the educational access and social mobility of families in the sending community.

More significantly, this book borrows from the gendered migration and racialization scholarship to conduct a comparative analysis of the experiences of women who lead their family's migration,[61] and the role of patriarchy as well as the state in the rising exodus of women from Latin America.[62] The findings extend an emerging scholarship on the resilience of women who head households in Latin America and in the United States,[63] with a focus on the migration strategies of more highly educated women and on how migration alters their status in the family, as well as their independence from patriarchal or oppressive communities of origin.[64]

Analytical Schemas

To describe how immigrants access resources that are vital for the settlement process, I borrow from *social capital* theories.[65] Social capital is rooted in Pierre Bourdieu's theoretical contributions of the intangible (social and cultural) resources of poor and isolated Algerian immigrants in France.[66] Gender and migration scholars document that men and women rely on different forms of social capital or networks for the migration and the settlement process.[67] My earlier work reveals that Dominican and Mexican immigrants rely on distinct gendered network structures for the migration and access to work.[68] Other earlier works have documented that gender, race, and class differently structure the access to social capital among racialized and poor minorities within inner-city structures.[69] This book expands on that previous scholarship with the experiences of immigrants in gentrifying neighborhoods within old and new urban destinations; it contributes new and theoretical insights on the social capital of Latina migrant women and how this affects their settlement and integration to New York City.

Racial Capital and Racial Capitalism. To explain how ethnic or racial identity, skin color, and physiognomy may function as a form of social capital in the middle-class ascendance of women in Latin America and in their immigration to the United States, I introduce the concept of *racial capital*, drawing on Nancy Leong's conceptualization of *racial capitalism* to describe both the commodification and devaluation of White and non-White identity in Latin America and in the United States. Almost a decade ago, Leong argued that White people benefit from diversity, or the inclusion and promotion of non-White people in their social circles and networks structures and in such institutional settings as the workplace. Her premise is that in a capitalistic society with a legacy of racism based on a system of slavery, a White identity has been commodified and considered more valuable than a non-White identity.[70] Leong draws on earlier literature rooted in Marxist thought[71] to argue that in the United States a White identity is a form of property or asset, based on the higher status and suite of legal rights given to White citizens and upheld through such legal cases as *Plessy v. Ferguson.* For Leong, as for most race scholars,[72] the commodification of racial identities entails both biological (phenotype, skin color, etc.) and social interaction (how race is performed and interpreted by different audiences) components. Depending on the audience, race can become a form of valued capital (i.e., similar to age, sexual, or even cultural forms of capital).

A very relevant point from Leong's analysis is the valued added to the identities of non-White minorities in recent decades as a result of the passing of the Civil Rights Act of 1964 and affirmative action jurisprudence and the Supreme Court's mandates for diversity quotas for institutions receiving federal aid.[73] Marxist scholar Cedric Robinson has counterargued that the commodification of a non-White identity has been part of U.S. history, as a system of slavery has served as the main foundation for capitalism.[74] Yet Leong proposes that racial identities are not commodified equally and that they depend on their use value on the dominant—typically White—class. I draw on Leong's analysis to further explore under what contexts and audiences the racial identities of Black and Brown immigrants are valued, commodified, and stratified in the workplace.

Unlike Leong, I conceptualize that the simultaneity or intersectional forms of social capital (e.g., gender, race, and class) may differently affect the racial valuation (or racial capital) of immigrant workers—especially those of mixed racial status, such as Latinos—and in turn their life chances for mobility. I make this argument based on certain caveats. While social capital has traditionally conveyed the levels of education, work experience, and social standing that immigrants import, *gender capital* connotes the access to material, social, and moral resources that immigrants (in this case, women) derive from family structures or civic status (such as being married or single or being mothers). This type of gender capital, I argue, is rooted in patriarchal culture but also enshrined within moralist and racist ideologies that may affect the roles and status of women in different contexts, such as in a small village in the Mexican state of Puebla versus the South Bronx in New York City. I also hypothesize that such institutions as the family or the workplace play a big role in validating the social capital and statuses of women. For example, marriage may increase or delimit the emotional, material, and social resources, including social status, of women. Marriage can affect women's access to education, work, or social mobility and—most important—the resources needed to engage in migration, as a typology of migrant women and case studies illustrate in chapters 2, 4, and 5.

Most central to Leong's work, I conceptualize racial capital in a framework that adds skin color and physiognomy and also the performance of a racial identity. This identity performance is manifested in the ability of immigrants to learn, assimilate, and adopt demeanors associated with a Black, White, or "proxy" White racial identity (as the case of the Mexican man working in the sushi bar and his adoption of an Asian demeanor while serving a largely Asian and White middle-class audience illustrates in chapter 6). Racial capital may convey different status to Latinos depending on the context, as Leong has argued; but I extend this framework to analyze the experiences of mixed-race immigrants in the service sectors as these jobs require the management of ethnoracial and gendered identities. Finally, I explore Leong's concept of the commodification of a racial identity or racial capitalism in the workplace with the use of an intersectionality lens to explore how the simultaneity of gender, race, and class affects the different valuation of a Dominican or Mexican identity in White and non-White workplaces and neighborhood contexts.

The Management of Emotions and Race. A scholarly journey often begins with a series of compelling observations. After joining Fordham University's campus in the Bronx, in 2004, I had the opportunity to gather longitudinal observations in the Northeast Bronx, near Little Italy, an ethnic White business enclave established in the 1950s by working-class European immigrants. For over ten years, I was able to gather ethnographic insights about the functions and positions of Dominican and Mexican workers in a few small service establishments there and in other neighborhoods in the Bronx, Manhattan, and Queens. To expand on my earlier analysis on the sorting of Black and Brown workers in service sectors, I draw in this book on Arlie Hochschild's classic insights on how service jobs require distinct forms of emotional labor, or "managing one's heart," to convey care for the clientele that is served.[75] I employ a social interactionist approach with a racial formation lens to explore how service jobs require immigrants to manage not only their emotions but also their gendered and racialized identities.[76] I note, for example, in chapter 6 how Mexican restaurant workers in Bronx Little Italy manage their emotions and ethnic identities when greeting customers or when tending to those customers' food selection needs. Often these workers, mostly immigrant Albanian and Mexican men, affect a working-class Italian accent and demeanor to market ethnic White appeal in the workplace and larger community; this also affects their own sense of belonging as hard-working ethnics—as opposed to racialized "others." Finally, I explore how this performance or the management of racial and ethnic identities affects the social mobility of immigrants in the workplace, as chapters 5 and 6 document.

Race, Ethnicity, and Racialization Processes. I draw on race, ethnicity, and racialization frameworks to analyze the migration and integration of Dominican and Mexican women in New York City. Scholars often distinguish between race and ethnicity, as both concepts tend to be confused in terms of identity and in the measurement of discrimination.[77] In this study, as in other relevant scholarship, race refers to biology, or traits that are immutable or cannot be easily changed, while ethnicity refers to more abstract concepts of national origin or connection to an ancestral culture that may change with migration and assimilation of the host society's mainstream culture. Racial identity, however, is conceived as fluid or a social construction that, it has been argued, has been stratified differently depending on the historical period and the prevailing ideologies of national ruling elites.[78] While in Latin America a hint of a White ancestry immediately connotes a non-Black identity, or being a member of the middle class, the same is not true in the United States. The history of Black and White segregation even after the Jim Crow era has always connoted that the "one-drop rule"—that is, a hint of Blackness—presupposes a non-White identity.[79] Thus, while in Latin America phenotypical and social status categories stratify mixed-race populations into a spectrum of identities that range from Black to White, in the United States a hint of a Black ancestry presupposes a non-White identity.

The racialization of people in the United States has also entailed the conflation of biology and class, leading to the common assumption that anyone who is Black is also poor or that all Whites are members of the middle class. Racialization theorists have assumed the association of a Black identity as a "burden" without considering how non-White Latinos, for example, may benefit from being confused with or passing as native-born Blacks or with more assimilated and politically empowered African Americans.[80] In chapter 3, I illustrate how a mixed-race, Black, or Indigenous identity positively affects some of my respondents' ability to find housing and work in traditional African American and Puerto Rican neighborhoods. I also show the contributions these new Brown and Black Latinos make to the revival of moribund economies in inner-city neighborhoods.

Analytical distinctions between race and ethnicity are hard to establish, as these tend to be conflated with geographical spaces and social standings.[81] For example, in New York, most people associate my last name, skin tone, or phenotype with Puerto Ricans; in California or Texas it is confused with Chicanas or Mexicans. Similarly, light-skinned Dominican immigrants in Puerto Rico may deliberately want to pass for Puerto Ricans, or as U.S. citizens, similar to the strategies used by Haitian immigrants in the Dominican Republic. Both racialized minority groups may benefit from a dissonant identity, especially given their more vulnerable status as undocumented or marginalized "others." Scholars argue that distinctions between ethnoracial groups will disappear through assimilation and adoption of U.S. bimodal racial identities.[82] Yet ethnic differences appear to racialize some groups more than others, as most people cannot distinguish among Latino groups, or Dominicans from other foreign or native-born Blacks, as is also the case for Guatemalans and other Central Americans, who are confused with Mexicans in the Southwest.[83]

Edward Telles and Christina Sue show that drawing distinctions between race and ethnicity is often problematic, as some individuals use the term *ethnicity* to refer to culture or national identity, while others use *race* to emphasize power relations, inclusion, exclusion, and racialization.[84] In this book I use *ethnoracial identities* to connote both the biological or physical (skin color, texture of hair, shape of nose, eyes, or lips) and the cultural (Spanish language, tone, demeanor in the presentation of self, etc.). I also use *ethnicization* to connote the process in which an ethnoracial minority is identified as an allied "ethnic" versus a problematized or racialized "other." My findings illustrate that service jobs require immigrant workers to manage their ethnic or racial identities to reproduce the culture and identity of the workplace. I argue that when immigrants engage and adopt the subjective or proxy ethnic or racial identity of the workplace or neighborhood, they partake in a process of racial capitalism that often benefits their mobility in the workplace but mainly their White employers or institutions, as illustrated in chapter 6. In gentrifying neighborhood areas with a strong African American and Latino presence, however, White employers benefit from hiring non-White workers as their racial or ethnic identities function as a form of racial capital, one that employers equally value as a commodity because minority workers help to attract other ethnoracial minorities as clients and often to legitimize the presence of White businesses in traditional minority neighborhood areas, especially during the early stages of gentrification.

Intersectionality and Migration. Intersectional frameworks have been used "to describe the location of women of color both within overlapping systems of subordination and at the margins of feminism and anti-racism."[85] Since the 1980s, an extensive line of work documents the multiple forms of inequality that women of color, especially African Americans, experience within the family, community, and larger societal institutions. An emerging and considerable body of feminist, intersectional scholarship and practice has documented the experiences of Chicana and Latina women in different social locations.[86] Yet despite the foundational contributions made to advances in intersectionality research by Chicanas and other Latina scholars, their works have been seldom cited by mainstream feminists. An emerging and critical Latina feminist scholarship has questioned whether intersectionality theories represent subordinate groups or instead cause the exclusion or misrepresentation of such groups.[87] This scholarship advocates the revisiting and expansion of earlier contributions made by Chicana feminist scholars to intersectionality studies, such as those in Cherríe Moraga and Gloria Anzaldua's foundational collection *This Bridge Called My Back: Writings by Radical Women of Color*.[88]

Drawing on this earlier feminist, Chicano Literature, *From Homemakers to Breadwinners to Community Leaders* conceptualizes four prominent themes in the study of intersectionality. The first is the border, examining how the crossing of the Mexican-U.S. border alters the experiences of immigrant women regarding race, class, gender, sexuality, and even citizenship. The second theme is identity or a reflection on how our own sense of who we are shifts or is shifted in different national contexts and for different audiences. The third theme is the analysis of structural or institutional inequalities and how they further complicate and reproduce the oppression and exclusion of Latina women of color, as Nancy López and Vivian Gadsden discuss.[89] The fourth theme is the concept of praxis, or an analysis of the "bridging, crossing, and resisting." These four major areas of study in the Chicana scholarship that, "add breadth and depth to the larger field and reveal many areas of social life that are unrecognized and unacknowledged in current intersectional work," help illustrate that feminist scholars can increase the inclusivity and connection of colored women with other women in similar locations and in other systems of domination and oppression.[90]

In chapters 2 and 4, I use the border analysis to illustrate how the domestic migration of women from rural to urban areas not only alters their sense of belonging and social mobility but also introduces new intersectional forms of gender, race, class, and sexual oppression. In chapters 4 and 5, I show how international migration increases the financial independence of women but also introduces other forms of vulnerability, such as class isolation, as well as new forms of precarity and abuse in the family and the workplace.

Finally, the methodological and analytical recommendations offered by López and Gadsden on the intersection of individual and institutional gendered and racialized inequalities that affect Latino minorities inform my analysis of the different forms of individual and structural inequalities that Afro-descendant and Indigenous women experience before and after migration. López and Gadsden draw on the experiences of Dominican youth in New York City, including López's own experience and that of her cousin, a youth close to her age but of much darker skin and different sexual orientation.[91] They reflect on the different treatment both receive in the health care system based on the intersectionality of gender, race, class, and sexual identity. I borrow from this scholarship to explore the intersectional forms of individual and structural inequalities that affect the factors pushing middle-class Dominican and Mexican women to migrate and the new forms of inequalities they experience in New York City. The applicability of a Latina feminist intersectionality framework helps compare the specific conditions of historically racialized minorities and, as Maxine Baca Zinn and Ruth Enid Zambrana suggest, will hopefully further an understanding of the process of "decoloniz[ing] knowledge production and activism" and the common experiences of inequalities that bind historically excluded ethnoracial women in Latin America with other racialized women minorities in the United States.[92]

Objectives and Design

A key objective of this book is to understand what drives the increasing migration of women from the Dominican Republic and Mexico to New York City. How are the premigration conditions of women who lead in migration distinct from those who follow family members (mostly spouses or conjugal partners)? Another objective is to document how different forms of social and racial, as well as class inequality, shape the social mobility, migration, integration, and racialization of Dominican and Mexican women.

Sample and Methods. In a descriptive, explorative study of the conditions that push and pull women to migrate, I principally draw on qualitative insights derived from focus groups, in-depth interviews, and longitudinal ethnographic observations. Drawing on Carol Stack's approach,[93] with the creation of dialogues between qualitative and quantitative insights, I supplement my qualitative insights with data on trends and patterns from the U.S. Census for 2000 and 2010, including international census updates.[94] As my analysis elsewhere suggests,[95] Mexican women obtain jobs through networks of male spouses or partners, while Dominican women rely mainly on webs of female friends and family networks; as such, the study's design was altered to include a handful of informal interviews with male spouse and partner respondents. The main interview questionnaire was revised so that the questions asked of women about their migration and work integration experience were also asked of their spouses or conjugal partners. I asked these additional questions only when respondents mentioned in their report that a spouse or partner lived in the home during the time of the study.

The findings in this book draw on nearly twenty years of field research conducted in New York City, beginning in 2000. I draw mainly on eighty-six semistructured interviews conducted with women (forty-four Dominicans and forty-two Mexicans) and fourteen informal interviews with employers (in five restaurants, one butcher shop, one nail salon, three beauty salons, two home attendant agencies, one dry-cleaning establishment, and two community-based migrant organizations); all interviews were conducted in Spanish and then translated into English. The first phase of fieldwork was conducted between 2000 and 2003. Fellowships from the Social Science Research Council, the Office of the President at Columbia University, the American Sociological Association, and the National Institute of Mental Health supported this first phase of data collection and writing.

The second phase of data collection, conducted between 2009 and 2010, involved follow-up interviews, ethnographies of workplaces and neighborhoods, and focus groups and was supported by a research grant for junior faculty from the Fordham University Graduate School of Arts and Sciences (2009–10). This phase also involved telephone and door-to-door recruitment efforts with the aid of one undergraduate research assistant and two Latino community organizations. The updated insights include in-depth follow-up interviews with twenty-five women respondents (fourteen Dominicans and eleven Mexicans) selected from the eighty-six women interviewed in the first phase of the study. I conducted additional informal interviews with employers and supervisors, as well as ethnographic observations, of five restaurants in the Bronx and Manhattan. The employers' selection came from a list of employment sites supplied by women and their spouses or conjugal partners when asked about places of employment. Additional insights come from informal discussions with a handful of maintenance workers, including two supervisors at my previous and current academic institutions. I also conducted participant observations with airlines and hotels during work- or family-related travel to the Dominican Republic and Mexico for a period of over fifteen years (2003–19) to inform the writing of this book.

Two ethnographies of households conducted intermittently for over a year, in the apartments of a Dominican family and of a Mexican family, allowed for the documentation of the living arrangements and strategies of middle-class women who lead their family's migration and those who follow or accompany spouses or conjugal partners. The insights increased my understanding of how family structures, class, race, and immigrant status affect access to housing and work. The insights also deepened my understanding of how undocumented women, especially mothers, cope with housing and work precarity and the networks of support that help anchor their and their children's lives. They also allowed me to better understand the tribulations that Black and Indigenous women face in a highly racialized context of reception and how these women cope with new forms of independence and also sexual, racial, and class oppression.

Intermittent field observations in one ethnic White neighborhood (Bronx Little Italy) and two legendary Black and Latino neighborhoods (East and West Harlem), conducted over five years (2014–19), helped further illustrate the larger contextual factors that affect the spatial integration and housing experiences of Dominican and Mexican families in New York City. Additionally, in-depth interviews and ethnographic observations helped document the living arrangements of Dominican and Mexican families in rapidly gentrifying neighborhoods within old inner-city and new immigrant destination areas. The findings illustrate the resilience of immigrant women and the contributions they make to the economic and cultural renewal of declining neighborhoods.

Finally, my updated fieldwork is supplemented by additional insights from a research study on remittances and transnational households in which I served as field director. The study, which was sponsored by Fordham University's Center for International Policy Studies and the North American Integration Development Center at the University of California–Los Angeles, involved interviews with heads of households in Los Angeles, a few municipalities in Mexico, and

New York City (2008–10) and included forty-six interviews with Mexican women who identified as heads or coheads of households in New York City. While directing the fieldwork, I conducted parallel focus groups with Dominican women in New York City and two communities of origin in the Dominican Republic to compare the immigrant experiences of the two groups and the role of remittances on families left behind in the country of origin.

Ethical Considerations. A few ethical considerations guided the gathering and reporting of findings. To safeguard the identity of respondents with an undocumented status, I personally conducted all interviews and focus groups. As a trained ethnographer and poverty scholar, I had the opportunity to work in poverty and immigration research while in graduate school through the longitudinal Yonkers Housing Desegregation and Health Community Study,[96] the Carnegie Endowment's Immigrant and Social Welfare Project,[97] and the Bailey House and HIV/AIDS Study,[98] as well as through my own dissertation project (with Herbert J. Gans as mentor). These experiences increased my sensitivity about fieldwork and safeguarding the identities of respondents. For this current study, none of the questionnaires asked for personal information. Respondents' personal information was kept on a separate list, and in a separate space from the completed questionnaires, and later translated into coded numbers for data entry into EndNote and SPSS Statistics files. The original list with names and contact information was kept in a locked filing cabinet in my home office.

Every respondent signed a consent form (CF) that explained in English and Spanish the nature of the study and its focus on the immigrant, housing, and work experiences of Dominican and Mexican women in New York City. Each respondent was asked to sign or initial the CF using a pseudonym, as at least half of the sample included people with a vulnerable immigrant status, some due to expired legal visas or having entered the United States without proper documentation. I left one copy of the CF with the respondent and also took a copy home. All CFs included my name and contact information and the name and contact information of my department's chair.

The research used a snowball methodology, with interviews continuing until a few main patterns became apparent. Respondents were recruited initially from two sets of focus groups conducted at a few immigrant organizations and churches. Each participant received an incentive (five to ten dollars) for every referral made to another coethnic who met the sampling criteria: being a foreign-born immigrant woman from either the Dominican Republic or Mexico, being between the ages of eighteen and fifty-nine, and having lived in the United States for at least five years prior to the study. The questionnaire included semistructured and other open-ended questions regarding seven themes or dimensions: (1) premigration household event histories; (2) demographic characteristics, including ethnic and racial identity; (3) mode of migration and networks of support;

(4) the settlement and spatial integration process, including living arrangements; (5) work conditions and relations with peers, employers, and supervisors, and the ethnic and racial composition of those coworkers, employers, and supervisors; (6) the impact of migration on the women's agency, relations with spouses, motherhood practices, and mental and physical health and well-being, including that of any children; and (7) the women's and household members' experiences of individual and institutional discrimination.

Interviews mostly took place in the respondents' homes, though respondents were asked where they would prefer to be interviewed; about one-third preferred a neutral place, like my campus's office in the Bronx, a migrant organization, or a church where they felt familiar or safe. I always asked if the respondent would prefer that I or another family member read the CF. I provided each respondent with a list of community agencies that serve immigrants, including medical centers that offered services to immigrants and other people using sliding scale fees. Whenever possible, I listed the names of social workers or service providers they could contact or directly made appointments or follow-up calls with service providers on my respondents' behalf. Each respondent was compensated for his or her participation in focus groups or a two-hour, in-depth interview; compensation included a New York City transportation MetroCard. During the first phase (2000–2003), respondents were given fifteen dollars and a two-dollar Metro-Card for their participation. During the second phase (2009–10) they were given twenty-five dollars and a $4.50 MetroCard if they traveled to the interview.

A few women reported incidences of abuse at the hands of landlords or *encargados* (lease holders who rent rooms in their own apartments to coethnics). They also reported being charged too much money for rent. One White couple refused to pay a Dominican single mother for the rental of a room and threatened to report her to the Department of Homeland Security or the Immigration and Naturalization Service, as I document in chapter 4. I explained to my respondents their rights to complain to the New York City Housing Authority and offered to advocate on their behalf; I also offered information about legal and mental health services offered by migrant organizations. On a few occasions, I witnessed the overcrowded conditions in which undocumented or poor families lived as boarders in other people's apartments or as extended kin of an apartment's lease holder. Because many of these respondents feared deportation, however, I weighed the damage that reporting a violation would have on the well-being of the family. During the first and second phases of research, I did not witness, or receive reports from my respondents of, any domestic or child abuse.

In weighing whether to disclose sensitive information about the lives of some of my respondents (as I do in chapter 4, when describing how one respondent was advised to pay a few thousand dollars as a cash advance to bump her up the waiting list in a public housing project), I consider the consequences these observations may have on the damaging of preexisting conceptions regarding immigrants. I aim, however, to emphasize the ways in which vulnerable immigrants (often the undocumented, but in this case a single mother of two and a legal resident) are taken advantage of by bureaucrats in underfunded government agencies. I find that it is the institutions that are often responsible for helping or protecting the poor or the vulnerable in our society that sometimes unwittingly reproduce their poverty or experiences of oppression. I find it important to remember that migrants are not infallible; they are people on the margins of society and must fend for themselves to provide for their families—sometimes under great material and psychological duress.

The Researcher's Position. Christina Sue has found that her status as a highly educated foreign scholar increased her ability to enter the Mexican community of her study in Veracruz, Mexico. Sue's mixed race (Asian and White), gender, marital status, and strong familiarity with the Mexican culture, including mastery of the Spanish language, facilitated her entry and the successful gathering of insights. In addition, she notes, most Veracruzans conceive highly educated or North American people as either influential or affluent, and this also increased her receptivity.[99]

Similarly, I believe that as the daughter of a working-class Dominican immigrant woman and having an elite education influenced my entry and receptivity among both my respondents and the gatekeepers in ethnic and mainstream institutions. My light-brown skin and Mestizo phenotype (more of a mix of Iberian and North African Arabic than Afro-Caribbean), and my fluent yet dissonant Spanish, without a demarcated Dominican or Mexican accent, increased but often challenged my initial entry into both Latino communities. As part of the so-called 1.5 generation—not fully part of my immigrant mother's or my own second-generation daughters' cultural worlds—I often elicited a bit of suspicion among respondents, leading some, especially the undocumented, to want to authenticate my ethnicity. Even among my own Dominican co-ethnics, when I said I was Dominican, I was often asked, "¿Y de donde?" (And where [on the island] are you from?) or "¿Y de que apellido?" (And what is the last name [of your family]?). My lack of a distinctive ethnic Spanish accent, mix of upper-class and working-class demeanors, and ambiguous mixed-race phenotype often led some people to be confused or feel uncomfortable, not knowing how to identify me or where to position me. Often I was confused with someone from the Middle East or North Africa (especially Algeria or Morocco), and often with Northern Indians; taxi drivers in New York City, as well as in Holland and Spain, where I have conducted research, have often reminded me that I look Punjabi or Syrian.

Generally, I believe that my status as a mother, more than that of a wife or a high professional, became the door opener, eliciting the trust and welcoming reception among Latina women respondents and female gatekeepers in community organizations and even Latino restaurants. However, I also noticed that when I visited restaurants alone I was treated differently, marked as a single woman, or not highly ranked as a client. Attending staff assumed frequently there was nothing else I needed before the check was placed on my table at the end of a meal. In the company of my husband, a 1.5 immigrant from Colombia with a strong Indigenous phenotype, our identities as Latinos were more anchored and our exclusion was even more evident, as we were often seated at tables near the kitchen or in other undesirable locations, even when we had reserved a table. I also observed that even though we were often given the worst tables in both Latino and non-Latino (Albanian, Asian, Greek, Italian, or Turkish) restaurants, most of the staff began to treat us deferentially and to give us better accommodations once we demonstrated an ability to pay for good meals and expensive wines. I gather that my dissonant (seemingly non-Dominican, non-Mexican) Latino identity worked in my favor in Latino restaurants more than it did in other (ethnic White) restaurants.

Several ethnic and mainstream organizations, including two Catholic churches in Harlem and two Protestant churches—one in the Washington Heights neighborhood of Manhattan and one in southwest Mount Pleasantville,[100] where my mother is a longtime member—increased my access to and recruitment of Dominican and Mexican participants in old and new immigrant destinations for the two ethnoracial minorities.

Although at first I encountered resistance in trying to gain entry into the emerging Mexican community of the late 1990s, participation in the Carnegie Endowment for International Peace's immigration and welfare reform project had already introduced me to the Latino directors of two immigrant organizations in Manhattan. With their mediation I organized a few focus groups and recruited respondents. In addition, the mediation of a Spanish-speaking priest who organized a support circle at his church in Harlem and a second Catholic church in Lower Manhattan for women experiencing domestic abuse further increased my reception in the community, including invitations to help with fundraisers and religious festivities. The leader of one of the oldest Mexican organizations in New York City (whom I had met through the Carnegie Endowment for International Peace's project on immigration and welfare reform) and one of my doctoral mentors put me in touch with a few diasporic bureaucracies. These diasporic bureaucracies helped arrange formal interviews with staff in the office of the Consulate General of Mexico and the United States' Mexican Chamber of Commerce in New York City, as well as with the heads of a few sports, entrepreneurial, and religious community-based organizations. Similarly, volunteering for two Dominican community organizations in New York City and participating in a few conferences—including one in the Dominican Republic, co-organized by Alianza Dominicana, in which over two dozen female academics, community activists, and artists participated—increased my entry into the community and local institutions. Finally, participant observation in one Mexican organization where I volunteered for several years and in another Dominican organization where I volunteered during graduate school has given me entry as well as increased my reception and trust among local and transnational community leaders, including several highly educated immigrant women volunteers. The experience furthered my interests in documenting the immigration and social mobility pathway of Dominican and Mexican women in migrant institutions, as foundational literature has suggested that men have historically controlled these ethnic niches.[101] Overall, my pregnancy and the raising of young daughters during the early stages of my dissertation research (2000–2003) increased my reception among most immigrant women, their families, and other women in ethnic and mainstream institutions.

The Women in This Study. The gathering of this qualitative data has taken over fifteen years, as it has included follow-up field gathering efforts and intermittent ethnographies of neighborhoods, businesses, and households. The first stage of data collection comes from my dissertation research, which included three years of interviews and ethnographic data. The second phase of data collection included follow-up interviews and ethnographic observations. This process included twenty-five women who participated in the first phase.

Table 1.1 shows the demographic characteristics of respondents prior to migration, as reported retroactively by the women. Thirty-three percent of Dominican and Mexican women came from working-class backgrounds or came to the United States with less than a high school education. Thirty-nine percent had between eight and twelve years of education. Twenty-one percent arrived with at least twelve years of schooling or some level of college education, or brought work skills with them. Among those importing little education, Mexicans are the majority; almost twice as many Dominicans imported at least one year of college education. Yet, notably, the follow-up interviews showed that among those importing professional or postgraduate degrees or equivalent work experience, Mexicans surpassed Dominicans by a slight margin—8 percent to 7 percent, respectively. On average, over one-third of women in both groups claimed middle-class status prior to migration. A good share of those with an undocumented status are included among those with a higher education, suggesting that most of these migrants entered the country legally and then overstayed their visas. Overall, a number of my respondents were hard to reach, as more than 55 percent of Mexicans and about 27 percent of Dominicans had an undocumented status. Yet while Mexican women's vulnerability was defined by their undocumented status, over 50 percent of Dominican women were the sole heads of households or acted as primary providers.

The bottom part of table 1.1 also illustrates the racial characteristics that Dominican and Mexican women reported when they were given a choice among

TABLE 1.1   Premigration Demographics

	Dominicans (N = 45)	Mexicans (N = 41)	Total (N = 86)
Age			
Eighteen to twenty-eight	32%	55%	44%
Twenty-nine or older	68%	45%	56%
Household structure			
Lived with spouse/partner	55%	78%	66%
Lived alone	45%	22%	34%
Family size (number of children)			
None	7%	—	4%
One or two	45%	49%	46%
Three or four	38%	39%	39%
Five or more	10%	12%	11%
Level of education			
Kindergarten to eight years	16%	51%	33%
Eight to twelve years	52%	23%	39%
Twelve years or more	27%	13%	21%
None	5%	3%	7%
Race/ethnic identity, as preferred by respondent			
Dominican/Dominicana	85%		
Latin American	5%		
Hispanic	6%		
Latino/a	3%		
Other race	1%		
Mexican/Mexicana		76%	
Latin American		8%	
Hispanic		5%	
Latino/a		1%	
Other race		10%	

SOURCE: Author's interviews, 2000–2003, and follow-up interviews, 2009–10.

the racial categories included in the U.S. Census. As the table illustrates, an over-whelming share of first-generation immigrants identified by their nationality or ethnicity, not their race (Dominicans at 85 percent, and Mexicans at 76 percent). Notably, more Mexicans than Dominicans chose the categories "Latin American" or "Other race," and more Dominicans than Mexicans chose the categories "Hispanic" and "Latino/a." Finally, and as is further discussed in chapter 2, more Dominican women immigrated alone, and almost half lived in a single-family home before the migration, compared with Mexicans, where a majority lived in an intact family both before and following migration.

Finally, as an immigrant adolescent, an "in-between" member of the 1.5 generation who was socialized outside of an immigrant Black or Latino community, I lacked the consciousness to cope with or navigate racially or class-based loaded messages or more sophisticated forms of institutional discrimination. On more than a few occasions, a professor for whom I worked as an undergraduate made fun of the way I used my hands to express myself; looking at the direction in which my hands moved every time I spoke, he reminded me that my mannerisms were indicative of uneducated people. He gave me a book to read on "class," sharing a few examples of the animated ways of dressing or speaking that gave away one's working-class origin. A latent internalization of an ethnic and racial consciousness, identity, and attitude allowed me to appreciate the protective effects of immigrant cultures on the psychological ravages of racial discrimination and oppression. This rebirth, or "coming out of the racial and ethnic closet," as I joke to my students, has also heightened a lifetime commitment to the study of migration and race, or how immigrants develop and adopt ethnoracial *identities schemas*, which are more context specific, fluid, and arbitrary and are not based on the polarized racial categories and experiences of Black and White Americans. I have grown increasingly interested in documenting the material and social mechanisms that mediate the inclusion and exclusion of mixed-race individuals in different neighborhood contexts and for different audiences. This book documents social mobility and exclusion in New York City and how this experience is inextricably linked to the workplace.

Organization of the Book

This book is organized into six chapters describing the premigration, settlement, and integration of migrant Dominican and Mexican women in New York City. Each chapter begins with a brief discussion of the subject to be addressed, a survey of the relevant literature, followed by an illustration and discussion of findings.

Chapter 2 details the individual and larger contextual factors that push Dominican and Mexican women to migrate. A typology organized by mode of migration, geography of origin, family structure, gender, race (skin color and phenotype), and class (education and work skills) describes the experiences of women who import a higher education. It also describes the premigration factors and different forms of inequalities that lead Afro-Caribbean and Indigenous women minorities to migrate from the Dominican Republic and Mexico to New York City. Chapter 3 documents shifts in the settlement and spatial distribution patterns of the two immigrant groups in the city. It then explores the paradoxes that emerge with the arrival of a new Brown and Black immigrant middle class and how the two groups navigate neighborhood spaces traditionally settled by poor, marginalized, and racialized co-ethnics. The insights help illustrate the nature, structure, and geography of the networks that facilitate the overlapping yet distinct spatial integration of the two immigrant groups in gentrifying neighborhoods within old and new destinations and the contributions these migrants make to the economic and cultural revival of gentrifying neighborhoods. Chapter 4 draws on longitudinal ethnographies to compare the living arrangements and housing strategies of undocumented migrant families and the precarious living conditions of middle-class mothers, the devastating impact that evictions have on poor immigrant families, and how they cope with the trauma of an eviction, sometimes followed by deportation (with long-term consequences for mothers and their children).

Chapter 5 describes the intersection of personal and structural inequality that leads middle-class women from the Dominican Republic and Mexico to migrate, and the role of patriarchy and the state in the repression and subsequent migration of poor women who gain access to higher education. It distinguishes the experiences of women whose middle-class status derives from their spouses or their families of birth compared with those who derive their status from their own education. The chapter then illustrates how migration transforms the status of women within the family, including relations with spouses and male authorities, and how it introduces new forms of oppression and agency impacting their mental health. The chapter ends by illustrating the mobility pathways of women in low- and high-skilled service jobs and how intersectional forms of social inequalities affect the mobility chances of Black and Indigenous women in New York City.

Chapter 6 documents how migrant women workers manage their ethnoracial identities in the workplace as part of a larger process of race formation and racial commodification. A handful of vignettes render a nuanced illustration of the ecology of the worksite and of the intricate interactions between service workers and their clientele. These detailed insights help document how mixed-race individuals manage their emotions as well as racial and gendered identities in the workplace to increase their mobility in service jobs. The insights also contribute new understanding on new processes of racial formation or racial capitalism that mostly benefits employers who hire minorities in gentrifying neighborhoods. The book's conclusion invites a discussion of the implications the findings pose for the design of public policies on immigration and labor employment that are sensitive to the vulnerabilities and contributions of Black and Indigenous minorities in the sending and receiving communities and in neighborhoods undergoing rapid demographic and economic transformation.

2 · THE MIGRATION OF WOMEN AND RACE
A Typology

With the implicit consent and a cash loan from her mother and an older sister in New York City, Berkis decided she would migrate and join them. She told Amado, her husband of ten years, that she could no longer live the way they did. She was determined to try her luck in New York. The final push came the morning that the promised promotion she had waited on for five years was given to a man she helped train. Amid tears, she told Amado she would go first, save money, then send for him and their two small sons. She had already spoken at length with her mother and older sister, who began preparing to take out a loan to help Berkis pay the passport and visa application fees. A large portion was deposited into the couple's savings bank account to show their middle-class solvency. Berkis's story begins to unravel the different forms of structural and social inequality that often push more highly educated women to migrate from the Dominican Republic to New York City—increasingly so since the 1990s. Her story also attests to the growing significance of migrant women in the educational mobility of family women left behind in communities of origin. Specifically, Berkis's premigration story and those of other respondents uncover the individual and institutional inequalities that push members of an emerging, yet vulnerable, Latin American middle class to migrate. This is especially the case of educated women in the Dominican Republic and Mexico, where Afrodescendants and Indigenous minorities make up the majority of the poor, while a White or light-skinned elite has ruled and controlled most resources since colonial times.[1] Despite sustainable economic growth in both Latin American nations, historically racialized ethnoracial minorities, especially women, experience the highest levels of inequality even after joining the middle class, as Berkis's case begins to illustrate.[2]

This chapter compares the premigration experiences of Dominican and Mexican women with the use of a gendered migration and Latina feminist intersectionality lens. Specifically, it compares the experiences of family women who lead their own migration with those who follow spouses or conjugal partners. Several questions organize this chapter: What can we learn from the increased immigration of Dominican and Mexican women into New York City, especially among those who import a higher level of human capital? What binds and yet distinguishes the migration experiences of both Latin American women groups? Finally, what can the simultaneous access to a higher education and to migration tell us about the links between development, social mobility, and racial inequality?

Nationwide, 36 percent of foreign-born Dominicans import at least one year of college education when they migrate. The growing U.S. immigration of women from middle-class sectors in Central America, the Dominican Republic, and Mexico has already been noted by gender and migration scholars.[3] Yet comparative studies about the immigration adjustment process of middle-class or more highly educated Black and Indigenous Latinas in New York City seem almost nonexistent. Drawing on insights from U.S. Census data,[4] structured interviews, and focus groups, one aim of this chapter is to explore how the financial and cultural remittances of working-class migrant women mediate access to the higher education or social mobility of family women in communities of origin. The conclusions invite a reflection about the mechanisms that contribute to the social mobility of ethnoracial minorities in Latin America and the inequalities and forms of institutional and social oppression that force many to migrate upon joining the middle class.

MIGRATING WOMEN, CLASS, AND RACE

Studies confirm that education increases the odds of migration for women, but not as much for men. They also demonstrate that more highly educated women lead international migration.[5] The United States has the largest number of migrant women in the western hemisphere; they come mainly from Europe and Latin America, the Caribbean, and Asia.[6] Figure 2.1 illustrates that out of twenty-two Latin American nations (including Puerto Rico), nations with the largest shares of Black and mixed-race populations tend to send mostly women to the United States; top among these are Panama, Colombia, Brazil, Jamaica, and the Dominican Republic.[7] Similarly, Latin American nations with a long history of military intervention on the part of the United States and/or internal civic warfare targeting Indigenous people in rural communities (i.e., El Salvador, Guatemala, Honduras, Mexico, and Peru) tend to send mostly men.

The immigration of Mexicans to the United States is part of a legacy of internal colonization that dates back to the mid-1800s. The sharing of contiguous geographical borders between two nations divided by asymmetries of economies and power has facilitated the U.S. appropriation of Mexican territory, and its importation of Mexican people to solve a labor problem, since the end of slav-

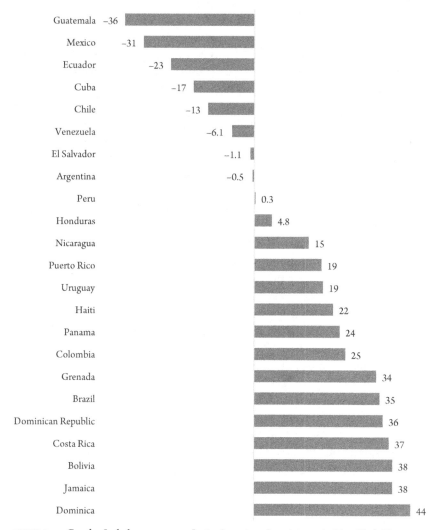

FIGURE 2.1 Gender Imbalances among Latin American Immigrants in New York City (ages 18–60). (*Sources:* Ruggles, Flood, et al., 2020; author's calculations using updates from the Integrated Public Use Microdata Series–USA, 2014–18, and the combined American Community Survey sample [5%]. Gender ratios obtained by taking the ratio of the female to male population and multiplying by 100.)

ery.[8] Although manual workers have composed the largest shares of this histori-cal immigration, in recent decades skilled people and the middle class have joined migrant streams, and increasingly since the early 1990s after the enact-ment of the North American Free Trade Agreement.[9] Indeed, by 2010, 16 percent of foreign-born Mexicans imported at least one year of a college education. Given this age-old legacy of labor migration, Mexican women have composed the largest share of females among all Latin Americans in the United States.[10] Since the mid-1990s this immigration has included the college educated and skilled professionals in search of career advancement,[11] but also women who follow or accompany professional, migrant spouses.[12] In the Northeast, however, Mexicans are relatively new as migrants.[13] In New York City, for example, numbers of Dominican migrants surpass Mexicans at a ratio of two to one.

While most U.S. migrant manual laborers come from Mexico, historical ties with the Dominican Republic have also involved the importation of migrant labor, and increasingly that of women.[14] In the 1800s the Dominican Republic became the most profitable Caribbean colony for Europe. Since the early twentieth century, its geopolitical location—situated on important waterways for U.S. commerce—has allowed U.S. investors control of most of its commerce, and specifically its sugar industry. U.S. occupation from 1916 to 1924 paved the way for Rafael Trujillo's ruthless dictatorship in the 1930s, maintaining a period of relative prosperity until his assassination in 1961. During the Trujillo era, the share of women traveling to the United States or abroad was minimal and limited to women traveling in the company of a spouse, father, or male family sponsor.[15] The United States passed the Immigration and Nationality Act in 1965, and Dominican immigration to the United States began in earnest in the mid-1980s, as chapters 3 and 5 illustrate.

To explain the causes of migration for middle-class Black and Indigenous minorities in the Dominican Republic and Mexico, I borrow from emerging research on development and racial inequality. A report published by the Economic Commission for Latin America and the Caribbean indicates that between 1990 and 2007 the Dominican Republic and Mexico were among the top ten nations experiencing the fastest growth in the share of households entering the middle class, defined regionally as households with income between $5,000 and $15,000, or with respective increases of 53.1 percent and 32.6 percent.[16] Increases in the share of middle-class households have brought corresponding increases in new middle-class individuals' consumption capacity and increased financial vulnerability. I argue that development and a virtual culture of consumption facilitated by the internet have also increased international migration. My qualitative insights illustrate that historically excluded Afro-Caribbean and Indigenous minorities, who are last to join the middle class in the Dominican Republic and Mexico, respectively, are the most vulnerable to the lures of migration. As new members of the middle class, Berkis and many others lack secure employment or social capital to validate their membership among members of the established mainstream middle class. This increases the vulnerability and subsequent likelihood of Black and Indigenous people new to the middle class to migrate in search of better economic or career opportunities.

Since the 1990s, Latin America (and most of the world) has experienced sustained economic growth, yet Afro-descendant and Indigenous minorities have not all benefited from such growth.[17] For example, even though the majority of Mexico's population (80.6 percent) is of Indigenous descent, and an even greater majority (almost 85 percent) in the Dominican Republic is of Black or mixed-race descent, these groups remain overrepresented among the poorest and the most marginalized in society.[18] Among both ethnoracial groups, women face the highest levels of poverty and intersectional forms of gender, racial, and class inequality, and this translates to significantly lower levels of opportunity and well-being. And despite research in Latin America documenting a historic gendered reversal in education,[19] only 6 percent of individuals who identify as Indigenous complete sixteen years of schooling.[20] In rural areas of Indigenous concentration, individuals face even greater levels of inequality, with almost 80 percent completing less than ten years of schooling.

In nations with the largest concentrations of Afro-descendants, Black women face the highest levels of inequality.[21] Scholars have documented how the multiple levels of exploitation and abuse that Black women have experienced through a system of colonization and slavery have led to a legacy of institutional and social exclusion as well as abandonment by the state. For example, in Brazil, Black women have always experienced the highest instances of marital instability and poverty. Black people receive less education, earn lower salaries, and experience the least social mobility, even when compared with White families with similar education and socioeconomic origins.[22] Black women also face the fewest chances of marriage, resulting in a long legacy of single parenthood and intergenerational forms of inequality among Black families.[23]

Similarly, numbers of Black families in the Dominican Republic, usually of Haitian origin or in Haitian regions and settlement areas, have always been high among poor immigrant households and those headed by single mothers. In fact, in Latin America and the Spanish Caribbean, the Dominican Republic ranks second only to Nicaragua among nations with the greatest shares of households headed by single women.[24] More troubling is that only 50 percent of highly educated women in the Dominican Republic, irrespective of racial or class origins, are able to marry someone with the same level or a higher level of education.[25] Yet not much is known about the marriage or mobility experiences of Black women. The qualitative insights suggest that Black women who join the middle class, such as Berkis, tend to marry men with lower education due (as the following typology illustrates) to a long legacy of racial and class exclusion in which family men and the state are often complicit.[26]

BERKIS: WHEN WOMEN COME FIRST

As Berkis's story at the beginning of this chapter illustrates, economic and emotional motives often push highly educated Latin American women to migrate. It also exposes the personal and professional barriers that Black women new to the

middle class experience in Latin America, unable to translate their higher education into gainful professional work. Berkis led her own family's migration from
the Dominican Republic to New York City in the mid-1990s, aided by the transnational networks of family women—in this case, her mother and older sister.
She is part of a rising, yet vulnerable, middle class whose emergence in Latin
America takes place amid sustained economic growth and inequality.[27] Berkis
joined the middle class in a nation with one of the highest wage discrepancies
between households in the middle- and working-class strata.[28] Her advanced
postgraduate education is also remarkable in a country where, on average since
2010, women between the ages of twenty-five and fifty-nine complete 9.9 years of
schooling. In 2017 the national average of education for women had increased to
10.2 years, while for men it lagged behind at averages of 9.7 to 10.1 years.[29] The
middle child of three, Berkis was born in a rural area and then educated near the
nation's capital, following her mother's separation from her father and domestic
migration. She was raised in a household in which her mother was a single par-
ent and the primary breadwinner. Berkis was the first in her family to obtain
both a college and a postgraduate professional degree.

Table 2.1 provides the premigration experiences of women selected for this
typology by phenotype and skin color, based on my respondents' self-
descriptions, including those for spouses or conjugal partners, following the categories used in Wendy Roth's qualitative study of racial schemas in the Dominican
Republic and Christina Sue's study of race and ethnic stratification in Veracruz,
Mexico.[30] I have translated the categories given by my respondents to the
equivalent use in the United States, using the methods employed by Edward
Telles and the Project on Ethnicity and Race in Latin America for their comparative study in Latin America.[31] I consider my role as the interviewer as a
proxy for how the larger U.S. society perceives the racial or ethnic identity of
my respondents in the United States. I include phenotype and skin color
because in the United States, unlike in Latin America, a hint of Black blood
immediately connotes a non-White identity.[32] The details, I hope, help evidence how race, gender, and human capital may combine in different contexts
to affect social mobility and exclusion in the sending and the receiving
communities.

Marriage to men with lower education or of darker skin is typical for highly
educated Black and Indigenous women in the Dominican Republic or Mexico.[33]
Yet a dearth of knowledge exists on the assortative choices or outcomes of highly
educated Black and Indigenous women in Latin America. This chapter makes an
initial contribution to this discussion, with qualitative insights gathered in communities of origin and destination. It also contributes insights as to the new
geographies from where educated women from the Dominican Republic and
Mexico migrate.

TABLE 2.1   A Typology of Migration and Race

Respondent	Respondent's Self-Identification	Interviewer's Identification of Respondent (Skin Color and Phenotype)	Respondent's Spouse	Spouse's Identification, as Reported by Respondent
Berkis	Negrita/morena (Black / dark-skinned)	Black skin with eastern European phenotype	Amado	Indio oscuro / moreno (dark Indian / dark-skinned)
Alejandra	Mulata/java (mixed race / white skin with Black facial or hair features)	Golden white skin with Black and White mixed phenotype	Tomás	Blanco / fino / Español del campo (White / Spanish from the countryside)
Maritza	Blanca/rubia (white/blond)	White skin with eastern European phenotype	Diogenes	Blanco / Español del Cibao (White / Spanish from El Cibao)
Magdalena	Mestiza/Ladina (mixed race / Central American)	Brown skin with Mestizo phenotype	Orlando	Mestizo / Piel Morena (mixed race / dark-skinned)
Gloria	Indigena/ Poblana (Indigenous / from Puebla)	Light skin with Indigenous/ Nahualt phenotype	Antonio	Piel clara Mestizo / Poblano (mixed race / from Puebla)

SOURCE: Author's interviews, 2000–2003, and follow-up interviews, 2009–10.

Berkis grew up in Herrera, an urban sector within Santo Domingo Oeste (SDO), the largest of seven municipalities in the greater Santo Domingo area. Located on the outskirts of the nation's federal district, SDO and its two largest sectors, Herrera and Manoguayabo, are key destinations for domestic immigration or the migration of individuals from the nation's interior (mostly rural regions affected by development and/or the commercialization of agriculture) to more urban areas. Berkis's mother immigrated to Herrera from a semirural area in the province of San Pedro de Macoris, after the failure of a marital union that had lasted over twenty years. When her mother arrived in Herrera, Berkis was still in elementary school. In the early 1970s, Herrera was an isolated working-poor community; most households lacked consistent water or electricity access.

Berkis's socialization in Herrera limited her relationships with members of the established Dominican middle class to superficial encounters at her university

and the private firm where she later found professional work. Social isolation ultimately led Berkis to marry a man with a high school diploma whom she had dated
on and off during her second year of high school. While she was in college, Berkis
accepted Amado's marriage proposal, but on graduation and employment,
Berkis assumed most of the household's expenses and financial challenges given
her taxi driver husband's unpredictable wages. Amado was a high school graduate, a native of Santo Domingo. As the firstborn in a large family, he had had to
work since the age of sixteen to help support his widowed mother and siblings.

Berkis had high hopes for Amado's dream of owning a taxi or livery business.
She also used to boast about Amado's looks, as his skin was a few shades lighter
than hers, though his nose and fuller lips, as well as his tight curly hair, made him
appear to have more African descent than he did. Both Berkis and Amado were
unusually tall, and Berkis felt that the two made an attractive couple. Her migrant
dreams were fueled by her mother's and older sister's wage-earning experiences
in New York factories and then as home attendants. Their working-class wages
had allowed Berkis to receive a private high school, college, and postgraduate
education. After she had worked in entry-level office jobs for about six years, she
enrolled in a graduate university program. But even after her degree and an
internship had allowed Berkis a high-end position as a certified public accountant, she could not afford a private education for the older of her two preschoolers. At times she could not even meet the mortgage payments for the new home
she and Amado had purchased in Los Rios—an up-and-coming middle-class
neighborhood also in SDO, a mere five minutes' drive from the poor community
of Herrera.

Gradually Berkis realized that her work situation was hopeless, despite her
education. On days she borrowed money to pay their mortgage—or when the
glaring reality of her "make-believe middle-class lifestyle" pierced her spirit—
Berkis talked with Amado about going to New York. She longed for the lifestyles
the women in her office enjoyed: gated homes with fancy SUVs or sedans, private schools for her children, and membership at a gym. More than anything,
Berkis dreamed of traveling and enjoying small escapes to tourist resorts. As she
put it to me one day when I asked what she expected of her education, "Por lo
menos, el lujo de decir que tome una pequeña vacación. ¡Aunque fuese en Boca
Chica!" (At least, the luxury of saying that we can take a family vacation. Even if
this meant at Boca Chica [the nearest public beach]!)

At thirty-eight, with ten years of work experience as a highly skilled professional, Berkis became resolute that New York would improve their lives forever.
During the first few minutes of our interview, when we spoke about her immigrant expectations, she quickly answered, "If my mother and my older sister, and
even my brother without a high school education, have made good money,
imagine myself!" She often repeated this to Amado when debts and other needs
stared her in the face. But her supervisor's fateful decision to promote a younger

and less experienced man, a new hire she had trained, "broke the camel's back," Berkis told me, nearly choking back tears, and ultimately spurred her migration.

That Friday evening Berkis felt the weight of her disillusionment. The long-held sadness about her career prospects led her to resolve leaving everything—a beloved husband of ten years; two small sons; a secure professional job; a newly purchased home; close friends; and extended kin who would guard her marriage and the "good upbringing" of her sons—for the unknown. On her way home, she practiced breaking the news to Amado. She was emphatic that New York City would change their lives forever, just as it had done for her semi-illiterate mother. Late that evening, after putting her two small sons to bed, Berkis sat on the edge of her bed to talk with Amado in "susurros" (a low voice) amid sobs. She spoke of her disillusionment with her job, which Amado had known about for years. She spoke of the limited chances of "becoming someone" or moving up in her profession owing to her age and her humble origins. She reminded Amado how hard it would be for a Black woman like her to find a better-salaried job were she to quit the one she had: "Tell me, Amado, who will hire me? At thirty, women are already too old for high-end jobs, especially Black women with high aspirations! Do you forget what it took for your sister to find work? People from the Ministry of Education needed to advocate for her! Imagine what would happen to me!"

Berkis reminded Amado of how her family in New York did not want her to migrate, but then, seeing her disillusionment, they insisted that New York City was the place where an educated woman like Berkis would thrive. She decided she would follow them. Her sadness at reaching this conclusion paled next to the dreams she had quietly harbored about New York for some time. "Wait, Amado!" she said. "Wait until I get there! If my sisters and brothers [in New York] bought houses here and if others with less education return loaded with jewelry and looking good, wait until I get there with my degree—you just wait and see!"

Within two weeks of Berkis and Amado's agreeing that she would go first, a corrugated envelope arrived from her family in New York City containing $5,000. Some of the money covered her visa application and medical exams, but the bulk of it was targeted for deposit in the couple's savings account to prove financial solvency beyond Berkis's letter of employment and payment stubs. Next to a visa application, she required a letter of good conduct from the police to confirm her lack of trouble with the law. Included in the visa interview were proof of the couple's mortgage payments, the title to Amado's taxicab, and a bank statement. These documents conveyed evidence of her family's solvency or middle-class status to the U.S. embassy, guaranteeing Berkis's incentive to return.

SDO has the largest share of women residents compared with the six other large municipalities in the national district, and while the average education of women in Berkis's age cohort (thirty-five to fifty-five) was a high school diploma, by 2010 SDO had the largest share attending college.[34] Additionally, this municipality is a major destination for women immigrating from other parts of the nation. Work lures many migrants to factories or industrial parks in Herrera and throughout the capital. More research is needed on the mechanisms that allow migrant women—and especially those of Indigenous or traditionally excluded racialized minorities—to obtain higher education or social mobility. Among Latin Americans in New York, the role of remittances and local development play a key role in both the access to education and middle-class mobility of contemporary Black and Indigenous minorities.

How does Berkis's story fit with the broader pattern of migration among educated women in this study? First, her migration is characteristic of educated women who lead in migration. She is also a Black woman in the Dominican Republic and the United States, two nations with long and sobering histories of social and institutional discrimination against Black and Indigenous minorities.[35] U.S. scholars ponder over why a majority Black or non-White nation would engage in racial discrimination against Black people. Centuries of interventions by European colonizers and by North American visiting elites, as well as a legacy of animosity and warfare against the predominantly Black neighboring nation of Haiti, explain some of this racialization historiography.[36] Dominican scholars concede that the triangulated history and influence that Europe, Haiti, and the United States have had on the Dominican Republic led to its citizens' socialization within a "Eurocentric" and a "negrophobic" culture, one that has led people to opt for a mixed-race or Indigenous ("Indio/a") identity.[37] This may explain why only 10 percent of Dominicans identify as Black and almost an equal share as White, while a majority opt for an in-between "Indian" identity, the way Berkis and Amado referred to each other, despite her ebony skin and his Afro-Caribbean phenotype. This in-between identity is also based on a spectrum of colors and phenotypes ranging from White to Black, denoting whether a person is a light- or dark-skinned Indio, and whether that person has a high or low social standing or class, dating back to the institution of the Casta System.[38] As a preeminent social stratification system based on biological and social markers, the Casta System functioned to stratify, separate, and control the much larger population of African slaves and Indigenous peoples by the smaller share of Criollos, or the descendants of the European elites.[39] Even though the end of a colonial period, independence, and modernization increased the integration and social mobility of Afro-descendants and Indigenous minorities in Latin America, research reveals that these groups continue to face the worst forms of inequality and discrimination.

ALEJANDRA: WOMEN WHO MIGRATE TO ESCAPE THE CONTROL OF MEN

As the plane lifted off, Alejandra closed her eyes and took a deep breath for the first time in a long while. Holding back tears, she promised God and la Virgen de la Altagracia, Our Lady of the Highest Grace, that if she made it to New York and got through immigration for the Dominican Republic and the United States, she would work so hard that her sons would never have to work in the *parcelas,* or wetlands, nor her daughter be forced into marriage or motherhood at age fifteen.

At forty-two, Alejandra had more than what many other women in her remote rice-growing village ever aspired to have: an extended and landowning family, a husband who provided for her and their children, a close-knit web of friends, a middle school education, and two years working in a multinational corporation factory, which took her away from her marital home a few days a week. Beyond her material capital, Alejandra's family also had racial capital as Whites in a mulatto or majority Black nation. They had been landowners and rice growers for generations—"everything that gives a woman security!" she said to me through dewy eyes during our interview in New York about a year after her arrival. So why did Alejandra choose to migrate?

Alejandra's migration extends an existing literature documenting how the migration of women is often driven by the need to escape a loveless marriage, an oppressive family, or even communities organized around men's lives and authority.[40] Women leading their family's migration play a key role in how their material and ideological remittances influence ideas about emancipation among family women left behind in the community of origin, and especially those who are able to achieve a higher education or work skills, as the case of Berkis—and now that of Alejandra—illustrates.

The "seed for migration" began growing in Alejandra's heart about a decade before her departure. In the apparent normalcy of her small village of Jabacao, the marriage and work aspirations of the young were shifting. Before the 1990s Jabacao had hardly been viable to outsiders, save for day laborers—mostly Haitians imported during the rice fields' planting or harvesting. Most people arrived by horse or on foot, given the few roads' ruggedness and the village's remote location in a valley between two mountains. The landowning and rice-growing families, and even the working poor, in Jabacao still traced their light skin and phenotype to Iberian ancestry. Despite most in her family having very white skin and sandy-blond hair, Alejandra and an older brother were exceptions: they had a mulatto or non-White phenotype, including tightly curled hair, full lips, and a wide nose bridge. This is why Alejandra's closest and younger sister, Julissa, used to call her "La negra de la casa" (the black one of the house), often as a term of endearment but during the skirmishes of their teen years as a final and egregious insult.

Women in Alejandra's family were among the village's first female migrants; all had left accompanying a spouse—except her youngest sister, who was pushed out by a failed marriage. Unlike her sisters, Alejandra went to New York to escape the oppression that marriage represented in her rural village. Since the age of fifteen she had envisioned traveling and meeting new people outside of Jabacao. She longed to have a job, to earn money and "become somebody," as she put it to me on the first day we met. She longed to escape the constant vigilance of other women and was especially determined to get away from her gossipy mother-in-law. A few months before Alejandra's departure, her mother-in-law started rumors about Alejandra cheating on her husband with a distant cousin while working intermittently at a sneaker factory on the periphery of Santo Domingo. Looking back, Alejandra shared—both in jest and with melancholy—that her mother-in-law had done her both an injustice and a big favor. She provided "the yellow canary that checked the dangerous mine tunnel" that was her marriage and her life in a small village.

Influencing her migration aspirations were Alejandra's sisters in New York City. The older one, Ana—also a middle sibling, like Alejandra—first tried her luck as a domestic in Spain, but then moved to New York prior to her European visa expiring. Five years earlier her youngest sister, Julissa, joined Ana in New York, who had guaranteed work with Ana's small maintenance crew. After a year of working night shifts, Julissa responded to her Dominican supervisor's advances and married him, despite a generational age difference of almost twenty years; it was Julissa's most viable option for regulating her undocumented status, as her tourist visa had already expired. Ana had also wedded an older man (twelve years her senior) in Jabacao, before the two of them migrated to New York. His stable construction job and her own night shift maintenance work allowed them to purchase a small home on Staten Island. Their largely African American and Puerto Rican community was mostly poor and working class, but this high concentration of Latinos, including immigrants from the West Indies, created enough of a client base that Julissa and Ana were able to open an informal hair salon in the basement of their private home.

Alejandra often received phone calls, letters, and photographs from her sisters in New York; they regaled her with stories about the ample work opportunities that New York City offered women. Once or twice a year Alejandra also received packages with fashionable jeans, sneakers, and the latest electronic games and toys for her kids. Along with these gifts, Alejandra coveted the cartons of Marlboro Lights cigarettes that Julissa always sent, a luxury that was elusive in Jabacao. Marrying at seventeen gave Alejandra legitimacy to smoke in front of men, including her family's elders. The men's stories about the challenges of the *cosecha* (the harvesting of the *parcelas*) and the sale and transport of "quintales[41] de arroz," her husband's control of the money, and her migrant sisters' stories about their work or business in New York City: all of these planted in Alejandra's heart the seed for migration.

Like her sisters, Alejandra married an older man (one who was ten years her senior). Tomás courted Alejandra when she was just fifteen; he asked her parents for her hand in marriage a day after her sixteenth birthday. Alejandra refused, but conceded when an accidental pregnancy followed a holiday night and a few rounds of beers with Tomás. As a wedding present, Alejandra's father gave his favorite middle daughter a piece of land and a few cows to make sure she could fend for herself, knowing her impertinent character and having his own premonitions about the nature of the marriage.

Tomás worked from dusk to dawn on the family's rice farm. As my grandmother would say, he was a man who supported his family "con el sudor de su frente" (with the sweat of his forehead). Tomás was a faithful husband and an old-fashioned provider; he was also a praiseworthy employer who worked on par with his workers, plowing and preparing the rice fields and tending the animals. On paydays he drank with friends or bet money on cockfights. Tomás did not want a divorce and promised he would wait for her—even if it took a long time. But Alejandra felt asphyxiated by her rough married life, toiling from morning to dusk, caring for four children, preparing meals on a charcoal stove and cleaning its hot ashes every morning and night, and tending to household animals and vegetable plots, all the while dealing with the gossip of her mother-in-law and her husband's imposing and arbitrary sexual demands, which resulted in his impregnating her five times. But what Alejandra resented most was his ultimate control of her life, their land and money.

Thus, early one morning when it was still dark, Alejandra left her home in the back seat of a *concho* (livery car) to supposedly get an X-ray at a clinic two hours away, having feigned a recurring muscle spasm in her lower back. Looking out from the back window of the car, she gazed at the river where she had once spent so many Sundays playing with her siblings and, more recently, with her children. Alejandra's stomach filled with trepidation as the car passed waves of moving rice sprigs in the fields where her father, brothers, husband, and now her oldest son toiled from dawn to dusk, their brown and golden backs bare to the sun, wet and with mud up to their hips. Alejandra clutched a small knapsack and reached for her fake passport and the several hundred-dollar bills her sisters had sent a few weeks earlier. As she boarded a plane destined for New York, her mind fixated on the small photograph of Patria, her youngest child and only daughter, that she carried in her wallet.

Until the mid-1990s, Jabacao, where Alejandra's family had lived for generations, was hardly known to outsiders—albeit located in a fertile and luscious valley in the northeastern Dominican Republic. Floods and perilous conditions on the area's only wooden bridge kept the village void of outside development or government investments, leaving the young deprived of a secondary education. Women worked mostly in the home or on family farms (though Alejandra prided herself that neither her mother nor her sisters had ever worked in the dirt). Young men often left in search of secondary or college education and for the better work and life opportunities they could find in touristic or urban areas.

But by 2008 the construction of a new highway, the Autopista Juan Pablo II, linked the southern coast of the Caribbean Sea to the northern coast of the Atlantic, reducing the time it took to get from Jabacao to the nation's capital from four to less than two hours by car. This highway gradually facilitated tourism to the area, with daily charter buses and private minivans transporting hordes of visitors to El Parque Nacional Los Haitises, a national park and major ecological landmark not too far from Alejandra's village. Such local development motivated the second husband of her youngest sister, Julissa, to purchase a sizable ranch-like house just a few blocks from Alejandra's home and make it into a hotel and a *gallera* (cockfighting place). The investment and the people it attracted brought new opportunities for Alejandra's husband and her brothers to also invest in similar small businesses. The opening of this small hotel and cockfighting enterprise also sowed new ideas in Alejandra's heart about the miracle of migration: a man with no land and no future, except that of his laboring hands could—after ten years in New York—buy large parcels of land and invest in two businesses back in his home village, thereby gaining the respect of his peers, elders, and of his much younger wife!

The opening of the Autopista not only reduced the travel time between the north and south but also eased women's migration away from rural communities ruled by men. Two years after the highway's completion, Alejandra boarded a commuter plane to New York. Thinking of her mother's warning that "no good woman would ever leave a good husband or their small children behind," Alejandra's departure represented a staggering transformation in her soul. When Alejandra shared her desire to join her sisters, her mother wearily consoled her: "Solo Dios sabe lo que él tiene para cada uno de tus hijos" (Only God knows what he has destined for your children). Without her mother's blessing, though, Alejandra could never have conceived of leaving. Unlike her sisters in New York, Alejandra left four children behind: Her oldest son, seventeen, already worked on the family's rice farm. Her two middle sons, ages fourteen and eleven, walked about a mile each day to school. Her only daughter, Patria—the youngest, at nine—attended a nearby elementary school. While her oldest son planned only on working on and inheriting the family farm, as his father and forefathers had done for generations, her middle son was fascinated by computers. After his aunts sent him a computer game from New York, he had desires to learn about graphic design and video production. Patria dreamed of becoming a nurse and of one day working in a large city hospital.

Where does Alejandra's story fit into the larger story of this chapter on the experiences of women who lead their migration? Scholars note that the Dominican migrant women of the 1990s were single mothers from rural areas; a good number first engaged in domestic migration, lured by low-wage jobs in the tourism and domestic sectors or in factories in urban areas.[42] In this regard, Alejandra's story represents those of more than one-third of the women in this study who come from rural areas and were married or had intact conjugal relation-ships. Many of these women migrate to seek economic or educational advance-ment, but many also migrate to escape the hackles of patriarchy. Alejandra's story also helps illustrate how local development contributes to the domestic and eventual international migration of family women. In a departure from much of the earlier scholarship on Dominican women's migration, Berkis's and Alejan-dra's stories suggest that Dominican migrant women from rural areas increas-ingly come from financially stable, landowning, or newly minted middle-class backgrounds after their families have migrated to urban or developing areas. New insights from national census files reveal that women are also leading the domestic migration in Mexico, as the case of Gloria illustrates next.

GLORIA: WOMEN WHO ACCOMPANY MEN

Gloria's story, like Alejandra's, demonstrates that larger contextual and house-hold factors lead women to migrate from rural to urban areas and then to the United States. Gloria's case is different from Alejandra's case insofar as eco-nomic advancement appears as a primary motivation for migration. Yet Gloria, like Alejandra, also migrated to escape the limited opportunities and delimited social lives that women face in small, rural communities.

Gloria grew up in Chila de La Sal, a small community in the Mexican state of Puebla that, since the 1990s, has attracted a good deal of domestic and interna-tional migration due to ecotourism. At age fifteen Gloria migrated to Santa Ana Chiautempan, a new destination for young people in search of work, higher edu-cation, or business ventures. Since the late nineteenth century—and fueled by President Porfirio Diaz's economic development through land reform—Santa Ana has been a magnet for international investors from Europe (mostly Spain) and the United States, as well as for local textile and wool industry barons. Since the early 2000s, the local economy has become diversified, including new wholesale and retail stores, co-owned since the 1960s by local factory owners, many of them transnational entrepreneurs living in the United States.[43]

The influx of investors and white-collar professionals has led to a diversity of local firms and development in Santa Ana Chiautempan. Some of the newcom-ers are national and international commercial banks like Bancomext and Scotia-bank. Migrant laborers from rural areas, mostly young, single women, come to meet the domestic and industrial maintenance needs of the new salaried gentry and of factory owners looking for cheap day laborers. Gloria, however, came to Santa Ana Chiautempan to work as a live-in domestic in the home of her *mad-rina* (godmother) and to seek an education.

Gloria had completed the eighth grade when she arrived in Santa Ana Chiau-tempan. When she graduated from middle school, her father asked her to help care for the animals and the harvesting of vegetables after her two brothers left to find work in Texas. Her godmother was recently widowed, without daughters or luck in retaining domestics, and it was suggested that Gloria could work for her. As Gloria told me, sort of mocking her *madrina's* complaints about her previous employees, "She says she never had luck with domestics, as no one is interested in working and living with her. The girls now are much more ambitious; many prefer factory work or to marry anyone simply to get their freedom or have someone send them dollars from the U.S."

Gloria's godmother believed young Mexican girls from rural or humble origins were no longer interested in domestic work given factory work's allure. This was a feeling shared by a handful of middle-class families and small business owners with whom I spoke informally during visits to the nearby Colegio de Tlaxcala, in the state of Tlaxcala, and Universidad Iberoamericana Puebla, in the state of Puebla, about two hours away. Gloria's mother allowed her to go to Santa Ana Chiautempan, and hoped that her daughter's relocation would offer her the opportunity to finish high school or find a good husband. Gloria herself had dreams about becoming a business owner or even a bank teller one day.

Separating from her parents at age fifteen left Gloria with a profound sense of loss and emotional dislocation, but it also fostered an unexpected sense of independence. The monthly wages she earned in late 1999—3,000 Mexican pesos per month (about US$100)—allowed Gloria to send money to her mother and her older sister. Gloria also determined that while working full-time she would complete her secondary education at a local vocational school that offered college preparatory training and certificates. More than anything, however, Gloria grieved leaving behind her boyfriend Antonio, who had courted her at the *plazita major* where her parents sold produce. As she recalled with bashful eyes yet a piquant smile, "He came to the plaza to buy food often, in the company of other young men. He would always stare at me. I knew from the first time, from the way he looked at me, that he had serious intentions!"

After starting evening classes in a vocational program in clerical work and bookkeeping, Gloria noticed that other girls interrupted their studies to help families with agricultural work or to care for younger siblings, just as Gloria had done. This was often the case in households where older brothers or fathers had emigrated. Sociologists Sean McKenzie and Cecilia Menjívar have documented similar findings regarding Honduran women who stay behind after the migration of spouses or conjugal partners: in the absence of men, many women perform both the domestic labor that is traditionally female and the heavy fieldwork that is traditionally male. McKenzie and Menjívar also find that when a male spouse or partner migrates, women eventually tend to migrate.[44] I find that the eventual migration of women—often educated daughters—happens in stages and involves the completion of higher education or engagement with wage employment. These experiences increase young women's independence from familial authority and an ability to fend for themselves, as Gloria's case will later reveal.

One night, following an invitation to enjoy some gorditas and churros in the park, Gloria sensed a new form of freedom: she realized she would have an hour of unsupervised time each school night, in between her three classes. "Me distraia al principio y no hacia los deberes" (I used to get distracted at first and could not concentrate on my work), she told me. The time allowed students to do group or individual work. Gloria opted instead to do her schoolwork at home; this gave her time to walk around the center of town, looking in store windows, listening to music coming from restaurants or small lounges, or treating herself to a small snack or an agua fresca. As she described it to me, "I realized I enjoyed just being on my own! In my village, I was never allowed to venture far from our house alone, without the company of my brothers—never at night." Her night school and the possibilities her education and small wages represented offered Gloria a taste of independence she had never before savored nor even imagined.

During the four years that Gloria worked in Santa Ana Chiautempan she came to see Antonio more regularly. He commuted by bus from San Francisco, a town in northern Puebla where the largest shares of Indigenous minorities historically have been concentrated.[45] Antonio worked alongside his father and siblings; his family sold and distributed agricultural products and livestock feed in a wooden shack near the center of town. After a year of long-distance courting, Antonio's intermittent visits to her night school, and love letters, Gloria decided that he would be an excellent life companion deserving of her *confianza* (trust) and *respecto* (respect).[46] They planned on eloping, but pregnancy pushed Antonio's decision to migrate. Gloria would stay behind, helping with "homework" jobs, such as tanning leather, that men in Antonio's family brought home for the women to finish—now including Gloria.

After taking Gloria as his common-law wife and relocating her to his parents' home, Antonio promised her father that he would go work for a few months in the United States and save the money to give his new wife a proper wedding and the home that she and their future child deserved. After three years of working as a dishwasher in an Italian restaurant in Chicago, Antonio came back for Gloria and their three-year-old son. A week later they reached the United States with the help of a coyote, a person who smuggles immigrants across the border.

When I first met Gloria and Antonio, they were not yet legally married. When asked about marriage, she explained that it was not their overriding goal; rather, "paying the coyote and other loans Antonio acquired to bring me here was a main priority." When she tried to guess my thoughts after noticing my silence, Gloria smiled, lowering her gaze and then adding, "I would prefer to wait until we return to Mexico, which is where being married counts! Besides, Antonio promised my family a *real wedding*." I met Gloria during the summer of 2003, during the first stage of my research. She was now twenty-four years old and a mother of two small children: a girl about three years old and a boy about seven.

Her basement apartment home was a few blocks away from the legendary ethnic White neighborhood of Mott Haven in the Bronx, known as Little Italy.

Gloria's dark brown skin, black hair, and Indigenous Mesoamerican phenotype set her apart from other South Bronx Latinos, who were mostly Afro-Caribbean from the Dominican Republic and the West Indies, though there was also a diminishing share of brown- and light-skinned Puerto Ricans. Most Mexicans arriving in New York City from the mid-1990s on came from the poorest states in the Mixteca Baja, the southern areas of Mexico with a history of Indigenous concentration, as Robert Smith's pioneering longitudinal research in New York City documents.[47] Yet Gloria did not consider her immigration to be motivated by poverty back in Mexico; her father and extended family had many landholdings and two small businesses in Chila de La Sal. As she explained to me, "Me vine porque me junte con Antonio porque quede embarazada. ¡Y, porque queria trabajar y salir adelante!" (I came [to New York] because I coupled with Antonio and got pregnant. And because I too wanted to work and get ahead!) While Gloria was pushed to migrate because her husband failed to provide the type of wedding and household goods she expected, she also migrated to improve her opportunities for work and life, as well as her education. Antonio also harbored higher aspirations. New York City had offered his older brother and a few cousins opportunities to save and to then build two homes back in Mexico. Antonio expected to do this, at least, for Gloria and their budding new family. What is evident from Gloria's case is that many women who immigrate internationally first engage in domestic migration. Many of these women are attracted to urban areas undergoing fast demographic and economic transformation; in the case of Santa Ana Chiautempan, this involved local development in the form of industry and tourism.

What distinguishes the premigration experiences of women who lead their migration from those who, like Gloria, accompany men? My interviews suggest that close to one-half of women from the Dominican Republic and one-third from Mexico lead their migration or arrive without a spouse (see table 1.1 in chapter 1). Yet women from rural or provincial areas in Mexico, unlike those from the Dominican Republic, frequently migrate with spouses or follow them to the United States. And migrant women from rural areas tend to be younger. Another factor that distinguishes the two groups is age at migration. As table 1.1 in chapter 1 illustrates, Mexican women migrate at a younger age than Dominicans. Of the Mexican women participating in the first phase of this study, 55 percent were between the ages of eighteen and twenty-eight at the time of their migration, whereas over 60 percent of the Dominican women were twenty-nine or older. About one-half of Dominican women, but less than one-third of Mexican women, said they had decided to migrate, as opposed to their spouse or other family members prompting their migration, as documented by Grasmuck and Pessar and other scholars among earlier migrant waves. Women with at least twelve years of education, originating from urban centers, or who are single mothers or the main providers for their households often lead their own and then their families' migration.

Additional insights from Dominican and Mexican national censuses suggest that Mexican women increasingly dominate rural-to-urban domestic migration.[48] Both the qualitative and census data reveal that Mexican women migrate domestically from the same states and municipalities from which men have traditionally led international migration to the United States. Many of these young female migrants, like Gloria, migrate from rural areas into developing urban areas, often in search of work, higher education, or both. Qualitative and quantitative insights suggest that the education these women receive is often paid for by remittances, usually from female relatives abroad. This then explains why, for women who lead their migration alone, many import at least a high school and more frequently a college or professional university education. Finally, the qualitative data, including interviews and focus groups in the two sending communities and in New York City, helps document that most women who lead their migration, irrespective of education or work experience, grew up in homes with a migrant legacy. Mexican migration, until recently, has been historically led by men. On the contrary, the migration of educated Dominican women often takes place in households with a history of migrant women.

MARITZA: WOMEN WHO MARRY TO MIGRATE

Maritza arrived in New York City with her husband Diogenes, a naturalized U.S. citizen thirty years her senior. Diogenes had lived in New York City for twenty-five years before marrying Maritza. In the early 1970s his mother sponsored him and three other siblings; his family emigrated from Santiago, the largest and second industrialized province in the Dominican Republic, when he was in his mid-twenties. Diogenes migrated with a business degree from a private Jesuit university in Santiago; he and Maritza also imported racial capital—light skin and a southern European, Iberian, phenotype. As I conceptualized in chapter 1 and have illustrated in Berkis's and Alejandra's case studies in this chapter, Maritza's non-Black skin and phenotype are highly valued in most of Latin America and in the Dominican Republic, a non-White nation. In large part the valuation of White skin is due to an anti-Black socialization and history dating back to the time of slavery and to centuries-old animosity with Haiti, also a Black nation with whom the Dominican Republic shares geographical territory and a common history of nationhood formation, colonization, and independence.[49]

After five years of factory work, Diogenes opened a small jewelry store in the Manhattan neighborhood of Washington Heights with a loan from a brother. He handled the business alone until he converted the store into a pawn shop. This increased his clientele as well as his revenues, allowing Diogenes to hire a distant cousin as an assistant to work the late evening and weekend shifts. By the time Maritza arrived, Diogenes had sold the store due to escalating rent, opting instead to work from home. But soon, realizing Maritza's desires for education and wanting to raise a family of their own, Diogenes found a full-time job as a security guard with a large storage company in Yonkers, a new destination for Dominicans in the 1980s and 1990s.

Maritza grew up in Rio San Juan, a prominent agricultural town in the province of Espaillat in the northwestern Dominican Republic. Maritza came from a home that included the love and protection of two older siblings, two living grandmothers, and an extended paternal and maternal line of kin. Maritza's family was traditional, her father the main head of the household and sole provider. By the time Maritza came of age, her mother had visited New York a few times, trying her luck working in factory jobs with other close female relatives. Maritza explained to me that her mother worked not because she needed the money but for the "wage-earning experience." As Maritza put it, "Para poder decir, 'Aqui esta. ¡Yo tambien puedo!'" (As an old saying goes, "Here it is. I too can [provide]!") Maritza was the second-youngest child, the only girl from her father's second marriage with a woman ten years his junior. By the time Maritza was born, her father had already been married once and fathered three children, two boys and a girl. He then left his wife for Maritza's mother.

Maritza attended a small private school in the main urban center of Rio San Juan. As the younger of two girls, she remembers being pampered by her father and half-brothers. She was also quite pampered by her distant maternal grandmother, who often brought her gifts from New York. Maritza's grandmother was her hero. After Maritza's father's health declined and income from his land holdings would no longer make ends meet, her grandmother paid, without hesitation, for Maritza's college education. Maritza was the first girl in three generations to complete college, as her older paternal sister had married and soon migrated to New York with her husband. Her grandmother and mother hoped Maritza would become a professional, but Maritza's heart remained set on the fashion and hair industries; at seventeen she dreamed of being a top hair and makeup artist in a famous salon. She also imagined life as an airline flight attendant—one who always looked beautiful and professional and had the freedom to travel, unguarded by men.

Maritza's story illustrates the new faces and geographies of women-led migration, precisely in areas where men originally led migration. Maritza's long line of kin had lived for generations in Espaillat, the tenth-largest province and one that, since colonial times, has enjoyed a reputation as a rich agricultural and cattle farming area in the El Cibao region. Due to the region's mountainous and isolated geography, as well as to centuries-old agricultural and livestock economies first begun by European colonists, much lower rates of miscegenation took place between White colonizers and imported slaves.[50] Their isolated existence led many Criollos from El Cibao, like Maritza and Diogenes, to migrate to New York in the 1970s and 1980s and to take advantage of the racial capital of their light skin and phenotype in the search for housing, work, and even small businesses in New York City.[51]

Scholars have argued that, following independence from Europe, a major modernization strategy of ruling elites in Latin America has been to buy White-ness or import European immigrants to incite development and "improve the race."[52] This contributed to European elites and their mixed-race descendants, including Criollos, deriving economic advantages from the control of land hold-ings and, increasingly, globalized tourist industries.[53] But for rural-born small landowners like Maritza's family, this meant gradual pressure to sell their lands to investors, many of whom tend to target commercialized agricultural production for international exports.[54] Since the 1960s this economic restructuring had led to the exodus of young men like Maritza's brothers from rural areas, and increas-ingly since the 1990s the migration of young, educated women in search of better work and educational opportunities, as Maritza's story reveals.

Although Maritza found a job at a luxury hotel before deciding to emigrate, her two older brothers did not fare so well. By the age of eighteen both had moved away from Rio San Juan—the elder to attend a private university in San-tiago, and the younger to work as part owner and part driver for a taxi company for which his father was a franchisee. Yet at the end of his first semester, Maritza's oldest brother found himself discouraged and overburdened in combining study and work as a front desk computer technician at a new resort. During the Easter break, Semana Santa, he met Julianna at a party, a tourist who was attending the wedding of her Dominican-born college roommate in Santiago. After a few months of long-distance romance, Maritza's brother sought a visa to visit New York. There he dated Julianna for about six months before they decided to live together and marry. Julianna, a technology-savvy Philippine American woman from Claremont, New Jersey, had a college degree in business management. Maritza's grandmother's and mother's traveling narratives of their intermittent migration to work in New York City, and now her brother's marriage to an Amer-ican woman, increased Maritza's resolution to migrate to New York City in search of a better life.

Before Maritza graduated from college, and two years before she left for New York, a female cousin helped her land a job in a luxury hotel in Puerto Plata, in the northeastern Dominican Republic. One of the oldest tourist resort towns in the nation, Puerto Plata was undergoing massive infrastructural and economic growth.[55] Maritza first worked in the hotel's beach café area, where she prepared food for the buffet; soon she was promoted to waiting on clients, mostly Euro-pean and North American guests, at the beach café and in the pool area. Occa-sionally she waited on a minority of native-born, Dominican middle-class landowning villagers who were visiting for family reasons, for business, or on holiday, including expatriates. She frequently met Dominicans living in New York City, colloquially known as Dominican-Yorks, who, thanks to New York factory wages, could indulge in luxuries denied to their class for generations. Maritza disliked their rudeness and attitude; she complained to me, "¡Pues se creen mejores que nadie!" (They think they are better than everybody!) Yet, Maritza also felt a different sense of resentment serving these co-ethnics, many of whom had lower education and less racial capital. She had also mentioned during our interview that her cousin who worked in the hotel's main administration and was now a supervisor had shared that Maritza's "good work" and "good looks" (meaning, her youth, education, and white skin) would help her move fast in the industry. "What this hotel and many others in the area want is for attractive workers to attract clients!"

After six months at the hotel's beach café, Maritza met Diogenes, a middle-age Dominican York who admired her from their first encounter. She describes how, when they first met, Diogenes called her "blondie," a name that her intimate school friends also called her. He would, for example, say, "¡Oye, Rubia, dame otra rubia, por favor!" (Hey, blondie, give me another blond beer, please!) After a year of phone calls and Diogenes's trips to the Dominican Republic to nurse their fast-paced long-distance romance, he proposed marriage. As Maritza explained to me, "I told him, What? You want to marry me? I thought of never marrying!" In the midst of nervous laughter, she added, "The first thing I did was call my mother. I could not believe it because she always told me that unless I changed my aggressive attitude and stopped hanging out in nightclubs or working in a bar, I would never find a decent man."

Although her mother was in favor of the union, her father had reservations about Maritza marrying a man almost thirty years her senior—closer to her father's age. The field data shows that, on average, fewer than three of ten young women who work in resorts and develop intimate relations with foreign clients marry them. Thus it is not surprising that Maritza recalled that she felt that "meeting and marrying Diogenes was a gift from God." A year from the day after Diogenes proposed, Maritza arrived in New York, accompanied by her legal husband. As Maritza's case and the case of Gloria earlier in this chapter illustrate, the rural-to-urban domestic migration of women often leads to international migration. It also shows that, typically, young women from rural areas often migrate in search of better work or educational opportunities, but also (and often) following their marital union with a foreign spouse or conjugal partner—frequently an older man who himself has a history of migration.

Maritza's migration also reveals that local development, including remittances, increases women's access to education and social mobility, including marriage, in what scholars conceptualize as the crossing of spatial, class, and racial boundaries.[56] I find that the crossing of spatial and social boundaries often lead women to engage in higher education, wage-earning work, and—

ultimately—international migration. This is evident in Maritza's trajectory: moving from a rural area to an urban resort town to work and study, finding a job at a hotel in a well-known tourist resort town, marrying an international migrant, and, finally, migrating to New York City. Based on conversations with Maritza and other respondents who worked in resorts, and also based on my own observations of the class and racial stratification of service workers at resorts that I have frequented during the past decade, I argue that the gender, class, and racial capital imported by migrants (as described in chapters 1, 4, and 5)—or what Pierre Bourdieu calls "cultural capital"—often increases the ability of young women like Maritza to cross class, racial, and ultimately geographic boundaries.[57] I have also observed that individuals with at least a high school diploma, basic English skills, and light or white skin color and a mix of European or non-African phenotype are assigned to functions with more direct access to hotel guests or clients, or placed in supervisory positions, as the case of Maritza exemplifies.

In the Dominican Republic, where over 85 percent of the population is of Black or Afro-descendant mixed race,[58] Maritza's European phenotype and white skin—her racial capital—increased both her work and marriage opportunities. In my many interviews and conversations with Maritza she explained how, early on, she became aware of how other children favored her in school because of her wavy blond hair.[59] As she explained in our first interview, "They—and later other people—always wanted to know if the color was real. They always called me blondie, or gringa, in school, and I always thought they were so funny! They always thought I was a *gringa* [female gringo]!" Today, at the hotel, most of her work peers and clients compliment her porcelain skin, despite her work in the Caribbean sun. And indeed, Maritza's Whiteness is what Diogenes celebrated when he first noticed her as a client.

How does Maritza's social mobility and migration story relate to the average experience of women's social mobility and migration in this study? Mobility in a high-end tourist resort usually entails work that requires some level of interaction with clients, as is true for domestics, restaurant workers, and in the entertainment, beauty, and sex industries. Depending on gender, age, and human and racial capital, many service workers in the tourism sector are often asked to assume dual roles—for example, as daytime hostesses and as nightclub entertainers. This can also include double duty both day and night in some form of entertainment and sex work. These functions increase the permeability of racial and class boundaries and the social mobility of workers, despite exploitation. Often Black workers—even the college educated—are assigned "backstage" office and administration positions, booking international sales and corporate/business events, where they are less likely to interact with clients and guests directly. But since completing the research for this book in 2016, I have observed that in some high-end resorts in the Dominican Republic, highly educated Black

Dominicans, often of Haitian descent or parentage, occupy "front-stage" supervisory positions requiring English- and French-language skills. These observations deserve further research to understand if these positions lead educated Black workers, and especially Haitians, to experience mobility or even the same level of salary compensation and benefits as other Black Dominican workers. For the most part, the higher the hotel's rank, the less porous the boundaries of class, gender, and skin color are. This is further discussed in chapters 5 and 6.

My qualitative insights suggest that a handful of my Dominican women respondents—five of forty-six—had a combination of white or light skin and non-Black phenotype, one that made them "pass" as ethnic Whites in New York City. Among Mexicans, the share was a bit higher, with eight of forty-four women having light skin due to being Mestizo (the mix of Indigenous and European phenotypes). In terms of work experience, the insights show that more than half of light-skinned respondents among both ethnic groups had worked in "front-stage" positions.[60] These service jobs often enable workers to closely interact with and get to know the clientele, improving the odds of building networks and of obtaining information and resources that lead to crossing class and racial boundaries or increased mobility, in both the sending and the new, host society—especially among those importing middle-class social and human capital. This analysis is further discussed in chapters 5–7.

MAGDALENA: WHEN WOMEN COME LAST

After nine months in a trailer camp—with intermittently available recycled water, exposure to pesticides (which Magdalena blamed for her daughter Julia's asthma and frequent bouts of whooping cough), and twelve-hour outdoor work shifts that turned her light skin a few shades darker (as Magdalena's mother joked, "¡Magda, pareces una pobre prieta!" [Magda, you look like a poor Black person!])—Magdalena threatened to leave Orlando, her husband of almost a decade, if he did not do something to change their lives. Three weeks later, on a sweltering late August evening, Orlando moved his small family by taking a bus from Pasadena, California, to White Plains, New York, the largest business hub and commercial city in Westchester County, New York, less than thirty miles from Manhattan. A paternal cousin had offered the small room he had rented for close to a decade to Orlando and his small family for free while Orlando found work and a permanent place to live.

Magdalena, like Berkis, considered herself a proud new member of the Mexican urban middle class. However, while Berkis led her and her family's migration from the Dominican Republic to New York, Magdalena followed her husband from Mexico City to California and then to New York. While Berkis had married a less educated man, Magdalena's husband held a similar level of education and work experience. Before migrating to the United States, Magdalena and her husband both held low-level, pink-collar, supervisory jobs within the large municipality of Nezahualcóyotl, a rapidly transforming *municipio* (municipality) in the state of Mexico that shares contiguous borders with Mexico City.

When Magdalena was an adolescent, her family migrated from a small village in Puebla to Nezahualcóyotl, or Ciudad Neza, as it is colloquially known. Both her father's and mother's ancestors hailed from San Francisco, a small village in northwestern Puebla, one of the towns with a large concentration of an Indigenous ethnic minority, the Nahua people. Magdalena's father had decided to migrate to Ciudad Neza in order to improve his children's educational opportunities.[61] And, as the only girl and the youngest of three siblings, Magdalena benefited the most from her family's domestic migration, as this chapter and chapter 4 will reveal. This rural migration is now increasingly led by women. Local development and access to education then mediate the secondary— international—migration of these now-educated women. Many of these women are of Indigenous origin and, increasingly, of Mestizo or mixed Indigenous and European progeny, and thus migrate importing both a higher education and racial capital to the United States.

Nezahualcóyotl is one of the largest and most diverse municipalities in the Distrito Federal (Federal District) that surrounds Mexico City. Established in 1963, Ciudad Neza sits within the *municipio* of Nezahualcóyotl, and the *municipio* oversees 111 *colonias* (neighborhoods). In the 1970s, the local government invested in Ciudad Neza's infrastructure and land regulations. In the 1980s, the city's leading administrative unit began major developments, including the redistricting and renaming of the *colonias*. And, since the 1990s, hospitals, municipal offices, schools, libraries, cultural centers, a sports facility, and new housing complexes have attracted a burgeoning middle class, established mostly by public service employment.[62]

Local and international investments have fueled the city's economic boom; many local investors are venture capitalists, such as Carlos Slim Helú, one of the richest men in the world. The boom in Ciudad Neza is most evident in its new commercial strips, shopping malls, and housing complexes. For example, part of a landfill in the Xochiaca area (declared the largest dump in the world by the World Bank)[63] has been transformed into a sports facility, a botanical garden, universities, and government offices. This development spurred employment and attracted migrant workers—mostly women in food service, retail work, and domestic work, serving as a first line of contact and support for visitors, students, and residents.

By 1995 the city's population had grown beyond one million. However, between 2000 and 2010 the population of its larger *municipio*, Nezahualcóyotl, dropped by 10 percent or from 1.2 to 1.1 million. Notably, while the city's overall population dropped, the population of women grew, driven by people who had lived in other municipalities and regions five years prior to a study conducted by the Mexican government's census. Migrant women, it appears, began leading the domestic immigration from the nation's interior into urban areas like Nezahualcóyotl.[64] In 2010, one-third of the population of Nezahualcóyotl held a high school degree, with women surpassing men by 9 percent. By then, 11% of the population had completed a university degree. Among these, a 1% differential between men and women significantly lowers the gender gap in higher education, which has traditionally favored men over women in Mexico.[65]

Before migrating, Orlando worked for nearly five years as a low-level manager in a printing shop near the center of Ciudad Neza. With a bit of luck, an associate's degree from a vocational college, and a maternal uncle's political ties, Magdalena secured a job as an office assistant. This was at the Tax and Revenue Office in the *cabezera municipal* (municipal seat) of Nezahualcóyotl, the second-largest municipality in the state of Mexico. Magdalena enjoyed job security and seemed to have prospects for professional advancement. As part of their new middle-class lifestyle, Magdalena and Orlando used their entire savings to purchase a condominium close to Orlando's work. The new development, owned by foreign-born American and Mexican investors in the United States, was part of a public housing experiment near the Xochiaca area, designed in the early 1990s to attract a burgeoning Mexican middle class to Ciudad Neza. It had also transformed what had once been a landfill area into a mix of residential and commercial facilities, including five condominium facilities built into modern duplex row houses.

Annexed to a large and modern shopping mall, the new housing complex included a public parking area, a gym, an array of fast-food restaurants, and a small indoor lounging and garden area that included a play space for children. According to Orlando's informal report (as he sat during the first interview with Magdalena), many of the new homeowners in the housing complex owed their education and social mobility to public jobs and government relations, but also to remittances from immigrant families.

Buying a condominium not far from a growing commercial area or private Catholic schools brought great joy to Magdalena, as well as high expectations for their young daughter Julia's education. They also hoped to raise a second child in their new home. As Magdalena explained in an interview, "I want Julia to have the best education, maybe become a doctor! As a child, my mother and I always told her she would make a fine doctor." With her voice breaking, Magdalena described the efforts she and Orlando had made to buy the condominium and to place Julia in a very good Catholic school.

Yet financial strains appeared once Orlando lost his job. Their mortgage went three months into arrears, and the bank threatened foreclosure. After repeated calls from the bank, Orlando borrowed money from his father to get the mortgage up to date and cover the cost of a coyote for his "crossover" to California. He decided to leave Magdalena and their small daughter behind. The separation, planned for one year, turned into three. After noticing infrequent phone calls and the diminished remittances Orlando sent back, Magdalena was more worried about the state of her marriage affairs than saving her home. Her mother urged her to consider joining her husband in the United States as soon as possible, cautioning, "If you don't go, Magda, you might lose not only your home but also the father of your child!"

Following her thirty-second birthday, and after a week traveling on foot, another week by bus, and a few days inside a truck, Magdalena and her seven-year-old daughter crossed the Mexican-U.S. border. Then, with the help of a third coyote, mother and daughter were bused to Pasadena. At the overwhelming bus terminal, Orlando waited impatiently for two days, nervous about their possible apprehension and safety. He had not eaten, save one gordita, since leaving the rural campsite where he lived and worked. For the past three years Orlando had worked on an orange farm in Pasadena, sharing a room with two male cousins in an isolated farming community of about fifty trailer homes. Orlando initially planned to work one year, maybe two, to pay the mortgage arrears and other debts, and then to go back home to Mexico. But by the time Magdalena joined him, these dreams had evaporated. They had had no choice but to rent out their condominium to save it from foreclosure by the bank.

Beyond the distinct family and economic pressures pushing Magdalena to migrate to New York, how does her immigration story relate to the experiences of other educated migrant women in this study? My interview insights reveal that upon arrival in New York, close to an aggregate 40 percent of Dominican and Mexican women migrate with at least nine years of education. Twenty-one percent have completed twelve or more years of school. In addition, international census data from the Dominican Republic shows that by 2010 the share of people migrating with a college degree was twice as high for Dominicans than for Mexicans.[66] In recent decades, the Dominican and Mexican migrant groups continue to increase in diversity, as more individuals import a tertiary or higher education and have origins in urban and industrial centers in Mexico or other nations in Latin America and the Caribbean.[67]

As the case of Magdalena reveals, since the 1980s, economic development and gentrification in Ciudad Neza led to the creation of new jobs but also the erosion of traditional work niches where most men predominated. Some men migrated because their domestic immigration and access to education, or even their new membership in the middle class, did not guarantee access to the opportunities available to the Mexican established middle class. This was the case for Orlando. Before crossing the Mexican-U.S. border as an undocumented migrant, Orlando worked at a printing shop. He lost his job when his employer could no longer afford to pay him, as hikes in the company's rent in Ciudad Neza, where it had operated for close to twenty years, required it to downsize. Demographic reports about Ciudad Neza's fast-paced development and social transformation reveal that gentrification and the higher costs of living have pushed members of households in Ciudad Neza's new middle class to migrate to the United States.[68] Since the 1980s, urban-based Mexican-U.S. immigration increased at a much faster pace compared with the earlier pattern of rural-based migration from traditional sending states, like Guerrero and Puebla.[69] This migration stream, according to both qualitative and census data, increasingly includes women, many of whom are from Indigenous and humble origins who join the middle class due to their families' prior migration to urban areas or remittances flows. Since the 1990s, many of these women who migrate from Mexico to New York City import an education.

CHAPTER SUMMARY

This chapter reveals that immigration from the Dominican Republic and Mexico is increasingly feminized and originates in new migrant geographies, in rural and urban sectors, with the latter undergoing fast development and demographic transitions. This migration includes a good share of women who import a middle-class status. Earlier literature has argued that economic and emotional desperations push women to migrate. Spousal and governmental abandonment (which deprives single mothers and the poor of public aid) pushes women with low levels of human capital to migrate. Many of the women that Ramona Hernández and Nancy López studied in the Dominican Republic in the 1980s and early 1990s came from rural areas, often embarking on perilous migration, such as on makeshift *yolas* (open raft boats), and sometimes even being forced to engage in temporary sex work to finance their costly undocumented migration.[70] The present study finds that these feminized migrant streams also include women who import a tertiary education or who are part of a growing, vulnerable Latin America middle class, as Hugo Ñopo argues.[71] This chapter has identified the faces and places of origin of some of the members of this new and vulnerable middle class in Latin America that—despite continued economic growth—lives on the margins of society and is ultimately forced to migrate, as the cases of highly qualified Afro-Caribbean Dominican professionals like Berkis and skilled, middle-class, Indigenous Mexican women like Magdalena illustrate. The intergenerational vulnerabilities that push ethnoracial minorities to migrate from Black nations like the Dominican Republic deserve further research.

Ultimately this chapter demonstrates that households with a legacy of female-led migration often fuel the migration of educated daughters and that of other women in the family.[72] Similarly, how education increases the social mobility of historically excluded Indigenous minorities in Mexico, and especially women, should be at the center of international migration and race scholarship. Mexican women, mostly of Indigenous phenotype but also those of Mestizo ancestry, like Magdalena, import higher levels of education than women among earlier cohorts. Many of these educated women lead their migration, first from interior rural or semirural villages and *municipios* in peripheral, urbanizing areas of Mexico's state. The increasing number of female migration may be explained by the new reliance of families on women's labor as the opportunities for men in agricultural work dwindle, but they may also be due to local government's targeted investments in their education. The qualitative and quantitative census data show that, since the 1990s, growing shares of women have attained a tertiary education, as the case of women in the municipio of Nezahualcoyotl earlier reveals.

The findings also attest to the key role of women's remittances in the increasing access to education among historically marginalized and racialized groups in the Dominican Republic and Mexico. Whereas higher education decreases the odds of male migration, for women it increases those odds.[73] A higher probability of employment also decreases the probability of female migration: in the case of highly educated Mexican women, the tendency has been for them to follow their professional spouses and partners in search of work in the United States and abroad, though they often experience downward mobility, unable to transfer their highly coveted education into similar professional work.[74] For Dominicans, the tendency has been for women to lead the migration, often leaving husbands of much lower education or social class behind for a later, often thwarted, reunification in New York, as Berkis's case illustrates.

Finally, gender and migration scholarship documents that women left behind in the community of origin do not gain much autonomy because absent spouses or conjugal partners maintain control of both the household and remittances sent from afar. Yet these studies took as their main premise the reproduction of patriarchy in the absence of men or in men leading the migration. Shifting the lens of analysis, I find that in households with a legacy of women-led migration, women are the main senders and beneficiaries of remittances. Remittances increase their education and alter their values about marriage and patriarchal ideologies. In addition, my earlier research reveals that undocumented migrants, especially women, tend to send remittances more frequently than migrants with legalized status.[75] An immigrant status may affect the control men can exert on women left behind or the money they send as remittances. The contributions of undocumented migrants and those of women to the community of origin have not been adequately explored, but this chapter suggests their importance.

Overall, the qualitative insights reveal that migration offers women new forms of freedom from the control and authority of males, substantiating the leading hypothesis of sociologist Pierrette Hondagneu-Sotelo that migration for women represents a rejection of patriarchal control or suppression within the family.[76] Indeed, the findings of this chapter reveal this to often be the case among women with low levels of education; yet, for highly educated women, labor market restraints present another form of oppression, increasing their experiences of intersectional inequality. These multiple levels of inequality push women to migrate, as many face a glass ceiling or are not able to transfer their education into gainful, professional work, as chapter 5 further documents. This chapter portrays the causes of migration for middle-class women who are also members of racial and ethnic minorities in Latin America, supporting the earlier works by Cecilia Menjívar, who finds that many Indigenous and Ladin women in Guatemala and Honduras, irrespective of education or social class, are also victims of institutionalized violence and sexual oppression.[77] How educated women cope with new forms of racialization or with the inferior status they are imputed in Latin America or the United States requires new forms of analytical schemas.

3 · THE NEW SPACES AND FACES OF IMMIGRANT NEIGHBORHOODS IN NEW YORK CITY

From the 1930s to the 1990s, African Americans mainly populated the New York City neighborhood of Harlem. But by the 1990s Latinos composed the second-largest population,[1] comprising especially Puerto Ricans in El Barrio in East Harlem.[2] Since the turn of the twenty-first century, immigrants from Africa, Asia, the Caribbean, and Mexico have dramatically altered the ethnoracial tapestry of this legendary African American neighborhood. Demographic shifts and economic redevelopment also brought the return of a young and professional White middle class, increasing the housing displacement of African American and Latino residents into poorer areas of the city. Notably, the arrival of new immigrants contributes to the replenishment of Harlem's Black and Brown population but also complicates the process of gentrification, one that until now has been explained mainly by a focus on the White middle class. Yet the arrival of Dominican and Mexican immigrants, as well as other Black and Brown immigrants importing a good education or equivalent business skills, also contributes to the gentrification and revival of inner-city neighborhoods like Harlem. Migration and gentrification also have contributed to the creation of new patterns of inequality and racial and class divides between older and recent cohorts of Black and Latino residents.

Ethnographic insights illustrate the settlement patterns of Dominican and Mexican immigrants from earlier and recent cohorts. Insights from interviews, ethnography, and census data portray the overlapping yet distinct spatial integration experiences of Dominican and Mexican families and the structure and nature of the networks that facilitate both the settlement and work and housing arrangements. The findings invite a reflection about the challenges faced by Black and Brown immigrants, including the undocumented, in neighborhoods undergoing rapid gentrification. They also invite the creation of new theoretical models on the contributions that non-White immigrants—especially those in the emerging middle class—make to the economic and cultural revival of poor inner-city neighborhoods.

BLACK AND BROWN LATINO IMMIGRANTS AND GENTRIFICATION

When I first met Berkis and Magdalena, both women lived on the impoverished periphery of Harlem. Berkis lived in West Central Harlem, at the poorest north-ernmost blocks of Hamilton Heights and the southernmost tip of Washington Heights, an area that is known as the home of Manhattan's Dominican commu-nity. Magdalena lived in El Barrio, the legendary community for Puerto Ricans, just a few blocks south of 125th Street and Park Avenue.[3]

Near Magdalena's East Harlem home, rows of ethnic delicatessens, low-end restaurants, takeout establishments, and fast-food joints traditionally owned by Black and Puerto Rican entrepreneurs were by 2010 owned by ethnic White investors, most of them foreign born. Some of these old-fashioned local ethnic eateries gradually transformed into panethnic establishments, with exotic decor designed to attract a professional class, including tourists from outside the neigh-borhood. Before their transformation, two small restaurants, El Aguila Taqueria and Caribbean Cuchifrito, catered mostly to African American and Puerto Rican residents; outsiders were limited to construction workers or taxi drivers en route to either LaGuardia Airport or one of two local hospitals servicing mostly the working poor.

By 2016, many Latino places in East Harlem already bore Pan-Latino names such as Camaradas, El Kallejon, and Lupita, attracting a mixed crowd of young, native-born White professionals and immigrant youth whose college education allowed them to reclaim a space in Harlem. These Black and Latino millennials play a central role in the economic awakening and cultural diversification of historically racialized inner-city neighborhoods. This is the case in Astoria and Long Island City in Queens, and the Belmont and Mott Haven neighborhoods in the Bronx. This is also the case of Bushwick, Dumbo, and Williamsburg in Brooklyn, where many members of my mother's family settled in the 1970s. In Magdalena's East Harlem neighborhood, the Black and Hispanic population's shares, while still the largest, decreased between 2000 and 2018 (from 34.9 percent to 27.3 percent and from 52 percent to 46.5 percent, respectively) while that for Whites steadily rose (from 7.3 percent to 16.1 percent).[4]

Harlem's socioeconomic transformation has depended on the arrival of local developers and an inexpensive immigrant labor force, mostly comprising "in-between" non-White and non-Black immigrants such as Mexicans. The group's robust far-flung networks increase the availability of jobs and housing in immigrant and mainstream Black and White middle-class neighborhoods. As my African American peer, another junior professor and ethnographer, once asserted while we had lunch in a Senegalese restaurant in East Harlem, "The Senegalese are the owners, but the Mexicans are the cooks. If it were not for these ethnic places and for all the work they have put into changing this neighborhood, I wouldn't even be living here myself!" Yet, like Magdalena, many Mexican immigrants are unaware of the contributions they make to their host neighborhoods' revitalization.[5]

Berkis lived in West Central Harlem. Twenty years earlier, her mother and her older sister Sonia had found housing in the more economically stable and demographically diverse northern community of Washington Heights. By 2016, in the northernmost areas of Washington Heights and Inwood, Hispanics made up 70 percent of the population. In contrast, in Manhattanville, on the periphery of which Berkis lived when we first met, the Black community was twice as large (25 percent), and the White community was in decline (7.5 percent). Here, as in East Harlem, Dominicans, Mexicans, and Puerto Ricans already made up a majority (62.8 percent).[6] A Puerto Rican mechanic, a distant relative of the superintendent of Berkis's building, had helped her sister Sonia to find Berkis an apartment in the same building, one that was rent stabilized. The apartment Berkis rented was initially offered for sublet by a Puerto Rican woman. Sonia, married with two children, had lived in Washington Heights for nearly two decades before Berkis arrived. She and her mother had arranged and financed Berkis' immigration.

Berkis lived a few blocks from City College, whose gothic towers were visible from her living room's window. Nonetheless, her immediate neighborhood, an area bounded on the west by the Hudson River and the east by Adam Clayton Powell Jr. Boulevard, was considered dangerous by students and other affiliates of the college. Sonia, who lived uptown in the rapidly gentrifying area of Washington Heights, also shared this perception. She wanted her sister to find another place to live. Across the street from Berkis's apartment, poor Black tenants lived in a large public housing structure encompassing an entire square block. Berkis and other residents on her block knew to keep a careful watch on some of the men who frequented the local deli, lingered idly under its awning, or kept busy on their cell phones for too long, which was likely an indication that they were unemployed. She was mostly concerned with finding work for her and her husband Amado, as they struggled with the money she earned through infrequent apartment cleaning or cutting and styling hair in her kitchen. She imagined that once Amado joined her in New York, they would move out in a matter of a few weeks.

Yet, while Berkis's disappointment about her marriage and opportunities festered, Magdalena's husband's new job led him to relocate his family to Astoria, Queens, in a more diversified and economically stable community. These different stories reveal the overlapping yet distinct network structures that facilitate contemporary Dominican and Mexican families' settlement. They also begin to reveal the different economic and demographic transformations of neighborhoods in Harlem and the life chances that new cohorts of Dominican and Mexican families experience. While two decades earlier Sonia was able to find an affordable apartment in Washington Heights, the traditional community of settlement for Dominicans, Berkis's choices were limited to the poorest areas of Central Harlem.

THE HISTORY OF DOMINICAN AND MEXICAN SETTLEMENT IN NEW YORK CITY: A GENDERED PERSPECTIVE

I met this Ecuadorian lady at the airport [in New York]. I had no one in this city. I was upset about my [marital] separation and only bringing my small child along. This lady rented me a room and told me I could pay for it after I had gotten a job. Her son helped me find a job in a brazier's factory, downtown. I felt relieved that I could pay my rent, my babysitter, and send money to my mother. This lady also cared for my little daughter. There were jobs everywhere, but it was difficult. I had never worked before. I got lost in the streets during my first week, so I called the landlady's son. He asked me where I was so they could pick me up. I was crying, and I kept insisting the street was named "One-way"!

As the above narrative from a sixty-one-year-old Dominican woman reveals, Dominican women from earlier immigrant cohorts (in this case, the 1970s) found work upon arrival given the plentiful availability of manufacturing jobs in the city. New immigrants like Berkis, however, experience declining work opportunities given the restructuring of the economy in older industrial cities like New York. This has led many immigrants, especially the undocumented, to concentrate in expanding, low-wage, service sectors like the food industry, as other narratives illustrate.[7]

Although scholars characterize the immigration of women among earlier cohorts as a consequence of the reunification of families, the next narrative—that of my own mother—illustrates the desperate economic and emotional motives that prompted some women among earlier cohorts to migrate. The narrative also evidences the low levels of education imported by women among migrant cohorts arriving before the 1990s. My mother's migrant story, from when she was about age twenty-seven, also helps illustrate the high diversity of the structure of the networks facilitating the spatial integration of Dominican families among the 1970s cohort:

When I arrived, the factory had few Latinos. My manager spoke Spanish. I think he was Argentinean. I stayed there about five years. After this, I made great money working in a fur company for about six years along with a few Puerto Ricans, Argentineans, Peruvians, and Americans. There were Dominican men and women in my factory. But my friends were mostly from Peru, Ecuador—South America. My boss's wife was an Argentinean Jew. She felt for me since I told her I was alone with a little daughter; she always looked out for me and helped me get training to work with fancy furs.

These narratives portray the experiences of Dominican women arriving before the 1990s. Despite the limited education with which they migrated, many found ample work opportunities in manufacturing, mediated by the access to a broader range of networks outside their ethnic group. The first respondent, and others, like my mother, found housing and work amid different Latino groups—mostly White South Americans, a good share of whom imported a middle-class status, some college education, or equivalent skills.

Interviews with members of earlier cohorts who participated in the Carnegie Immigration and Welfare Reform Study (described in chapter 1), and the emerging literature,[8] allow me to gain preliminary insights on the experiences of Dominican and Mexican women in New York City and other destinations. The immigration and adjustment of these earlier groups was facilitated by the availability of industrial jobs and the access to Spanish-speaking networks among more established immigrants—mostly Argentineans and other South Americans as well as White Cubans—of different class origins. The comments of a Mexican community leader at the Consulate General of Mexico in New York City render a more nuanced reality about the price paid by Mexicans from humble origins and their distinctive work and housing experiences in a changing context of reception, one that affects the resources available to different immigrant cohorts.[9] "I lived in the Cuban and Colombian community of Elmhurst, Queens, in 1982," he told me. "The fact that everyone spoke Spanish was great and helped me find housing. But, at the time, the gradual disappearance of factories forced many Mexicans to find work, mainly in restaurants. This is the first generation in New York, the 'sparring generation,' which takes all the punches. Until the children of this generation study and learn the language, Mexicans will remain abused and offered the lowest jobs. This is a capitalist city, and now the target of capitalist exploitation is the Mexican." As this respondent suggests, since the 1980s, Mexicans—like many other immigrants—have experienced declining work opportunities in New York City's industrial sector. This has led many of them to concentrate in low-wage service sectors.[10] As another informant, the twenty-eight-year-old Mexican husband of one of my female respondents who insisted on being present during her interview, explained,

My father came before, and then his three brothers followed. He left us with our grandmother. My father sent money, but we remained poor. I was not yet conscious of my poverty, since my father sent money for food and clothes. I watched out for my grandmother and did not want to abandon her, since her entire family left for New York. My aunts lived near us but were doing well economically. One of their business was supplying coyotes. Finally, [in 1992] I became desperate, I wanted to have my own money and own things. I called my father, who arranged the trip. I arrived in Upper Manhattan. My father lived on 137th Street and Broadway [in the Dominican community of Central and West Harlem]. I got a job that same week in this restaurant that my cousins owned.

As his narrative reveals, in the two fastest-growing cohorts of foreign-born Latino migrants, Dominicans and Mexicans, spatial integration has overlapped. This has facilitated the gradual integration of the groups into neighborhoods in Manhattan and the Bronx, including mostly the poorest areas of East and West Harlem. It is precisely in these economically deserted inner-city areas that new Black and Brown immigrants make the greatest contributions to the revival of the local community through the opening of small businesses, like the restaurant owned by this Mexican respondent's relatives. These small, embryonic developments set the stage for White middle-class investors and residents to return to inner-city areas, as Black and Brown immigrants and their small businesses serve as a symbolic socioeconomic buffer between middle-class White residents and their historically impoverished Black neighbors.

GENTRIFICATION AND IMMIGRANTS IN OLD AND NEW DESTINATIONS: EAST AND WEST HARLEM

At the intersection of 126th Street and Amsterdam Avenue, a long-established Puerto Rican, and then Dominican, live poultry store, or *vivero*, has had a face-lift: wooden chicken cages holding live chickens are no longer on view in front of the main entrance. The chickens are now delivered through the building's side entry, sparing clients the noise and distraction at the front door. Inside, behind a new counter, a few Brown men in their late forties and fifties perform "front-stage" functions: greeting clients, taking orders, ringing up sales, keeping things tidy. The newly refurbished countertop in the front spares clients the view of the poultry, which is now safely hidden in the back. The biting smell that used to make them rush their orders while holding their breath is now gone. The store's sign—towering above the front facade and facing west onto Amsterdam Avenue, across the street from a small African church—now reads "Halal." The faded old "Vivero" sign that used to be in front now teeters above the side entrance. An older, light-skinned Puerto Rican man in his late sixties, whom I recognize from my graduate school years, is still working there, at both "front-stage" and "back-stage" shifts, but for the most part a new cohort of immigrant men, mostly Black and Brown, has replaced the previous African American and Puerto Rican staff—as well as the ownership—of the *vivero*.

Scholars have argued that gentrification is mostly driven by development and the influx of young professionals—mostly, members of a White middle class socialized in the suburbs. Yet qualitative and quantitative insights reveal that Black and Brown immigrants partake in the larger and stealthy process of Harlem's gentrification. Ethnographic insights allow a new and nuanced understanding of the new demographics of Harlem and its housing and work integration, as well as contributions of middle-class Dominican and Mexican immigrant women.

On a drizzling and cold October morning, around 8:30 a.m., at the busy intersection of 125th Street and Amsterdam Avenue, a young Mexican traffic guard, with dark brown skin and Indigenous phenotype, blows a loud whistle. She moves her right hand with authority, signaling to a cluster of African and Latina mothers with small schoolchildren to cross the street. A few men hang idle, leaning against the wall of a once legendary secondhand furniture store, its main door and windows boarded up with discolored wooden planks. I make a left turn onto Amsterdam, then a quick right onto 126th Street, headed east. I find a parking space three blocks from the *vivero*. Across the street, a Verizon cable distribution factory extends eastward for almost half the block. Directly across from the main business entrance of the building are rows of two- and three-story attached old brick buildings that once functioned as factories where African Americans, Puerto Ricans, and, later, Dominicans once found work. The factories have been replaced by office space, including a medical center for renal diagnoses and ambulatory dialysis.

Beyond attracting immigrant workers from outside the local neighborhood, the architecture of new or renovated buildings and businesses in Harlem seems designed to attract new employers and entrepreneurs, including both foreign- and native-born professionals as apartment renters or owners. Across from the renal center, a few large apartment buildings nearing final construction cover the next few blocks. Across the street, rows of BMW, Volvo, and Lexus sedans and SUVs fill most parking spaces, bearing witness to the presence of a well-salaried gentry, most of them of White European stock. I park my compact car at the end of the street and walk westbound toward the *vivero*'s side entrance, where a delivery truck is parked. I pretend to use my cell phone while instead noting the demographics of the men unloading wooden cages packed with chickens into the *vivero*'s back room. I smile at one of the delivery men. I walk a few steps past him to check out the new coffee shop just past the poultry store.

Like most new or renovated structures in West Harlem, the coffee shop's front facade has wide floor-level windows with ample views of its interior, with comfortable lounge chairs and cushioned corner booths. Inside are the White, but also Brown, gentry, and some with Asian, Latino, Middle Eastern, or ambiguous phenotypes—mostly young men in comfortable, sporty clothing. They foretell their status as graduate students or "superfluous" independent contractors of the new knowledge economy and online, internet-based, digital and social media business.[11] Most sit hunched forward, gazes fixed on small computer screens, large coffee mugs by their side. The Zen aura of this seemingly "safe space" invites onlookers like me, leery of the luxury of quietness and the comfort of this place, amid a street heavily trafficked and in a neighborhood scarred by the legacies of poverty and the abandonment of the government. I think of the juxtaposition of the two classes of people, mostly new residents of Harlem, and how each class contributes to the development of this gentrifying neighborhood.

I walk back to the *vivero*'s side entrance to take a better look at the "backstage" workers. Two Black men in their mid- to late thirties are busy unloading wooden cages packed with contorted chickens. One man, dreadlocked and dressed in comfortable attire (designer sneakers, matching dark jean jacket and pants, an Apple wristwatch, and headphones), listens to house music loudly. We make eye contact as I walk by, and he acknowledges me with a nod in the way immigrant Black and Latino youth are taught to acknowledge an older member of their group. A few Brown men in their late twenties and early thirties, with dark hair and Indigenous Mesoamerican phenotypes, work hastily in the back room. A honey-skinned middle-age man stands in the back of the room. He is about five foot eight, thin-framed, in his late forties or early fifties. In a loud but friendly tone he gives orders to the two men in broken Spanish. The shuffle and noise of scared chickens and a large ventilator's engine muffle what he is saying, but his heavy Middle Eastern accent and Arabic phenotype suggest that he is possibly from the southern part of the Arabian Peninsula.

I notice that the Middle Eastern man is talking with one of the delivery men. As I walk by, his curious eyes try, I believe, to discern my identity. My light brown skin and mix of North African and southern Iberian phenotypes adds to the puzzle. I gather he is trying to discern if I am an old client of the *vivero* or a new member of the imported middle- and upper-class gentry that works, owns businesses, or has apartments in the immediate block. He gives me an affected smile, or what scholars argue entails the "management of emotions."[12]

Amsterdam Avenue from 135th to 145th Streets exemplifies this type of economic and social transformation: bodegas, delicatessens, and supermarkets owned by Chinese, Yemenite, Dominican, and, of late, Mexican entrepreneurs bare new facades with signs reading "Gourmet," "Green Bar," "Healthy Delicatessen," "Tea Room," "Mediterranean Cuisine," "Asian Cuisine," and the like. At the corner of 135th Street an old liquor store has also had a facelift: Above large windows, a scripted-letter sign with the name "Wine Vine" has replaced the older neon sign that used to simply read "Liquors." All of these changes seem designed to attract a new type of clientele: the area's new residents, or students and faculty from the two nearby universities who venture out in search of ethnic foods and other cultural attractions.

Rows of businesses with redesigned facades reflect the larger economic and demographic transformation of West Central Harlem, meant to attract a new Latino middle class—mostly upwardly mobile millennials. With the help of higher education and technical jobs, many of these Black and Brown Latino youth carve their way into the middle class. Many live as boarders in the affordable apartments of parents or grandparents. Others, like the second-generation millennial Latina I met at a community organization in the Bronx, are natives of Harlem and new homeowners. Her medium-light brown skin and Mesoamerican Indigenous phenotype and humble demeanor contrasts with her New York matter-of-fact middle-class way of speaking. When I told her about my research in Harlem, this young Mexican American woman shared how she and her fiancé, a White man she met while attending college upstate, had, before marrying, decided to buy a co-op apartment not far from the apartment where she grew up, right there, in the poorest area of East Harlem. As she explained, "One day, I walked from my parents' apartment to the train [subway] at 125th Street and Lexington Avenue and noticed apartments for sale inside a building in the same block. The building had been in renovation for a while. I told my fiancé, and then he asked his parents, and I asked my parents. We borrowed the money and qualified immediately!"

Similarly, not far from this millennial Latina's new East Harlem home, a college-age second-generation Latino, the friend of my college-age daughter, rented an apartment with two other college friends. His neighborhood is ranked top among the most dangerous in Harlem, yet, even though he is an outsider from an elite college in Downtown Manhattan and originally hails from the Southeast, he was undisturbed by this news. His remote family found the apartment for him with the help of a Manhattan real estate broker. A deli on the first floor of his apartment building has a new sign that reads "Gourmet Grocer."

A block away, a large public housing structure is home to generations of African Americans, Puerto Ricans, and other working-poor Black and Brown minorities—including an increasing number of Dominicans. At the deli inside a nearby building and supermarket, young Dominican and Middle Eastern women work the cash registers. A few Mexican men do "back-stage" jobs, preparing foods and making deliveries. My visits to stores in the area, insiders' reports, and my longitudinal research in the area reveal that Korean and other Asian families have replaced Jewish families as owners of delicatessens, supermarkets, and a few renovated apartment buildings.

THE RACIAL CAPITAL AND LIABILITIES OF IMMIGRANTS AT OLD AND NEW MIGRANT DESTINATIONS

In 2016, one of my daughter's friends moved to a gentrifying Brooklyn neighborhood settled by Puerto Ricans, many of whom are in the process of being displaced by gentrification. He is the progeny of immigrants from Colombia's coastal region and Mexico, and his dark brown skin, mixed-race phenotype, and tight curly hair help him blend in with the broader demographics of this old Black and Puerto Rican neighborhood. He shares with me how most Hispanics or even Middle Easterners working at the delicatessens near his apartment—or on the streets of his neighborhood—immediately speak Spanish or acknowledge him as Latino. Explaining how comforting it is that the locals identify him as one of their own, with bright eyes and a broad smile he declares, "This is really awesome!" Such observations make me further question how higher education and the mixed non-Black, non-White identities of Dominicans and Mexicans affect my women respondents' integration in gentrifying neighborhoods of New York City. I am also curious as to how the imported human and social capital, including the racial capital of middle-class Dominican and Mexican immigrants in Harlem, improves my women respondents' opportunities or creates barriers in the access to housing in traditionally African American and Latino neighborhoods experiencing gentrification.

Back in Harlem, across from the *vivero*, a small Catholic church has all of its windows shut, and large wooden planks are nailed across its two front doors. I wonder if houses of prayer can fall victim to spiraling rents in the larger housing displacement process, which has transformed inner-city communities of New York City, and especially Harlem.[13] The sound of children's voices comes from a jungle gym behind the boarded-up church. Two clusters of small Black and Brown preschoolers are busy at play. A few steps away, African immigrant mothers wearing traditional djellabas,[14] some also with headscarves, and others with dreadlocks pulled back, clutch fancy pocketbooks and remain carefully on guard from a nearby corner.

On this early summer evening, rows of police cars dot the street corner by the church and the local precinct at the corner of Broadway and 126th Street. On most summer and autumn days, poor African American, Puerto Rican, and, increasingly, Dominican families sit alongside the playground. Men in their twenties and early thirties stand on corners smoking, checking their phones, or engaging in conversations, on alert. A light-skinned Latino man in his late sixties or early seventies holds onto a cane. He stands aimlessly in front of the only bodega left on the block, at the corner of 126th Street and Broadway. He seems startled by the grinding noise of an arriving subway car's brakes on the elevated tracks above.

At the other end of the block, at the intersection of 125th Street and Broadway, the newly painted, penitentiary-looking dark green color of the elevated IRT subway tracks seems part of a larger plot: the dark paint covers all the graffiti at one of the few spaces where the local youth expressed creativity or dissent. On the other side of Broadway and 125th, across from a Bank of New York branch (now Bank of America), a long-standing McDonald's is undergoing demolition. The fast-food spot was the only "safe space" for local families to take their children to after school, for the elderly who lived alone, or for public school teen-agers to gather on cold and gloomy days. One respondent, a fifty-five-year-old Dominican mother of three who lives in the public housing building across the street, laments the changes in her neighborhood: "This McDonald's was key for taxicab drivers to repose in between shifts; the only place where outsiders grabbed a fast meal or took a quick bathroom rest."

A couple of other residential buildings nearby are boarded up. My respon-dent has lived in the area since she arrived in the United States twenty years ago. Her two daughters used to work at the McDonald's, but both were laid off about three years ago. She feels sorry about the change but remains hopeful, uncon-cerned about meeting the same fate as the families that lived in those boarded-up buildings, as she lives in public housing: "¡Gracias a Dios que no es facil sacar tanta gente de edificios del gobierno!" (Thank God that it is not easy to displace people from government buildings!) By 2018, 16.3 percent of rental units in Central Harlem were public or government subsided. The median housing rent had increased from $820 in 2006 to $1,160 in 2018. Several reports reveal that close to 25 percent of households in Harlem are severely rent-burdened (spend-ing more than 50 percent of household income on rent).[15] As chapter 4 reveals, Dominicans face the highest risks of housing eviction and rental burdens in the Bronx and Manhattan, the two boroughs in which Dominicans are most concentrated.

Gentrification has brought new opportunities, as well as new forms of inequality, or liability, for Harlem residents. This book's findings reveal that undocumented families in Washington Heights pay the highest rental fees, even though the neighborhood has the highest concentration of rent-stabilized apart-ments in the city. Dominicans appear to be the most affected given the group's lower-than-average household incomes.[16] For example, in 1999, out-of-pocket rent expenses in the neighborhood averaged $777 per household,[17] but by 2014, this had increased to $1,040.[18] The qualitative insights reveal that four of ten Dominican families relocated from Washington Heights to the Bronx and into other poorer areas of the city. Many of these families, especially those headed by single mothers, are forced to seek public housing or other forms of government-subsidized rent, for which only migrants with legal status can qualify. As chapter 4 shows, Mexicans have a much higher incidence of undocumented immigrant status, and this leads many to rely on group-living arrangements, often renting rooms as boarders or sharing an apartment with other coethnics.

Scholars have documented how local development, the rising cost of rent, and the arrival of the White middle class contribute to the displacement of local Black and Latino families in inner-city neighborhoods.[19] Yet little is known about the role played by local developers as well as public housing structures and other public institutions in this social and economic transformation. The follow-ing ethnographic insights engage this conversation:

At Broadway and 125th Street, commuters rush up and down escalators, to and from the elevated tracks. The sounds of the arriving and departing IRT trains, the busy traffic, and the hurried pace of a pedestrian horde, in and out of new stores, symbolize this neighborhood's gentrification. Positioned less than a block from each other, two large banks compete for the new gentry that will be affiliated with Columbia University's new satellite campus, which is still under construction. A couple of pharmacies seem to divine the financial ventures that will be derived from the contrasting health care needs of the new Columbia campus and the old public housing. A MetroPCS cell phone store, a few new remittance establishments, microfinanciers, and gourmet delis have pushed away a once-popular cuchifrito establishment, a Chinese restaurant, a fried chicken take-out place, and a check-cashing store that in the past served the working poor or the unbanked.

New real estate and business developments compete to attract middle- and upper-class residents to West Harlem, including the children of immigrants. For example, a few blocks west of the old McDonald's, the legendary Cotton Club lies almost desolate, open only for private entertainment. Across the street, two of three postmodern, large, square-shaped behemoths owned by Columbia stand unresolved, still under construction. The large windows allow a panoramic view of one of the building's first-floor interior. Inside, minimalist, colorful furniture reaffirms an inviting, open community space with cayenne-pepper-colored lounging seats and small futuristic canvas chairs, some bright red and others yellow, lined up, facing a postmodern island-shaped reception desk. A man in his early- to mid-thirties, with dark ebony skin, sits at guarded attention behind the desk. A scattered number of about ten Brown and White college youths work, some alone and some in groups, their eyes affixed to phone or laptop screens. Some sit at single tables lined up against the large windows, while others lounge on squishy sofas, as if almost submerged in a cloud. In this vast room with high ceilings and transparent walls, most chairs remain unoccupied. The vastness and the few motionless bodies give the eerie feeling that something that should be about to happen may never happen. The farthest of the ultramodern behemoths bears the same light shade of gray as the cumulus clouds floating above it. The building's water-like, grayish fiberglass wall panels seem to mimic the colors of the nearby Hudson River and the metal columns that hold up the elevated highway, obscuring the building's presence, like a Romulan spaceship would cloak itself to avoid detection by the USS *Enterprise* on *Star Trek*. I cannot help but wonder if this building's architectural design is intended to disguise the larger transformation, displacement, and gentrification of West Central Harlem.

The building directly facing the public housing projects on Broadway bears a sign reading "Columbia University's Jerome L. Greene School of Environmental Sciences." Until about five years ago, part of this space was a Valero gas station that was first owned by an African American, then a Puerto Rican, and then a

Dominican Black man in his mid-sixties—my mother's step-uncle, who had been a local resident for about thirty-five years. Working as the shop's main mechanic, he was invited to become a *socio*, or part owner, by the Puerto Rican owner. In the late 1990s, when I was in graduate school, knowing that a relative worked at the gas station gave me a sense of pride but also of safety and support. My future husband and I frequented the shop for gas or when we had car troubles. This entire area of approximately four square blocks, except for the New York City's Metropolitan Transit Authority bus depot, was purchased by Columbia University, one of the largest real estate holders in the city, through the city government's process of eminent domain.[20] In recent months, the police presence has increased across the street from the new Columbia buildings; invariably, one or two cars remain parked around the clock in front of the public housing projects, facing the newly installed instructional and community-based facilities of Columbia University.

These larger developments attract new cohorts of foreign-born Latinos but also new Blacks, whose racial, class, and cultural capital allow them to navigate both inner-city poor and middle-class neighborhoods, as well as housing and business spaces. A block east of Broadway, at the busy corner of 125th Street and Amsterdam Avenue, African immigrant mothers in their mid-thirties to early forties, some in djellabas and others in stretch jeans, spandex, or other modern attire, walk small children to school. On 125th Street past St. Nicholas Avenue, new hair, health, and clothing stores with African motifs speak of a new succession by Black ethnics from the middle class or more financially solvent origins. Scholarship documents that a key and negative outcome of gentrification has been the displacement of immigrant and native-born poor Blacks and Hispanics, and then that of the White middle class from inner-city neighborhoods.[21] But the qualitative insights reveal that immigrants and the return of a new Black and Brown middle class now contribute to the redevelopment of Harlem. Many of these new immigrants enter economic niches and social spaces that have historically excluded native-born African American and Latino residents. The insights also show the new faces, racial and class origins of these non-White newcomers, including a new Latin American middle class from the Dominican Republic and Mexico and its second-generation millennials who, equipped with a college education and technological savvy, can contribute to the revival and cultural diversification of older immigrant destination areas like Harlem.

GENTRIFICATION IN NEW DESTINATIONS: MOUNT PLEASANTVILLE

Since the 1990s, Harlem and other inner-city neighborhoods like Bronx Little Italy have been transformed by urban development and gentrification. The transformation has pushed native- and foreign-born Black and Latino families to seek housing in cheaper areas that often have higher rates of poverty and crime. Others fall into poverty, as in the case of mothers who are primary providers and who, after qualifying for public housing, must relocate to areas with higher poverty. For Mexicans, however, far-flung networks and an informal system of group living leads them to find housing in new migrant destination areas.

The case of Gloria, a light-skinned single Mexican mother, illustrates the network mechanisms that allow Mexican families' widespread spatial integration in both older and newer migration destinations. Her mobility from a neighborhood on the periphery of Bronx Little Italy, a working-class ethnic White community, into downtown Mount Pleasantville, a new destination for Latinos since the late 1990s, increased her housing and work opportunities. In 2010, by the time of Gloria's arrival in Mount Pleasantville, her new neighborhood already showed the first signs of gentrification. Mexican families in the area were already visible at work both inside and outside small stores mainly owned by Chinese, Indian, and Korean families.

White young urban professionals living in newly built condominium apartments along the Hudson River often ventured as far as Gloria's building, about six blocks toward the southwestern blocks of Main Street, perpendicular to the Hudson River and the Metro-North commuter train station. A good share of these new professionals were Albanian and Ukrainian millennials, often of the "1.5 generation," in their thirties to early forties, who came as far as Gloria's building to buy fresh bread at a Mexican bakery or to the Chinese green grocery on the first floor of her building. Some of them came to fetch taxis after missing the hourly Metro-North train bound for New York City.

Gloria's apartment looked down on rows of parked taxicabs and the hustle of pedestrians heading to catch nearby transit. At the intersection of Main Street and Broadway, the heart of downtown Mount Pleasantville known as Main Square, lines of people—mostly poor African Americans and Latinos—waited patiently for buses or for their turn to pick up Medicaid prescriptions from the corner pharmacy. On most weekends, however, the Black and White population became invisible or receded, while the Mexican and Middle Eastern groups gained visibility. Gloria's immediate block experienced a discernible transformation, apparent in the clusters of Mexican laborers, many of them enjoying their Sunday or only day off from work, with children in hand, drifting in and out of the Mexican bakery directly across from Gloria's building. The smell of vanilla cakes, breads, and coffee, and the bright colors of the papayas, avocados, green plantains, yellow bananas, and other Asian and Latino produce lined up in rows outside the Chinese green grocer, attracted both daily shoppers and onlookers at all hours of the day and evening.

The latest newcomers and entrepreneurs, bearded Middle Eastern taxi drivers, some in light-colored summer djellabas and leather sandals, waited for pedestrians in need of their services. While on their cell phones, many kept a watchful eye on approaching pedestrians, and especially the cluster of unemployed middle-aged African American and Latino men who loitered on the sidewalks on their way in or out of the local alcohol and drug rehabilitation center, which distributed methadone. Along with the homeless, some of these regulars would, on very cold nights, find refuge in the entryway of Gloria's building. Their presence made Gloria wary, especially at night, when she came home from work in a taxi or by bus, or when she was with her young children.

The alcohol and drug rehabilitation center opened in 2005, in the early stages of this neighborhood redevelopment, as a main feature of the local government's investment in doing a facelift of the area, putting away the "undeserving" members of local society. The center's sign loomed across the street from Gloria's building, drawing working poor or destitute clients, their social workers, and mental health professionals. Rehabilitation centers, ethnic eateries, and the sight of in-between, non-Black and non-White immigrants provided the first symbolic racial and class boundaries, cushioning or narrowing the long-standing divide and systemic exclusion that has separated poor African Americans and middle-class Whites in southwest Mount Pleasantville for generations.

Renting rooms to coethnics allowed Gloria, a single mother of three, to live rent-free for a few years following her husband's deportation. During the first stage of my field research in 2002, I interviewed Gloria in her Bronx apartment in the Belmont neighborhood, not far from the legendary Italian working-class community of Arthur Avenue and Bronx Little Italy. About six years later, Gloria and I met again for a follow-up interview in Mount Pleasantville. When I mentioned how delighted I was to see the large size of her new apartment, she proudly shared, with a broad smile, how she had become the *encargada*—the person who leases the apartment and then rents rooms to coethnics.[22] With the help of one of her uncle's Mexican employees, she turned the living room into a bedroom and living space for her and her three small children. She rented three other rooms to boarders: the first to her brother-in-law (who followed her from the Bronx) and her younger sister, who had recently crossed the border; the second to a middle-aged Dominican woman and her husband, both with an air of self-importance and a bureaucratic demeanor; and the third to an Ecuadorian woman in her early thirties with black hair, porcelain-white skin, and Ladino phenotype (a mix of European and Indigenous ancestry) who was a domestic laborer and single mother.

I estimated that Gloria received, on average, $150 weekly per room for a total of about $600 per week, in addition to the earnings at her full-time job as a manicurist in a local salon. These fees did not include the money she received for two people in one room, as in the case of the Dominican couple, or the additional fees she charged for a tenant's use of the kitchen and refrigerator or other amenities, such as a heater, fan, air conditioning, or ironing board and iron. Gloria was an expert nail and skin worker, employed in an Asian salon for over ten years, but she also worked at home on the nails, skin, or hair of some of her Latino tenants and clients, as chapter 6 details. Overall, collecting all of this rent while paying the market rate allowed Gloria to keep her apartment for over six years and to still send money to her parents in Mexico. Eventually her Chinese landlord sold the building to an Albanian immigrant developer who owned a restaurant in the area and wanted to rent rooms to his staff of mostly Albanian Mexicans from rural origins. Having Gloria as a secured tenant allowed both the previous owner and the new one to derive income from apartments that attracted only the most vulnerable of tenants, such as the undocumented or single mothers on limited budgets, given the lack of repairs and substandard living conditions that most tenants were willing to tolerate.

THE GEOGRAPHIES OF IMMIGRANT WOMEN'S NETWORKS: PARADOXES OF INTEGRATION AND RACIALIZATION

This section renders an analysis of the network structures that have allowed Dominican and Mexican women and their families to experience spatial dispersion to improve their own opportunities and those of their children. The findings also expand on my earlier work with Marta Tienda on the paradoxes apparent in the growing spatial integration, as well as segregation and racialization, of U.S. Latinos and immigrants,[23] this time with a focus on women.

Changes in housing markets, population shifts, and local development limit Black Latinos' and poor minorities' ability to hold on to housing in gentrifying neighborhoods. Among these, single mothers like Berkis face the greatest housing instability. While members of previous migrant cohorts, like my mother, were able to move from the poorest areas of West Harlem into areas with better work opportunities and networks, including suburban destinations, Black Latinas like Berkis and others are often stranded in poorer neighborhoods.

Since the 1990s, Dominicans have concentrated mostly in neighborhoods of the Bronx with the highest poverty levels; among these are Crotona Park, High Bridge, Melrose, Morrisania, Mott Haven, and Tremont. Table 3.1 illustrates that Dominicans have experienced the highest indices of poverty concentration among all Hispanic groups since 2000.[24] By 2008 all Hispanic groups had experienced declines in poverty rates, but Dominicans have continued to rank at the top among the poorest Hispanics.[25] Between 2010 and 2015 the share of the foreign-born population in the Bronx grew by 500 percent. Follow-up interviews and new census updates reveal that Dominicans experience higher poverty shares than Mexicans in New York City.

Dominicans' higher concentration in poor inner-city neighborhoods has also increased social isolation. Table 3.1 also shows that next to Blacks, Dominicans experience the highest indices of isolation, or racial and class spatial segregation, from Whites. Black Latinos share lower indices of social interaction with Whites,

TABLE 3.1   Segregation Indices for New York City Community Districts

Ethnic/ Racial Group	Poverty Concentration		Dissimilarity from Whites		Interaction with Whites*		Isolation Index	
	2000**	**2006–8	2000	2006–8	2000	2006–8	2000	2006–8
Mexican	27	25	43	50	42	40	4.3	7.2
Dominican	31	28.5	62	65	32	29	18	21
Black alone	26	23	63	65	24	24	52	50
Colombian	19	17	52	50	45	47	3.7	4.1
Cuban	23	21	37	37	37	37	0.9	0.7
Puerto Rican	29	26	48	49	37	35	18	17
Spaniard	22	18	32	28	50	56	0.2	0.3
All Hispanic	28	25	46	46	37	36	41	43

SOURCES: **Author's computation of Integrated Public Use Microdata Series–USA Census 2000 data for poverty concentration by community districts and of combined 2006–8 American Community Survey data for measures of spatial segregation and interaction between the different Latino and White groups.

NOTES: Segregation indices are dissimilarity indices; both measure, for example, the degree to which a Latino/Hispanic group is distributed differently from Whites across census tracks. These indices range from 0 (completely integrated) to 100 (completely isolated or segregated—or, in this case, that most Blacks or Dominicans live largely among their respective racial/ethnic groups). Each index is derived according to the average share of a group in a census track or neighborhood. For further information, see Frey, 2012 and Frey and Myers, 2005.

* The interaction index is sometimes referred to as the exposure index.

next to Blacks, while White Latinos, like Cubans and Iberians, experience the highest levels of interaction with mainstream White groups. Table 3.2 shows that between 2000 and 2005, the Dominican population's share declined in three of the five New York City boroughs, but not the Bronx and Staten Island. Since the 1990s, the share of Dominicans in Staten Island has been insignificant.

The spatial integration of the Mexican population in the city has, since the 1990s, overlapped with that of Dominicans, mostly in Manhattan and the Bronx, the boroughs with the largest concentrations. Between 2000 and 2005, the foreign-born Mexican population in the Bronx grew by 78 percent. Notably, the Mexican population has continued to grow the most in boroughs where the Dominican population has declined: Queens (54 percent), Staten Island (33 percent), and Brooklyn (15 percent).[26]

Although the greater numbers of Dominican women reside in Manhattan, by 2015, the largest shares of the female Dominican and Mexican immigrant population (56 percent) were concentrated in both Manhattan and the Bronx. Dominican women in the Bronx experience the highest levels of poverty. Even when the Mexican population is more evenly distributed throughout the boroughs, coethnic women tend to concentrate in Brooklyn (44 percent) and the

TABLE 3.2 Share of Foreign-Born and Female Populations in New York City Boroughs

	Dominican Immigrants								
	Borough Share (%)				Female Share (%)				Percentage Change, 1990–2015
Total (N)	227,000	375,000	392,000	258,000					
Borough	1990	2000	2010	2015	1990	2000	2010	2015	
Bronx	27	34	41	46	56	55	57	56	70
Manhattan	42	34	28	25	56	55	58	56	−59
Brooklyn	16	15	16	13	55	55	58	60	−19
Queens	15	16	14	14	56	57	60	58	−6
Total population	100	99	99	98	56	55	58	57	13

	Mexican Immigrants								
	Borough Share (%)				Female Share (%)				Percentage Change, 1990–2015
Total (N)	13,000	50,000	78,000	75,000					
Borough	1990	2000	2010	2015	1990	2000	2010	2015	
Bronx	23	22	29	29	39	41	42	45	26
Manhattan	17	15	10	7	39	37	36	39	−59
Brooklyn	36	35	31	28	40	42	44	35	−22
Queens	22	27	29	33	33	37	39	42	50
Total population	98	98	99	97	38	40	41	43	576

SOURCES: Author's calculations using decennial data from the U.S. Census for 1990, 2000, 2010, and updates from the Integrated Public Use Microdata Series–USA and the American Community Survey 2015.

Bronx (42 percent). My earlier analysis and new qualitative and quantitative insights show that the Mexican labor force is concentrated mostly within White-majority work establishments and neighborhoods.[27]

The geography of Dominican and Mexican networks also tells an interesting story about the different and overlapping spatial integration of the two immigrant groups in New York City. Table 3.3 shows that networks of support for Mexicans concentrate mainly in Queens (20 percent) and in Manhattan's East and West Harlem (27 percent). In comparison, for Dominicans, these links have increasingly moved to the East Bronx (39 percent), diminishing in traditional areas of settlement, such as Manhattan's Washington Heights (30 percent) and Queens (6 percent).

Comparing the network structures and their function in the settlement process reveals that Mexican women rely on the support of friends and family who

TABLE 3.3   Women's Network Links and Locations

Location of Link	Dominican Women (N = 46)	Mexican Women (N = 30)	Total (N = 76)
Washington Heights, Manhattan	30%	13%	23%
East Bronx	39%	23%	33%
Harlem, Manhattan	20%	27%	23%
Queens	6%	20%	10%
Dominican Republic / Mexico	11%	3.3%	8%
Other	0%	6.7%	3%

SOURCE: Author's interviews, 2000–2003, and follow-up interviews, 2009–10.

live in the same building or on the same immediate block. In contrast, around one-third of Dominicans' close links of support live in the same building or neighborhood. Another difference lies in the formal and informal links the two groups rely on for finding work, housing, or essential services for their families. Figure 3.1 shows a heuristic representation of the network composition and location of the two immigrant groups. For example, more Dominican (45 percent) than Mexican (29 percent) women rely on formal links, such as community organizations, real estate agencies, homeless shelters, and public government agencies, for services. Additionally, the composition and structure of their networks remain gendered. Figure 3.1 shows that Dominican women depend mainly on other women, while Mexican women mostly depend on men to find housing or work. The qualitative insights suggest that a higher share (close to 60 percent) of undocumented families among Mexicans, compared with less than one-third (29 percent) among Dominicans, may explain variations in the composition and location networks. Middle-class women tend to have wider networks, often with greater access to more formal institutions than their lesser-schooled coethnics, as chapter 4 illustrates. Overall, rent was usually the main reason why Dominican and Mexican women relocated to a neighborhood, and not the need to live next to families, as scholars have assumed.[28]

More Dominican than Mexican families chose a place to live because of the access to affordable housing. When asked why they moved into a particular neighborhood, most Mexicans answered that it was because of low rents. Meanwhile, less than half of Dominicans considered rent to be the determinant factor in finding a home. Poor, single heads of households were the exception; for them, relocation was usually based on the access to public or affordable housing. When Carmen, a thirty-six-year-old Dominican woman of middle-class origin, was asked why she moved from her apartment in Washington Heights, near her mother and family, to a public housing structure in the

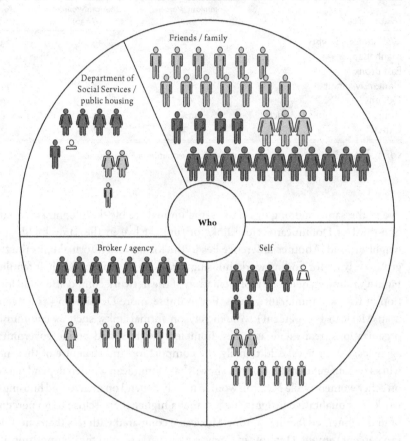

WHO HELPED YOU FIND HOUSING?
HEURISTIC MODEL
Gendered links

Friends / family

Department of
Social Services /
public housing

Who

Broker / agency

Self

 Mexican women who found
housing via other women = 8

 Mexican women who found
housing via other men = 26

 Dominican women who found
housing via other women = 28

 Dominican women who found
housing via other men = 10

Who helped you find housing?		
	Dominican women	Mexican women
Total sample (n =)	(37)	(34)
Friends / family	40%	47%
DSS / public housing	16%	8%
Broker / dealer	29%	21%
Self	15%	24%

FIGURE 3.1 Housing Network Structures of Dominican and Mexican Immigrant Women. (*Source*: Author's analysis based on survey and interview data gathered in 2002–3 and updated in 2009–10.)

southeast Bronx, she quickly retorted, "Because this is the only place that accepts Section 8!"[29]

Another proxy of social integration is the reach of immigrant women's networks outside the ethnic group. Female respondents traveled outside new areas of settlement back to their previous neighborhoods to attend church, buy ethnic foods, or (mainly) to obtain childcare. For example, Magdalena continued seeking pastoral services in her old church, visiting friends, and sending money in a remittances store owned by a coethnic in her old neighborhood in El Barrio despite having moved to Astoria. This was also the case for Carmen, who, after relocating to Morrisania, sent her teenage daughter to school in her old neighborhood for fear of crime and often took her children to a babysitter in the old neighborhood too. Similarly, despite her involuntary move to the South Bronx, Berkis continued to see two close friends in her old neighborhood near City College in Harlem. Most important, Berkis had established close relations with a social worker, her children's teachers, and her mental health therapist in Harlem. She found it hard to reestablish these professional ties in her new, impoverished, and isolated community in the Bronx, and the transportation from her new apartment in the South Bronx to Harlem was limited, forcing Berkis to opt for walking or taking taxis with her two small children, thus increasing her financial burden.

I gauged the network structures and composition that helped my respondents with their initial settlement. I also examined social integration in their building and immediate neighborhood and if they knew the landlord or property manager. I asked how they paid the rent (if in person, by mail, or through a third party), and to whom it is paid. The analysis reveals a consistent finding: twice as many Mexicans as Dominicans knew other coethnics in their neighborhoods; they also knew the landlord/building superintendent; and a majority paid the rent in cash, usually in person. Doing so in person provided opportunities for families, especially conjugal partners, to inquire about housing availability for prospective coethnics—mostly family members. It also provided Mexican men an ability to legitimize their status, even if they were vulnerable and undocumented, as main providers, heads of households, or "middlemen" (mediators) for their families and, chiefly, for their wives' access to housing and employment.

CHAPTER SUMMARY: PARADOXES OF DISPERSION, CONCENTRATION, AND RACIALIZATION

Several paradoxes emerge regarding the spatial integration and distribution of Dominicans and Mexicans in gentrifying inner-city neighborhoods. One unintended consequence has been the arrival of a new Black and Brown middle class and the boundaries these residents draw to separate themselves from poorer and historically marginalized coethnics. The economic and demographic restructuring of inner-city neighborhoods like Harlem is driven mainly by powerful institutions, such as real estate conglomerates, academic institutions, banks, and local government. Other players take part in this larger transformation, too, such as small business owners, new apartment owners and lessees, and most of my middle-class respondents, who live as boarders. Middle-class immigrants who act as *encargadas*, like Gloria, also play a role in this larger process, as chapter 4 documents. Working-class migrants also partake in the economic and cultural revitalization of moribund economies.[30] Without the wages of Mexicans and other working-class Black and Brown immigrant workers, small enterprises like the *vivero* or restaurants or stores owned by middle-class Koreans, Senegalese, and Yemenites, as well as Latinos, would not thrive in Harlem. Much of the literature on gentrification has focused on the role of White upper- or middle-class residents and local developers of new businesses, including real estate enterprises and banks.[31] This literature has argued that the concentration of poverty in inner-city neighborhoods is due to the flight of capital or jobs, as well as that of the middle class. This chapter has prescribed as a solution the return of industry and the middle class. It reveals that local development contributes to the housing displacement, concentration of poverty, and isolation of residents and immigrants whose class, gender, and race vulnerability intersect to increase isolation in historically racialized and poor neighborhoods. Yet the return of a new Black and Brown middle class, including that of Black and Latino foreign- and native-born millennials and their small and midsize business ventures, contributes to the economic, class, and racial and ethnic revival of inner-city neighborhoods at old and new immigration destinations. Not much of this contribution is documented; nor is how gentrification and the growth of a Black and Brown middle class in these neighborhoods will lead to improvements in the lives of poorer multiracial and multiethnic communities.[32]

Missing in the urban renewal literature is how immigration and demographic shifts contribute to the revival of declining local economies and cultures. An earlier study by Leah Schmalzbauer examines the effects of Mexican families' migration and work integration in rural Montana. The author finds that Mexican families' adjustment is quite different in rural Montana, where the White population experiences growth and where jobs are plentiful and then disappear, following the boom and bust of the housing market. Schmalzbauer finds that women from rural origins feel better in areas with an ecology similar to that of where they lived before migration.[33] Yet these women also experience higher levels of isolation than those in urban settings. This chapter examines the experiences of highly educated migrant women at old and new destinations undergoing gentrification. Many of these women benefit from the availability of an informal system of group living first conceptualized as the "encargado system" by sociologist Sarah Mahler in the mid-1990s.[34] I further detail this type of analysis in chapter 4. The encargado system increases the social cohesion and network resources of immigrants in their attempts to find and retain housing, especially in new destinations experiencing gentrification, as the case of Gloria in this chapter demonstrates.

Another key finding of this chapter is that Dominicans' longer tenure in New York City and their higher levels of poverty lead many to seek government subsidies in public housing. This increases their class and race spatial segregation and isolation, especially among middle-class women, who, despite the importation of high human capital, face high levels of precarity and isolation as single mothers. The case of Carmen and that of Berkis in chapter 4 will further document the experiences of Black Latinas. While Magdalena was able to move from one of the poorest communities of East Harlem, owing mostly to her husband's powerful networks with a Greek employer and her own network with her local church in Astoria, Queens, Berkis remained in the poorest community of Central Harlem. She faced eviction and subsequently was forced to transplant her children and herself into a shelter and then into a poorer isolated neighborhood of the South Bronx. The qualitative data helps the documentation of the paradoxes of gentrification, development, and racialization. Despite the imported levels of human and social capital, and the contributions new immigrants make to the revival and economic and cultural diversity of marginalized inner-city areas at old and new immigrant destinations, Black and Indigenous immigrant women experience the highest—and worst forms of—vulnerability.

4 · "UNOS DUERMEN DE NOCHE Y OTROS DE DÍA"
The Living Arrangements of Undocumented Families

In Mrs. Uraga's apartment,[1] a small preschool girl emerged from a bedroom, passed the entryway, and came with us to the kitchen. She found a place under the table near my chair. The elderly white-skinned Latino couple that rented out their apartment, or the *encargados*, had their gazes fixed on a small black-and-white television tuned to the afternoon's news in English, occasionally turning to look at us. I sensed that the presence of a stranger was of concern in an apartment with several undocumented boarders. While interviewing Mrs. Uraga, I would at times put my hand under the table to wave hello at the little girl. Toward the end of the two-hour interview, I felt a small hand holding mine.

On my way home, I thought about how well behaved this three-year-old was to have sat quietly under a kitchen table for so long. For the first time I wondered about the age at which undocumented children begin to distinguish which spaces or symbolic boundaries never to cross as boarders in someone else's home. And, more specifically, how do undocumented families find housing in New York City at a time of a heightened backlash against immigrants? Equally important, how does a group living arrangement affect motherhood or even relations with spouses or conjugal partners? What distinguishes the housing of documented and undocumented Latino families, and how do migrant women and their children cope with the shock of eviction or even that of deportation?

My observations stem from two intermittent, longitudinal ethnographies and interviews with Dominican and Mexican women that were focused on undocumented families' housing experiences, as close to 50 percent of the aggregate sample of women respondents in this study have undocumented status. Extant literature on undocumented Latino families concentrates mostly on California and the Southwest. In comparison, this chapter portrays Latino subgroups' housing experiences in the Northeast,[2] specifically in New York City, a long-standing destination for Dominicans but a relatively new one for Mexicans.

I first draw on intermittent, longitudinal ethnographies conducted in one Dominican and one Mexican household and explore how the intersection of family structures and immigrant status inequalities affects access to housing. Next, and drawing on in-depth interviews, follow-up updates, and neighborhood census data, I compare the housing experiences of immigrant families from middle- and working-class origins and their strategies to find and retain housing in the midst of gentrification.[3] I then explore how the living arrangements of undocumented families affect women's lives—specifically, their motherhood practices and intimate relations with spouses or conjugal partners. Next I document how mothers cope with the shock of deportation or eviction and the networks of support that help buffer the shock of homelessness. Finally, my analysis is guided by the findings of Mathew Desmond on the impact of eviction on the lives of poor Black families in isolated, rural and marginalized urban areas.[4] I compare the experiences of eviction for Black and Brown immigrant women in New York City, equally documenting the impact of losing a home on the mental health of poor mothers and their children.

THE HOUSING STRATEGIES OF MIDDLE-CLASS MOTHERS

The first time I visited Berkis's apartment building, she met me downstairs. She immediately offered me something cool to drink, a *refresco* of my choosing from the deli on the building's first floor. Upon entering the store, she introduced me as a fellow coethnic and new friend to the owner, a light-skinned Dominican man in his early fifties with an eastern European phenotype and amenable demeanor. He was a nice "family man" Berkis whispered as we readied to leave the store. While the proprietor packed our drinks in a small brown bag, Berkis murmured, eyes downcast, "Apuntemelo ahi, por favor, señor" (Write it down on my tab, please, sir). I was reminded of the humble yet stoic strategies my family had employed when I was a small child. My grandmother was a widow, and poor, a new rural immigrant in Santo Domingo. One of my two uncles, the oldest but only an adolescent, would often be in charge of getting food staples for my grandmother from the local *colmado* (deli). He knew how and when to ask the store owner, without others noticing, to please add the cost to my grandmother's tab. Witnessing Berkis's deli interaction made me reflect on how running tabs, getting credit, or establishing trust in a local food store must also be a key survival strategy of immigrant mothers or the inner-city working poor, and especially key among the undocumented.

Berkis's apartment was on the top floor in a building with no elevator. Four flights up, the climb was a bit of a challenge for me and for Berkis's small sons. As I entered, the kitchen was the first room on my left, and the largest room in sight.

Berkis asked me to sit at a table in the right corner, near the kitchen's entrance. From this corner I observed Berkis's family life, intermittently, for over a year. I witnessed how she made ends meet for her home, and how she handled her marital tribulations and parenting challenges. But mostly I observed the protean resilience of an immigrant mother with an inner drive to work toward getting herself, and especially her children, a secured future despite her undocumented status.

Old, faded pastel green and gray linoleum covered the floor and most of the apartment's floors. A simulated wood Formica counter wrapped around a large, faded, cream-colored enameled kitchen sink. At the end of the counter, a small black stove with four gas burners was the life of the kitchen. Berkis always used a match or piece of burning newspaper to light one of the burners. A standard-size refrigerator, with chipped enamel, about ten years old, stood at the farthest right corner, not far from the only window in the kitchen. A small withering bromeliad hung above, striving to survive the heat that fumed from a cast iron radiator beneath the window. In the corner next to the window and the refrigerator, a small, portable hair dryer box, partially used bottles of hair care products, boxes of rollers and pins, and other hair styling paraphernalia, orderly stocked on top of a thin two-foot-by-four-foot table, especially captured my attention.

Under the kitchen's dining table, a cardboard box with Avon beauty products and Amway cleaning products stood as a reminder of Berkis's multiple efforts at making ends meet, as an undocumented migrant and the main breadwinner for her family. She often sold cleaning products from a friend's discount store. A cousin who lived in a South Bronx public housing project was her main client, along with a handful of women who, occasionally, came to have Berkis wash and set, but mostly straighten, their hair. Many informal clients also participated in Berkis's monthly savings societies, known as SAMS, including raffles. The money gathered helped cover her rent, which took from 60 to over 80 percent of her family's monthly income.

On late Friday afternoons and weekends, Berkis played music on a small radio in her kitchen, often at her hair clients' request. On these days she would skip one or two meals to make extra money washing or drying the hair of a few close friends for half the price they would pay at the local hair salons. Her South Bronx cousin also came to earn a few dollars, helping Berkis wash or set hair with a blower or the large dryer and sweeping, cleaning, and washing towels and utensils by hand. On most weekends Berkis's husband, Amado, would eat and hang out at the deli downstairs until late at night, or until the last of Berkis's hair clients had gone. The boys, ages six and nine, would watch television in their room or visit their only friend in the building, the superintendent's son.

On busy Fridays or Saturdays, I would often volunteer to run to the deli, feigning my own hunger, to pick up lunch for Berkis and her children and sometimes beer for the women clients or Amado. I once had the pleasure of having my hair washed in Berkis's kitchen sink, and then set and blown out with her new portable dryer. This, I felt, brought me closer to Berkis and the other women, some of whom ultimately volunteered to participate in my study. From time to time, when business slowed, Berkis's older sister Sonia would help her find part-time gigs cleaning homes in Queens or New Jersey and filling in for Sonia's home attending assignments in the apartments of retired, impoverished, or infirm Latina women who did not mind the informal replacement.

Despite these efforts, Berkis struggled with her monthly rent of $1,000 at the time—an especially burdensome amount, as her combined family income fluctuated between $1,200 and $1,500 per month. I would often help her read or interpret letters from her children's school or serious warnings from utilities about interruption of her electric or phone service. Later, eviction warnings came from her building's management office due to her late rent payments.

Often an older Puerto Rican neighbor would place copies of *El Atalaya*, the Jehovah's Witnesses magazine, under her door, knowing of Berkis's need for prayers given her recent filing of an immigration petition to regulate her undocumented status as a victim of domestic abuse. Five years before Amado, her legal husband in the Dominican Republic and the father of her two sons, came to New York, Berkis had married a U.S. citizen, a Dominican man introduced to her by a close friend of Sonia, to help regulate her immigrant status. Berkis had asked Amado to accept a legal divorce and this temporary decision, only to secure the petitioning and reunification of her with her children in New York. Amado accepted with heaviness in his heart and a deep sense of shame, as he would later tell me. But he trusted Berkis, the more schooled of the two, the one who had always guided the family's decisions, especially for the sake of their children. But two years after Berkis had contracted into this marriage, the man began to visit Berkis's home without warning, demanding food and/or money, as well as sexual favors, and threatening to call off the deal if she did not comply. Berkis's mental health began to deteriorate, forcing her to seek counseling with an immigration agency's help. The agency also tried to help her obtain temporary legal status based on a domestic abuse case, mental health needs, and the fact that her current U.S. husband had abandoned his promise to endorse her as a legal immigrant. He later returned to the Dominican Republic, taking the money she had paid him.

Six months later, Sonia and her husband helped Berkis secure the money needed to bring her two small sons from Santo Domingo. To do so, they borrowed close to $10,000 from a loan shark to cover the airfare and the cost of two passports and visa stamps. The boys joined their mother in New York three years after her own migration. Amado joined them a year later, after nearly six years of conjugal separation.

Housing and the Tribulations of Marriage and Motherhood

In her kitchen, Berkis and I often talked as she cooked meals, did dishes, or hand-washed her sons' school uniforms in the kitchen sink. Outdated issues of

El Diario La Prensa that Berkis had picked up for free from the deli before it closed, topped a pile on the kitchen's only table, along with her children's school papers, neatly stacked, with the orderliness of an accountant. I would often notice Berkis's struggles to divine her children's homework in English, a language she knew only on a minimal level. Sometimes she would ask for help to understand the assignments so that she could explain them to her sons. She wanted to make sure her children did not fall behind, and that they could reinvent themselves through school in the way she had done. But her nine-year-old son, bespectacled and with somewhat of a stoic countenance, rarely smiled in my presence, and he often insisted that he did not need either my or his mother's help with his homework. As the older sibling, he had already interpreted his role as his little brother's keeper and made it a point to keep himself and his brother in check, tucked away in their room when I or other adults visited. His dark brown eyes, too serious for a boy his age, would avoid mine. They seemed to have already internalized his mother's anguish about her precarious immigrant status or his father's self-effacing sadness at not being able to rescue his family from an imminent descent into poverty.

Amado, Berkis's husband of almost twelve years at this point, did not know English and was "not a man of many words or letters," as Berkis frequently joked. He begrudged having completed only a vocational high school degree and then marrying a professional, someone he secretly knew expected more out of life than what he could offer. Meeting Amado and taking occasional glimpses at their interactions as a couple allowed me to reflect on the tribulations of educated Black or Brown Latinas whose limited assortative mating options lead them to marry men with lower education or prospects. Witnessing Berkis's motherhood joys or frustration at not being able to help her children with their homework also led me to reflect on the tribulations of educated immigrants who are not able to transfer their valued, imported human and cultural capital on to their children, especially in such a competitive host society.

A low and narrow hallway led into Berkis's living room, a frugal room with a somewhat desolate aura. The building's superintendent had given Berkis an old brown couch and a small black-and-white television set after learning of her two children's arrival. The two bedrooms, one on each side of the living room, offered Amado and the boys a bit of privacy, as none of the women that visited, including me, ever ventured that far. The smaller of the bedrooms, a space shared by the two boys, included a single wood-framed twin bed, pushed against the left wall. An old Nintendo console took up the rest of the space, on top of a small, black-lacquered corner table. In the late afternoon the scattered sunlight that often filtered through the windows warmed the living room's old wooden floor. The distant sounds of cartoons or of the old Nintendo games were in the air, and the enticing aroma of rice and beans and *cafecito con nues mozcada* (coffee with nutmeg) filled the room. Berkis and the women shared stories about the last time they visited, or the next time they would be visiting, their families in the Dominican Republic.

When the children finally reunited with her in New York City, Berkis immediately insisted they share the larger bedroom with her after nearly three years of not being able to hold them. Ten years before the smartphone and the social media age that allow visual interaction from a distance, her youngest son had been only two and her oldest five when Berkis had last seen or held them. Two years later, when Amado arrived, the sleeping arrangement changed. They had been married almost twelve years, but migration and financial issues had separated them, physically and gradually from the heart. A full-size bed with a modest wooden frame and a mirrorless dresser took most of the space in their bedroom. Two pillows and two portraits chronicled their conjugal union as well as Berkis's social mobility. The first portrait captured Berkis and Amado in a rapture, beaming with smiles, holding their first son, on his baptism. The second showed Berkis alone at her graduate school investiture, in full academic regalia, face glowing, holding up to the camera her diploma, almost six years before her migration. When I first became acquainted with Berkis, when her children and Amado were still in the Dominican Republic, I asked her if she had pictures from her wedding. She told me they were saved back home, as she had left them behind for her children. Besides, she was hoping to renew her marital vows in New York City when Amado arrived, as they had divorced as her last resort to change her legal status—a memory they wanted soon to forget.

I usually visited the apartment in the afternoon, when Berkis suggested I was most likely to find her home. During these times, I observed her interactions with her sons. Schooled only in raising daughters, I was delighted to see Berkis talking to her boys, especially when they came home from school. She would religiously ask what they had learned that day, demanding an inspection of their lunch boxes and, sometimes, an explanation of why one of the boys had not eaten his lunch. She insisted that boys needed discipline of both the mind and body to make them into strong yet considerate men, "¡Que valgan la pena! Y, que se valgan por si mismos; pero con piedad del projimo!" (boys that will be worthwhile! And, that will become self-reliant or successful but with compassion for others!!) Raised Catholic, Berkis lamented not being able to prepare her oldest son to receive his Holy Communion—"¿Y con que dinero?" (And with what money?) She would grieve about her inability to provide for the ceremony and festivities for this rite of passage. Even so, the boys prayed every night before going to sleep. I was most impressed with the neatness of their beds, surprised as to how these small boys managed to make them before going to school, when my own daughters could hardly manage to get dressed on time. On most weekend evenings Berkis had the boys walk with her to nearby apartment buildings, door-to-door, to sell Avon products, cleaning supplies, or numbers for her monthly raffles. But on most weekday evenings the boys kept to themselves in their room or in the small living room. While doing hair or cooking, Berkis watched from the kitchen, oversaw homework, intervened in fights over the TV or toy allotments, scolded the boys, or reminded the boys it was time for a bath or bed.

Amado was often absent from home, as sporadic work and long commutes delayed his arrival until the middle or late evening. But even when he was present, Berkis complained, he often kept to himself, at a distance from the kitchen, a space he viewed solely as Berkis's domain. On most evenings or weekend days Amado sat in the living room, transfixed in front of the small television. Of late he spent time with the men who loitered in front of the deli, many of whom had recently joined the unemployed or disabled, to play or watch games of dominoes or engage in the intricacies of taxicab mechanics. Berkis mustered her courage to tell me that Amado had been acting a little strange in the past few months since he had started working. He would not say if he had worked for a full day or for how long—let alone how much he had earned. Back in Santo Domingo, after he had toiled most of the day, and often evenings and weekends, in his taxicab, she knew the minimum or maximum he would have earned. In New York his work opportunities and his routines were different and unpredictable. Until recently, when he would come home after work, he would give her all the money he had earned. But now Berkis had no way of knowing his earnings. Every time he went out, Berkis worried that something would happen to him, since he had little knowledge of the language or how things worked in the new society, but mostly she worried about his undocumented status.

On the day of their younger son's fifth birthday celebration Amado shared his plans for going back home. We stood next to each other, at a distance from the mothers and small children surrounding the kitchen table and the cake. While Berkis eagerly urged her son to come close to the cake and pay attention to the camera while the children sang "Happy Birthday," I asked Amado what he thought of New York. I believe this was the first time I saw him with a relaxed smile. With his gaze straight at the cake and his youngest son's elated yet worried face, as Berkis fussed, insisting her son must make a birthday wish before blowing out the five candles—"Love, ask for something very special you would want from God!"—Amado smiled and kept his eyes fixed on his small son. As the boy struggled to keep his eyelids tightly shut while he whispered a wish, Amado mustered, "Esta ciudad está llena de sorpresas, de sueños, pero también de muchos sinsabores" (This city is filled with lots of surprises, of dreams, but also with some bitter disillusionments). Savoring the last sips of his beer, eyes downcast, he told me that when Berkis was finished with her immigration papers, he would go back home. He would buy another taxicab, and then a fleet, coming back to work in New York City if necessary, but only to save money to expand the business and eventually take his family back to Santo Domingo. He lowered his head, leaning it toward me, and then looked into my eyes for a moment, as if seeking solidarity. I sensed that Amado hoped that, since I had become close to Berkis and was the only one of their close connections who could navigate the larger society, I would help Berkis fix her immigration papers, and that that would get her to understand his sojourning, or dreams about going back home. Years later I would learn that Amado had gone back to Santo Domingo and never returned and that Berkis had ultimately resolved her immigrant status and sent her children to private schools, one of them to a highly ranked Catholic university.

The Scattered Spatial Mobility of Mexican Immigrants

Beyond their new status as working poor, undocumented immigrants, both Berkis's and Magdalena's fates in New York City were delimited by their vulnerable housing experiences in historically racialized neighborhoods of New York City. However, very distinct networks led middle-class Dominican and Mexican families to find housing or escape poverty. Magdalena and her husband, after a few years of living in East Harlem, moved into a more integrated neighborhood of Astoria, Queens. Berkis, however, remained in one of the poorest areas of West Harlem, eventually losing her husband and later being evicted, with long-term consequences to her and her children's mental health. These situations illustrate the multiple forms of intersectional inequality that undocumented families, especially Black immigrants like Berkis, confront despite migrating with high human capital.

I met Magdalena through a Spanish-speaking priest who organized support groups for domestic abuse victims in East Harlem. At the time, Magdalena lived in the first-floor apartment of a four-story row house tenement on the eastern periphery of El Barrio. In the late 1990s, this legendary Puerto Rican neighborhood had become known as Little Puebla for the many Mexicans from the state of Puebla who either lived, worked, or owned small businesses there—including taquerias, bakeries, and remittance agencies.

When we first met, Magdalena worked in a pocketbook and leather goods factory owned by an Egyptian family that operated in a basement apartment in East Harlem. Her husband, Orlando, had worked in this factory before finding a different job with his cousin's help. His cousin had worked as a handyman and assistant to a Puerto Rican building superintendent. After finding a better job at a Greek diner in Astoria, Queens, his cousin passed down the handyman job to Orlando. In this new position, Orlando earned about $200 a week (in 2004 dollars). In exchange, he also had access to his cousin's previous studio apartment in the basement of the apartment building. Orlando paid his cousin $250 a month rent, even though the apartment came free with the job. Orlando did not mind paying rent, as the average rent for a studio apartment in the area at that time ranged between $550 and $650 per month. Besides, his cousin had done him many favors, including helping Magdalena find work.

I believe Magdalena accepted being part of my focus group and doing an in-depth interview because the priest in her local church had endorsed my research on undocumented families' hardships. After a preliminary interview that was part of a focus group conducted in the church's basement, Magdalena agreed to a follow-up visit and an in-depth interview at her apartment. About a month later, my empathic responses to both her domestic abuse and her precarious living conditions built trust and willingness to allow me to document her life and that of her family for a year.

The week of the first interview, Magdalena showed me the eviction notice Orlando had found under their door. The notice came from the property's management office, addressed to her husband's cousin, whose name was still on the apartment lease. It terminated the studio's one-year lease due to a violation of occupancy codes: serious overcrowding by three people, including a child, in a studio limited to a single person's occupancy. The Puerto Rican superintendent suspected that some new non-Latino tenants, or "gringos," had reported the couple's precarious living arrangement and the superintendent's implicit consent to the management office.

The priest at Magdalena's church intervened on the couple's behalf. He pleaded with the property owners, a Jewish family on Long Island, to allow Magdalena's family to stay for another month or until the church could help them find a new place to live given the couple's small child. But before the church or even I could intervene,[5] Orlando found a new job and a place to live in Astoria. His cousin had learned of a handyman job in one of the buildings owned by his Greek employers, near Ditmars Boulevard. The Greek brothers who owned the diner rented apartments and rooms, mostly to coethnic families, but also a few to Mexican single men who worked for them and a few to single, White professionals.

Orlando's new job in Astoria led him to work with a coethnic superintendent, a Mexican man about his father's age who was also from Puebla. His job as a handyman also came with a free small one-bedroom apartment. Orlando only had to worry about paying for the electricity and his phone, and being on call seven days a week and twenty-four hours a day, in case the superintendent was unavailable or needed a hand with any emergencies for repair or maintenance work. This was above and beyond keeping a work shift of ten to twelve hours, six days a week. The move to Astoria also gave Magdalena access to a new set of Mexican women friends with better-paying jobs, and it expanded her networks to include working-class ethnic Whites such as Albanians and Greeks. Many of these newcomers attended a Greek Orthodox church with free English lessons for adults and summer programs for their youth. Magdalena's new apartment building was two blocks away from Ditmars Boulevard and Thirty-First Street in Astoria, near a commercial strip that also brought her new hopes for work. The immediate radius of her new community had a distinct demographic ebb and flow. It offered better housing and opportunities than those Magdalena had found in her racially and spatially isolated older neighborhood of East Harlem. As she explained, "I like it here; everyone seems to be busy at work, and people look really good. Besides, I am not too far from my old neighborhood, only twenty minutes by train. I can continue to attend my women's [domestic abuse] group, as I have close friends there already."

Since the 1990s, Astoria—just like Harlem—has experienced a gradual demographic and economic boom. This transformation has included the arrival of young White professionals from the suburbs or outlying areas of the city. This internal migration has paralleled new waves of immigrants from Asia and Latin America, with Chinese, Dominicans, and Mexicans among the groups with the highest populations. Concomitantly, real estate developers have now come to this traditionally ethnic White, working-class community. Astoria and many other immigrant neighborhoods undergoing fast transformation also attract *encargados*, or immigrants who rent rooms in their apartments to other coethnics. Longtime residents, including more assimilated immigrants and the native born, are more likely to become *encargados* like the immigrant Greek brothers who employed, but also rented an apartment to, Orlando. These middle-class businessmen play a key role in the demographic and economic transformation of Astoria. Often long-term citizens, including retired individuals or "empty nesters" with long tenure in rent-regulated tenements,[6] also rent apartments to immigrants, contributing to the ethnoracial and class diversity of gentrifying neighborhoods. (This is the case of the elderly Puerto Rican couple, retired civil servants, who rent a room to Mrs. Uraga and her family in East Harlem.) The only way these older residents manage to hold on to their housing and not lose it to the higher rents imposed by gentrification is by renting rooms to immigrants and young single professionals—often their adult relatives who, despite their professional salaries, cannot afford contemporary housing market prices.[7]

The next section illustrates the housing experiences of undocumented immigrant families who have few skills and little education. I reintroduce the living arrangements of families and their effect on motherhood practices and relations with spouses or conjugal partners and children.

LIVING IN SOMEONE ELSE'S HOME: THE TRIBULATIONS OF UNDOCUMENTED MOTHERS AND WIVES

When we first met, Mrs. Uraga had lived for about four years on the periphery of the fading Puerto Rican community of East Harlem. Unlike women like Berkis who lead their migration, Mrs. Uraga had followed her husband to New York City, without having any input about the selection of her housing or group living arrangement. The neighborhood where she lived had initially been settled by several cohorts of Puerto Ricans, and later by waves of Dominicans. In the early

2000s, Mexicans, mostly immigrants from rural villages like that of Mrs. Uraga's family, began to rent single rooms as boarders. Young professionals, increasingly from eastern Europe, the Middle East, and West Africa, were already apparent as new occupants in half-renovated buildings.

On a rainy afternoon around 3:00 p.m., I visited Mrs. Uraga's apartment to conduct an in-depth interview.[8] As soon as I rang the bell, I heard someone struggling with the door's lock and metallic chain. The door opened only a quarter of the way, and a woman with a soft voice greeted me in Spanish. She was not quite five feet tall, with dark brown skin and Indigenous Mesoamerican phenotype, in her early or mid-forties. With a gentle and apologetic smile, she asked if I was the person sent from the church. I nodded. I saw a small girl peeking out from what I gathered was a bedroom door very close to the entryway. In a low voice and using her hand, Mrs. Uraga signaled for me to follow her inside, then stopped to get the girl, about three years old, from the next room.

As Mrs. Uraga opened the bedroom door to get the child, I took a quick look inside. I noted that four adults were sleeping either on the floor or on thin mats. One middle-aged man slept on a bunk bed. I tried to speak with the little girl in Spanish and reached my hand out to her. With a nervous smile Mrs. Uraga whispered, looking down at the girl, that we must speak quietly so as not to wake anyone, as her family had worked the previous night. As we walked to the kitchen, I noticed an elderly couple, the apartment's *encargados*, seated in the small living room with the lights off, their gazes fixed on a small black-and-white television. They appeared to be White Latinos in their late sixties or early seventies.

In the kitchen, where we sat to do the interview, we talked for a while about her small granddaughter and the inclement winter weather, and then I asked Mrs. Uraga how she managed living in someone else's home. She explained, "It is like living someone else's life! In someone's home one feels disoriented, estranged; but one must be also grateful for others are worse off." What Mrs. Uraga missed most was a kitchen for cooking. To prepare meals she had to use the kitchen of either a male relative who lived in the neighborhood or a close family friend from her village in Puebla who lived in the Mott Haven area of the Bronx, about thirty-five minutes away by public transportation. She shrugged her shoulders and gave me a resigned smile. While looking down at her hands and avoiding my eyes, she calmly explained how she coped: "¡Yo no sabía que este lugar no tiene cocina, o que nunca puedo preparar comida para mi familia!" (I did not know that this place did not have a kitchen or that I would not ever be able to prepare food for my family!) I gathered later that even the use of the bathroom was limited. Only two people per day could take showers; otherwise, the landlord might notice too much water in use and the elderly couple who rented the apartment would be in trouble.

I noticed at this point that Spanish was not Mrs. Uraga's native language, so I asked what other language she spoke. She told me Nahuatl, the language spoken

by a large share of Indigenous people in Puebla and in the Mesoamerican southern and central regions of Mexico. I told her I had visited the small town of San
Francisco in Puebla, where one of the largest Nahuatl communities resides. She
smiled and seemed very surprised and also pleased at this disclosure.

When I asked Mrs. Uraga how many people lived with her in the apartment,
she lowered her eyes again, looking at her right fingers, and holding each one
with her left hand as she did the count: "My husband, our oldest daughter . . . ah,
my son and daughter-in-law, and their only son; he is in school now; and, yes, of
course, my little granddaughter!" (the three-year-old girl under the kitchen table
who tightly held my left hand). I asked Mrs. Uraga how her family managed the
sleeping arrangements in one bedroom. She looked at my eyes this time, with an
amused smile, and answered, "Gracias a dios que unos duermen de día y otros de
noche" (Thank God, some sleep in the daytime and others at night).

After the interview, I noted that five adults, one adolescent, and a preschool
child lived as boarders in a single room in a two-bedroom apartment. The couple
who held the lease had lived in this rent-stabilized apartment for over thirty
years. Mrs. Uraga and her family paid fifty dollars per week for each adult, for a
total of $250 per week; the *encargado* Latino family did not charge fees for the
two children, a boy of twelve and the girl of three. This was a generous gesture,
but even so, they were limited as to how they could eat or even bathe, as they had
no access to the kitchen and only two family members could take a bath daily.
The children were not allowed to play or lounge freely in the small living room
space and were restricted mostly to their one room.

On my way back home, I better understood the nervous stares of the older
Latino couple who rented the room to the Uraga family. I also understood why
Mrs. Uraga had hesitated to open the door to a stranger and cleverly introduced
me as a "teacher" she met in her church to the *encargados*. I realized I was lucky
to have witnessed these living arrangements and the unique challenges and survival strategies that came with them, as well as the remarkable strength of the
poor mothers in undocumented families. The practice of Latino immigrants
subletting rooms to other coethnics was first documented by Sarah Mahler in
what she calls the "encargado system," where more assimilated immigrants with
longer tenure in the United States tend to rent rooms to their more vulnerable,
immigrant coethnics.[9] These arrangements often lead to intraethnic competition
and exploitation, as *encargados* tend to rent rooms at twice the going market rate.
Yet these arrangements also provide undocumented immigrants and the working poor—mainly, single mothers—the only way to avoid homelessness. The
findings in this chapter contribute new, nuanced insights into children's lives and
how group living arrangements affect parenting and relations between mothers
and their children, which have not been explored in previous works, including
Mahler's. For example, Mrs. Uraga said the *encargados* would get very nervous
whenever her small granddaughter would pass near their shelf with the TV and

small knickknacks, quickly discouraging her from sitting on the couch or playing on the floor. The children have no legitimacy to claiming a space or watching the small TV, which is often the only diversion of the poor. They had no access to a refrigerator or a kitchen. Children do not understand their status as illegitimate boarders nor the limited spaces in which they exist.

Group Living Arrangements and the Health of Children

Despite the benefits that immigrant women derive from group living arrangements, such as paying lower rent and having access to readily available networks of support, undocumented families face the worst of housing health risks. As the case of Mrs. Uraga reveals, the older couple who rented her family a room as boarders would not allow use of their kitchen, despite the presence of a preschooler and a school-age adolescent. This violates the housing health codes for occupancy imposed by the New York City Housing Authority.[10] Additionally, children older than two years should not sleep with adults, and only with siblings or parents when emotional or physical limitations require such accommodations.[11] In this case, five adults, an adolescent, and a preschool child all shared a single room.

Berkis and many other respondents found roaches and other bugs inside their food pantries, on their clothes, and even on their own or their children's bodies. As Berkis explained,

> There were so many roaches in this apartment that I grimace at the thought. There was no money or room to fit another bed. I used to sleep on the floor with my children on the couch. Roaches used to walk all over us. They even bit me inside my private parts. A friend of mine came to the room one night to bring me a raincoat. We were already sleeping. When I turned on the lights, I was covered with roaches. I just cried and shook the entire night. It was the end of the summer, and I used the only sheets we had to cover my sons, head to toe. I had to sleep with a coat on, covering myself from head to toe. I was sort of traumatized!

A few undocumented boarders and tenants complained about their fears of roaches or moths going inside their babies' or small children's ear canals, a phenomenon that was reported by a Mexican woman to have happened to a four-year-old living in the South Bronx. One of my respondents had a son who suffered from intermittent asthma attacks. During one attack she rushed him to the emergency room at Lincoln Hospital, and the doctor discovered a dehydrated moth inside his ear canal. She began sobbing, thinking how she and her small son would have to go back to the same dark, humid, and windowless basement room: "When I understood what he [the doctor] was saying with an interpreter, I felt panic about taking my son back to sleep in that horrible place, but what are our choices?"

In 2009, when I met Gloria again, she had relocated to a new apartment at a new immigrant destination, Mount Pleasantville. She was now an *encargada*. Yet her apartment's abysmal conditions forced her to spend an entire year, including a harsh winter, with her two bedroom windows covered with plastic wrap. Her room was so cold that she had to keep an electric heater running all the time to keep her small children warm, and this doubled her electric bill. But the property managers, an elderly Chinese couple, were fighting a contracting company they had hired to do building repairs, including Gloria's windows. Gloria and her younger siblings knew that they could not complain to the Municipal Housing Authority of Mount Pleasantville due to their undocumented status and because her Chinese landlord had allowed Gloria to informally rent rooms to other coethnics as an *encargada*.

Another woman respondent's precarious housing conditions further substantiate that the undocumented, especially single mothers and their children, experience the worst forms of housing abuse and health risks. This woman was a forty-two-year-old Dominican mother of two elementary school girls. When we met, she had been living in the East Kingsbridge neighborhood of the Bronx for about six years. Her apartment was on the top floor of a six-floor walk-up building. Upon my entering her apartment to conduct the interview, and knowing of my interest in immigrants' housing conditions, she stopped to show me her bathroom. There she had placed an open umbrella hanging above the shower ceiling and most of the toilet area to prevent leaking water from falling into the floor. Luckily, she said, with humored resignation, "at least when it rains, we get fresh water directly from the sky. Sometimes I collect it in buckets to water my plants!" After I explained the threat of mold and its possible effects on her children's lungs, she said she was planning to move. Otherwise she would have to assume the cost of repairs, as the superintendent had said there was not much he could do. "He and the owner knew I was undocumented," she explained, "so they abused us!" Besides, she had already had some run-ins with the superintendent because he had sexually harassed her a few times. When he drank on weekends, he would text, call, or even come knocking at her door. One day she asked a cousin to call the police. So she knew it was time to find another place. She lamented that her two small daughters were attending an excellent Catholic school a few blocks away from her building—the only luxury gained from renting her daughters' bedroom to another woman boarder.

Besides housing abuse, undocumented Mexican immigrants are three times more likely than Dominicans to live as boarders or in group living arrangements. The undocumented also experience higher overcrowding indices. Longitudinal census data analysis indicates that most Mexican households include an average of three to five adults per housing unit, while among Dominicans that number is only 1.5 adults per unit.[12] My qualitative findings (see table 4.1) reveal that these estimates may be low. On average, Mexican households include three or more

TABLE 4.1   Number of Adults per Household

	Dominican (N = 45)	Mexican (N = 41)	Total (N = 86)
1–2	75.5%	53.7%	65.1%
3 or more	24.5%	42.3%	34.9%

SOURCE: Author's interviews, 2000–2003, and follow-up interviews, 2009–10.

adults (ages eighteen and older) per *room*, not per housing unit. This does not include the at least 2.2 nonrelative coethnics who either rent rooms or live in group arrangements when Mexicans rent apartment units and become *encargados*. The same pattern holds among Dominican households. On average, Dominican apartments include one or two adults, and sometimes also an additional roommate or boarder, especially in single mothers' households. Yet a larger share of Dominican women, especially those with a legalized immigrant status, engage in the "encargado system" than do Mexicans.

When Employers Are Also Landlords

In 2003, when I first met Gloria in the northeastern Bronx, she shared a two-bedroom apartment with her husband and her two younger brothers, both in their early twenties. The two young men shared one room, and Gloria, her husband, and their children shared the other. All of the adults were undocumented, but two children, a boy of about six and a girl of about four, had been born in Chicago. Gloria's apartment was owned by the same Italian family that owned the meat store where her husband, Antonio, and his older brother worked. The building's superintendent, an older Mexican man who had emigrated from Puebla in the mid-1990s, lived in another basement apartment, across the hall from Gloria's, in the back of the building near the storage, garbage, and maintenance room. A dark metal emergency door led into a side alley and then onto the street. Antonio's older brother had sponsored the couple in New York and helped them find this apartment. Upon their arrival, he instructed them that the landlord preferred tenants in the basement to exit the building from the back alley. The same was asked of immigrants who worked in the meat store's basement floor, just a few blocks away.[13] Antonio knew well the cautionary implications of new spatial boundaries, as all the men who worked with him in the meat store's basement, where they cleaned and prepared all the carcasses, cutting and packaging the meats for display in the store's main-floor counters and window, were undocumented. Antonio was soon promoted, which meant that he would drive with the Italian men and another younger Mexican man to pick up the carcasses at wholesale distribution plants.

In Gloria's basement apartment the faded grayish paint on her living room walls was peeling, and many tiles were missing or cracked in the bathroom and the kitchen. The living room and the small kitchen where Gloria and I met on a few occasions had poor lighting, and it seemed the heat was never on. Before the interview we drank *horchata* (a milky drink made from nuts and/or rice) while we talked and shared stories about my new baby girl and Gloria's preschool daughter. She felt the proximity of her kitchen window to where the garbage was stored and incinerated was the reason there was often a disagreeable smell of burnt refuse in the small dwelling.

During our long interview in the small kitchen, which took two visits, Gloria's older son, a very mature boy for his age, frequently interrupted our talk to ask me questions about who I was or if I was coming back for his forthcoming birthday or during Christmas. Her two younger brothers, ages twenty and twenty-five, sat motionless in front of the TV. Gloria explained that they were timid. I surmised they had just arrived and were cautious about whom to trust or crossing different social boundaries given their extra vulnerable status as undocumented migrants and tenants. With the superintendent's implicit consent, Antonio, Gloria's husband, used Sheetrock to divide the living room into two smaller rooms: one in which the family could eat meals and/or watch the small TV, and a second one with two bunk beds where Gloria's younger brothers could sleep.

Gloria and Antonio's apartment was just a few blocks away from Grand Concourse, a major thoroughfare lined with gracious buildings erected during the 1890s and the early twentieth century.[14] In Berkis's West Harlem community, a twenty-minute drive west and across the East River, similar tenement structures were built in the same period. Both neighborhoods had large apartment buildings with high, decorated ceilings and elegant marble stairways reminiscent of a distant past when wealthy European immigrants and the middle-class professionals that served them kept at a prudent distance from the urban poor. Today it is mostly the working poor—Black and Brown immigrants from the Dominican Republic, Puerto Rico, West Africa, and the West Indies—who rent apartments from absentee landlords. African American and Latino superintendents, custodians, and floor managers now act as middlemen, tending to the needs of their majority White property-owning employers and those of their Black and Brown coethnic tenants.

A few weeks after they migrated, Gloria's brothers were already busy at work in the same butcher shop where her husband, Antonio, and his older brother had worked for years. Upon arrival, Antonio told her brothers that they did not have to pay rent for a while but would be expected to help pay for food, especially when Gloria and Antonio did the monthly *compras*, or big shopping. Sharing food expenses allowed Gloria and her brothers to pool together money to send to their mother back in Mexico. The group living arrangement also allowed Gloria and Antonio to save money and send larger remittances to their families.

Most important, Gloria was able to stay at home, caring for her two small children, until they entered school.

Documenting how employers—mostly, ethnic Whites who own businesses in gentrifying neighborhoods—are also landlords alerted me to a new and intersectional pattern of inequality vulnerable immigrants experience in housing as employers play dual roles as both landlords and employers. This housing/work integration represents an advantage for immigrants, as their integration into mainstream middle-class neighborhoods increases, but it can also be a double disadvantage: if a worker is fired, he or she also is evicted.

The Housing of the Poor

Gloria's case illustrates that group living arrangements come with overcrowding and often living in substandard conditions, such as her basement apartment, which was usually filled with smoke coming from the incinerator. When Gloria moved to this apartment, her new landlord refused to replace her windows, forcing her to sleep with plastic on two windows and an electric heater on all the time. As the case of Mrs. Uraga has illustrated, group living arrangements often limit the relationships of mothers with their spouses and, more than anything, their child-rearing practices. Although public housing increases women's housing security and agency, it also tends to increase their class and racial isolation, as the case of Carmen will now illustrate.

Upon arriving in New York City in the early 2000s, Carmen, her husband of ten years, and their eight-year-old daughter shared a room in her mother's rent-stabilized apartment in Washington Heights. Most of her extended maternal family had lived in this neighborhood for over twenty years. After a few years of renting a room from her mother, Carmen and her husband moved to a one-bedroom apartment down the street. The couple managed to pay rent at market prices, or $750 per month, for three years. An abrupt separation from her husband diminished Carmen's income, forcing her to apply for public housing. She learned about the opportunity to apply for public housing in the southeast Bronx through maternal relatives who had lived in the same housing structure since the 1980s. Thus, unlike Gloria's relocation to an ex-suburban city in the periphery of New York City, with better chances for finding work, Carmen's relocation into public housing increased her isolation from extended kin—and her mother's function as chief babysitter for her two children—in Washington Heights.

In the fall of 2009, when I reconnected again with Carmen, she had lived in public housing for close to six years. She shared that she had been placed on a waiting list that would take between four and six years for her to receive housing. Her maternal aunt who had resided in the housing projects for about ten years encouraged Carmen to submit her housing application only to a specific agent who had helped the aunt and one of her daughters to secure an apartment in the same building. Six months later, Carmen moved into a one-bedroom apartment, bumped ahead on the waiting list for a fee of $2,500 paid in cash to this insider. This took all her savings, as well as $500 borrowed from her mother. This type of informal strategy allows immigrants with good network resources to compete for housing and other resources; it also allows these "public agents" to exploit poor and vulnerable immigrants, especially single mothers, thus depleting their meager resources through fraudulence. Carmen, like many immigrants, was afraid to report these abuses for fear of losing her housing or getting her family in trouble.

Although the move increased her housing stability, public housing proved to be a double-edged sword. For example, to meet the income cap that would qualify them for housing subsidies with Carmen as a working-poor mother, she had to quit her full-time job and maintain a part-time weekend job. These same income caps qualified her for much-needed Medicaid benefits for her asthmatic son. For several years Carmen had held two jobs as both a weekend home attendant and a domestic babysitter, but neither one of these jobs provided health insurance for herself or her children. Her teenage daughter complained to me that her mother kept her like a prisoner in their new apartment. When her mother was not around, she was forced to spend most afternoons and nights at home, mainly on the phone with friends and family in Washington Heights. She was not allowed to hang out outside, not even with cousins that lived in the same building. Carmen was afraid her teen daughter would get mugged or hang out with the wrong kids, some of whom sold or used drugs.

As Carmen's case illustrates, a common housing strategy of the working poor who have legal immigrant status is to apply for public housing. Scholars find that public housing increases women's housing stability and their children's permanence in neighborhood schools.[15] However, my qualitative findings show that poorer coethnics than Carmen and the permanent poor experience in public housing intersectional forms of social, class, and racial isolation. This problem is exacerbated by the increasing concentration of families with women as primary breadwinners, which often limits their ability to move out of public housing. Despite these barriers, public housing reduces housing displacements so that children stay in neighborhood schools.[16] Yet my insights reveal that support is needed for single mothers and their children, and especially adolescents, who often experience the most social and class isolation, which leads to intergenerational poverty and racialization. A study by Ramona Hernández and colleagues indicates that Dominicans have the lowest of all household incomes, increasing the share of displacement from the Manhattan neighborhoods of Washington Heights and Inwood to resort to public housing due to increasing rent.[17] But for the undocumented, who are ineligible, this means homelessness.

HOUSING INSTABILITY AND MENTAL HEALTH

Housing abuses also affect the mental health and daily functioning of families. In one case, Alicia, a twenty-eight-year-old undocumented migrant and manual laborer, rented a Queens apartment from an Ecuadorian woman whom she met at work in a bakery shop. Upon learning that Alicia was looking for a place to live, another coworker, also an *encargada*, referred her to the woman coethnic, in East Harlem. Alicia ultimately ended up losing her security deposit of $2,500, but with the help of a social worker at her daughter's school she was able to get her rent reduced by almost $300. As she explained her housing story to me,

> I got this apartment through M, this Ecuadorian woman I met who held the lease. She rented the apartment to us for $1,000 per month. I asked for less, but she refused. The social worker from my daughter's school came home one day to work with my little one. She heard about my rent and the conditions and she intervened for me. The [Ecuadorian] woman had to leave me the apartment and then we paid the owner only $783, which is what he was charging her; but she kept the $2,000 I had given her as down payment. What can one do? She said she would report me to the *migra* [immigration services] if I insisted on the return of my money.

This narrative illustrates how vulnerable, undocumented migrant workers can also become victims of more assimilated minorities, as Sarah Mahler found to be the case in the early 1990s.[18] Like most of Mahler's vulnerable, undocumented Salvadoran immigrants in Long Island, New York, Alicia thought she had no right to seek protection from the local housing authority or the police. After her child's social worker intervened with the housing management office, Alicia was able to put the apartment lease in her name. This again validates the positive benefits of intracommunity networks for immigrant families, and especially for single mothers. I also find that undocumented tenants paid the highest rents among all my respondents. During the first stage of this study, in 2000–2003, the average monthly rent paid in New York City by Dominican and Mexican immigrants with a legal immigrant status was $1,000. But undocumented tenants paid an average of 30–40 percent higher fees, or between $1,300 and $1,400 per month. Room boarders paid an average of $300–$450 per month. By 2010, room rentals had increased to $600–$750 per month, averaging $150–$200 per week per adult.

The case of another respondent, Monica, helps illustrate the intersectional forms of inequality that undocumented mothers experience. When we first met, Monica, a forty-four-year-old Dominican single mother of two and also an *encargada*, had been renting rooms mostly to coethnics or distant relatives for about five years. She lived in an apartment building in Kingsbridge, the Bronx.

Apparently an Albanian immigrant couple to whom Monica had rented a room for about a year fell six months behind in their rent payments. The couple claimed money shortages due to a family death in the home country and a reduction in the husband's work hours. Six months later, when Monica demanded payment, the husband threatened to report her to the police or housing authorities because of her undocumented status. As she explained,

> I was renting two rooms in my apartment after borrowing money from a relative to paint and fix them. An Albanian couple was referred by another Dominican woman who always helped me get cleaning jobs in the Pelham area [of the Bronx]. But, about two months after moving in, the couple stopped paying rent. The husband claimed he lost his job at a mechanic shop. Then, when he found a new job, I asked about the rent payments. They owed me three months, but they had another excuse this time about a death in the family. One day the wife came to the kitchen. She told me in sort of a threatening tone that if I kept putting pressure on them, her husband who had a bad temper was going to call the police. She said I was not supposed to even be in this country! One day, when I came home from work, I found the two plants I kept in the kitchen dead, as if someone had placed acid or done some *brujeria* [witchcraft] on them. The room was empty, and they were all gone. They had taken all my kitchen knives and other appliances, even my food!

Beyond illustrating the abuses of vulnerable, undocumented families in substandard or deplorable living conditions, the above narrative also connotes the networks that help frail families find housing. In the first case, a Mexican respondent befriends an Ecuadorian coworker who links her to another Ecuadoran *encargada* in East Harlem. In the second case, a Dominican woman's narrative further reveals how undocumented immigrants' work and housing networks often overlap, as an Albanian family is referred to Monica by a coworker. Like the cases of Berkis, Gloria, Magdalena, and their spouses or conjugal partners, these findings show that immigrants' housing and employment networks tend to overlap. The experiences of immigrant women who often rent rooms from coethnics or who act as renters or *encargados* reveal the housing strategies of vulnerable migrants, often undocumented individuals or mothers who are main breadwinners, irrespective of migrant status. Their housing and work experiences illustrate the price many of these women pay for access to housing, and the different forms of abuse and risks to their physical and mental health, as Monica's narrative reveals.

The Injuries of Deportation

During our follow-up interview in her new destination of Mount Pleasentville Gloria described to me the painful experience of her husband's deportation and her eventual heartbreaking divorce. In 2008, the police had stopped Antonio on his way back from his weekly drive to Union City, New Jersey. He was picking up wholesale animal carcasses at a distribution store for his employer, a trip he had made regularly, but not in the driver's seat. Apparently, one of the delivery van's headlights was burned out that evening, and the police used this to stop the van after it crossed the George Washington Bridge into Washington Heights. Because of his expired temporary driver's license and because the headlight was broken, Antonio was given a summons to appear in court. As the police did not allow him to drive the truck, his boss had to send his most senior coworker and coethnic to pick Antonio and the van up. Antonio spent six weeks in an immigration detention center in Elizabeth, New Jersey, and three months in El Paso, Texas, where a judge ruled that Antonio would be deported back to Mexico, despite his employer's intervention and Gloria's efforts to borrow $5,000 from her uncle and other relatives in Mexico and the United States to pay for an immigration lawyer.

To save the $3,000 that she would need for coyote fees for Antonio's possible return, Gloria took a day job as a domestic in Pelham, an upper-middle-class neighborhood in the northeast Bronx. Antonio's previous employer and his wife helped Gloria find this job and continued to show support for her and the children after Antonio's deportation. But the pressure of a full-time job, shifts in schedules, and being the sole caretaker for her children and housekeeper for her younger brothers began to take a toll on Gloria's physical and mental health. Uncertainty about Antonio's return and fears about her own possible deportation gave her chronic anxiety, causing a lack of sleep and bouts of depression. Amid tears, on the first day we met for the interview, Gloria shared how she had pulled it off on her own, with two small children and no papers: "I don't know how I did it. It all seems like one long nightmare. Thank God my younger sister [from Mexico] came to help me. I had already offered for her to come many times before, but she was scared of crossing the border. At first she helped me take care of my children, but then she wanted to work."

Although Antonio and Gloria had planned for his impending return to New York, the plan never materialized. The *pasada* (border crossing) was postponed a few times due to rising apprehensions at the Mexican-U.S. border and the staggering number of deportations during the administration of President Barack Obama (2009–16). A year after Antonio's return was thwarted, Gloria heard that he was drinking and spending nights outside of his parents' home. She was distraught when he was not there to take her calls. Even when her older son asked to speak with him and Gloria left messages with his mother, Antonio did not return their calls on time, and when he did, he sounded emotionally distant. Two years later, with the help of a social worker and her employer, Gloria filed a petition in Westchester County Family Court to claim full custody of her U.S.-born children.

Overall, Gloria's case illustrates the precarious living arrangements of undocumented families and deportation's scarring impact. The interview insights reveal that at least four of ten Mexican families and 2.5 of ten Dominican families had experienced deportation or apprehension. Overall, Dominicans were apprehended at a higher rate than Mexicans, but the latter were deported twice as often. Of the nearly ten out of eighty-six families who had experienced deportation in my original study, men were deportation and incarceration targets. Research now confirms a new pattern of gendered deportation, one that targets mostly Black and Brown immigrant men.[19] Qualitative insights from my interviews reveal that deportations also increase the share of households headed by women.

The deportation shock also introduces new anxieties and psychological pressure on the families of the deported—especially fears of another imminent apprehension and/or deportation.[20] Most notably, as Gloria's extended story will later show, deportation and housing instability also hinder the educational and emotional development of children. Despite her son's qualifying to attend an elementary school program for gifted children, he fell behind in school for a few years, needing counseling after his father's deportation. Gloria's story is similar to those of many other women respondents in my study who also faced increased anxiety after a spouse or close family member experienced deportation. The enactment of the USA PATRIOT Act after 9/11, designed to combat terrorism, put limits on the court's ability to review detentions and deportations. Other ordinances put in place during the administration of President Donald Trump increased immigrant backlash.[21] Deportations of Latin American groups have occurred at unprecedented rates.[22]

The Toll of Eviction

In my research, close to 30 percent of Dominicans and about 22 percent of Mexican women experience housing instability including eviction and homelessness. Homelessness, however, is more common among Dominican than Mexican families. This finding correlates with a 2018 report by the Association for Neighborhood Housing and Development (ANHD; see table 4.2).[23]

Updated insights support earlier findings about more Dominican women than Mexican women having to exchange sex for a place to live or to spend a night in a homeless shelter.[24] Overall, single mothers and undocumented immigrants face the greatest risks of rental and housing abuse, irrespective of ethnicity, race, and class of origin.

Three years after her arrival in the United States, Magdalena moved from East Harlem to Astoria, an established working-class ethnic White neighborhood in Queens. Her husband's network helped the couple find a new and better place to live, in a small building owned by his Greek employer. Berkis, meanwhile, remained in the poorest neighborhood of West Harlem for another few years

TABLE 4.2   New York City Housing Stress Indicators, by Race and Ethnicity (2016–17)

| | Hispanic_Latino Groups | | | | Non-Hispanic_Latino Groups | | |
	Mexican	Puerto Rican	Dominican	Colombian	White	Black	Asian
Number of evictions by marshal	339	388	470	239	194	433	213
Percentage with severe crowding of 1.5 or more persons per room	5.7%	4.4%	5.3%	5.6%	3.7%	4.3%	4.6%
Serious housing code violations	11	13	15	8	10	12	8
Number of DRIE or SCRIE apartments*	1,202	883	1,761	1,225	1,112	892	1,138
Threats to affordable housing	11	13	15	8	10	12	8

SOURCE: Block, 2018.
NOTE: * DRIE = Disabled Rent Increase Exemption; SCRIE = Senior Citizen Rent Increase Exemption.

until her eviction. After Amado, her husband, had tried (to no avail) to find work and adjust to life in New York City, he became depressed and despondent. One day Berkis asked him to move out. Later that year, her physical health deteriorated, and she found it hard to keep the pace of holding different side jobs to make ends meet as the sole caretaker and provider. When we met for a follow-up interview, she shared how her rent in her apartment in West Harlem fell into arrears for two consecutive months; she was evicted and forced to move into a shelter with her two small sons. Her sister Sonia had refused to bring Berkis to her apartment, telling her that things had changed and there were warnings of evictions in the building.

Amid painful sobs, Berkis shared how after just three weeks in the shelter she had suffered a nervous breakdown and required counseling and medical treatment by a psychiatrist. Five months later she relocated to the South Bronx, near the Hunts Point area, where her cousin had allowed Berkis to sleep with her children on a sofa bed in the living room. But, as the mattress springs were in such bad shape, she had to lay it flat on the floor. The roaches and other pest conditions made it hard for Berkis to sleep, as she was afraid her children would be bitten by the roaches or would develop asthma from sleeping on a floor treated with pesticides. Though Berkis was unable to obtain a permanent legal residency status based on her domestic abuse experience, her mental health counselor advised that she take advantage of her temporary legal status to take

English classes in her children's public school. And a social worker with whom Berkis had developed a close relationship during her stay at the family shelter helped her enroll in a local community agency's program to gain a home health attendant certification.

With the help of her paternal uncle, Gloria moved to Mount Pleasentville a new Latino immigrant destination, after her husband, Antonio, was deported. This move increased Gloria's economic opportunities as a single mother and as an *encargada*. Things did not turn out as well for Berkis, however, as a Black single mother, and despite the advanced professional degree she imported. While Berkis had only managed to find a series of dead-end jobs, her temporary legal status allowed her to qualify for training as a full-time home attendant. In addition to selling cleaning products and beauty items and washing other women's hair, Berkis also conducted weekly raffles and carried a rotating savings society with a group of family women and friends. Even so, none of it covered her $1,200 monthly rent, especially after she and her husband permanently separated.

One evening, upon returning home after selling Avon products door-to-door on foot with her two sons, Berkis found a large wooden plank nailed across her apartment door and an eviction notice from the New York City Marshals' Office. Because Berkis had missed one single appointment at housing court, her landlord had won the case to evict her and had ordered the superintendent to remove Berkis's belongings. The superintendent, who knew Berkis and treated her as a friend, asked for clemency on her behalf but was mandated to proceed. A few feet away she saw all of her belongings in a large pile, in plastic bags and crates, in a corner of the storage room. The superintendent had no authorization to let Berkis or anyone else into the room, and the management office had prepared an itemized list of her property, which was to be conferred by the Marshals' Office as property to the landlord in lieu of Berkis's rental payment. Unable to afford a temporary place or to secure her few belongings (her and her children's clothes, the portraits of her children's christening and of her own graduation, and their school report cards), Berkis became clinically depressed and unable to function, forcing her to seek temporary refuge in a homeless shelter. The last time I visited Berkis, she told me she had suffered what her therapist considered a nervous breakdown. She stared at me with a measured and stoic, yet courteous, look, while I tried to reconcile the woman she used to be with the one she was now, making sense of all that had happened to her in the last few years. She had again secured an apartment of her own, this time in the South Bronx in a large prewar building near Yankee Stadium. She held her head high—the way she used to, dignified—and shared something the therapist told her that had stuck with her: "When problems attack your mind and your heart at the same time, this leaves you feeling you are no longer the person you thought you once were . . . but I had to think of how far I had come and how much more lay ahead for my sons and me." This made her reflect about her need for healing. Berkis sobbed uncontrollably while I struggled to wipe my own tears from my face and note-pad. She told me that only after her therapist had explained what happened to her was she able to mourn the loss of her immigrant dreams: "¡Lloré como el día que se murió mi madre!" (I cried the same as the day my mother died!)

The mental health counseling Berkis received at an immigration center was key to her slow recovery. At a public clinic she received weekly advice, strong directives from a social worker at her children's school, and a temporary court-appointed legal guardian. Her therapist told her she needed to learn how to cope with her immigration, the failure of her fifteen-year marriage, the residual effects of working three or four part-time jobs while never making ends meet, and the stigma and fear of having lost control after a nervous breakdown. She had to learn how to cope with this injury and the intermittent depression while also making sense of her new life as a highly educated, yet impoverished, single Black mother. She had to make new plans, get better, and reinvent herself for her two small sons. One in four of the women participating in this qualitative study had experienced eviction or displacement. One in ten had experienced or had a close family member who had experienced deportation.

Sociologist Mathew Desmond's acclaimed ethnographic work *Evicted* documents the consequences of housing evictions for striving and working-class families in Milwaukee, Wisconsin. Desmond captures the devastating cumulative effects that the experience and stigma of eviction leave on individuals. It eventually leads some to suicide, which is more common among those who are Black single mothers. Desmond concludes that losing a home leads poor families to suffer for years, and children are not spared. When a mother fails to keep her home and her belongings, the act saps any joy and strength she has to care for her children. The experience, therefore, can also scar the children for life. "Then there is the toll eviction takes on a person's spirit," Desmond adds. "The violence of displacement can drive people to depression, and in extreme cases, even suicide. One in two recently evicted mothers reports multiple symptoms of clinical depression, double the rate of similar mothers who were not displaced from their homes. Even after years pass, evicted mothers are less happy, energetic, and optimistic than their peers." Eviction can cast families "onto a different, and much more difficult, path," yet "for poor women of color and their children it has become ordinary." Additionally, Desmond notes, "the substandard housing and unsafe neighborhood to which many evicted families must relocate can degrade a child's health, ability to learn, and sense of self-worth."[25]

Similarly, I argue that evictions convey a painful yet more complex sense of loss and dislocation for immigrant families, as homes are material and symbolic sanctuaries of all that was already left behind in the nation of origin. Immigrant mothers have already borne the emotional price of leaving behind not only a place that was once most meaningful but also, at times, their own children. Losing one's home means diminished hopes for family reunification. Beyond hopes for improving their and their children's economic and social conditions, immigrant mothers bear the responsibility of transplanting the home as traditional bearers of culture. Beyond holding a combination of poorly paid jobs, immigrant mothers must also make magic by transforming bleak, empty basements or overcrowded rooms into warm and safe spaces, with symbols and delicious aromas that appease the longing for what is no longer discernible to the soul. For Berkis, losing her home meant not only losing material possessions but failing to keep her children away from the abyss of poverty despite her education and best efforts. It meant never seeing the few things that gave her and her sons a sense of continuity: baby pictures, wedding and graduation mementos, school pictures, or the earrings her mother had given Berkis on her graduation day.

Statistics show that one out of every five women experience eviction or involuntary mobility. On average, Dominicans experience more court-ordered evictions than Mexicans, though Mexicans tend to experience more housing transience or instability given the higher share of the population that is undocumented and/or living in informal group arrangements.[26] Table 4.2, from the ANHD report, reveals that in New York City, Dominican and Black tenants experience the highest numbers of marshaled evictions, followed by Puerto Ricans and Mexicans. Next to Mexicans, Colombians have the highest percentage of housing with serious overcrowding. Despite facing the most evictions, Dominicans have the largest share of rent-controlled apartments, and some controls protect the disabled and seniors from facing displacement due to escalating rents.[27] But these rent controls do not protect families in the prime years of their lives or those immigrant mothers who are increasingly overburdened with high rents.

Further analysis of neighborhood rankings (not shown in table 4.2) from the ANHD report shows that the Bronx has the highest evictions. Three Bronx neighborhoods are at the top of this list: Highbridge / South Concourse, University Heights / Fordham, and Kingsbridge Heights / Bedford. Finally, the ANHD report reveals that these neighborhoods also include the highest shares of the unemployed and tenants facing rental burdens. Similarly, Washington Heights has the highest rent burden among all Manhattan neighborhoods, though it also has the highest numbers of rent-stabilized apartments in Manhattan.[28] Except for two Brooklyn neighborhoods listed in the ANHD report, families in the Bronx experience the highest incidence of evictions among all boroughs.[29] Latinos make up more than 50 percent of evicted families in New York City, with Dominicans and Mexicans, the two largest immigrant groups, making up a majority.[30]

Unlike Berkis's spiraling housing trajectory, Magdalena's took a different path. Her husband's new job in Astoria, Queens, gave the couple access to a rent-free one-bedroom apartment. With the superintendent's informal consent, Orlando, Magdalena's husband, used Sheetrock to build a small room in a corner of the living room for their nine-year-old, Julia. There they placed a donated cot from

Magdalena's previous church in Harlem, along with a two-drawer plastic container that served as both a dresser and a table. This building was owned by the same Greek family for whom Orlando's male cousin worked as a dishwasher in two restaurants they owned, one in Astoria and another in Midtown Manhattan; three Greek workers also lived in the same building where Orlando and his cousin lived in Astoria.[31]

Berkis's eviction is part of a larger economic and demographic transformation that has affected Black and Latino neighborhoods in Harlem since the mid-1990s, when the cost of housing accelerated. Between 1999 and 2014 the average cost of housing in Washington Heights increased by 25 percent.[32] Dominicans have suffered the largest housing displacement in Washington Heights, though my qualitative insights document some of the strategies that Dominican and Mexican immigrant families use to hold on to their apartments in the midst of gentrification.

Five years after completing my degree, and working at my first job as a newly minted professor in the Bronx, I returned to Berkis's old block, this time invited by a White European peer and college friend, also a recent PhD, who with her boyfriend had recently purchased an apartment in the area. To my dismay, her apartment was on the same block, just three buildings away from where Berkis had lived. I shared with my peer and her boyfriend, a White Gen Xer affiliated with Columbia University, that a half decade before I had visited this block for close to a year for very different reasons. In Berkis's old building, the Dominican deli was gone, replaced by a juice bar; the building's facade was now a glass entry with private buzzers and an eastern European doorman. Berkis did not get to witness the changes already apparent in the class and racial makeup of her building or in the bulk of her old neighborhood. Now only the public housing projects, a few ethnic delis, some small restaurants, and a pawn shop still stand guard as symbolic cultural boundaries against urban development and housing displacement of the working poor.

CHAPTER SUMMARY

As is shown in this chapter, Dominicans experience higher levels of spatial segregation and isolation than other ethnic and native-born groups. New York City's Mexican population manages to move sooner out of poor and racialized neighborhoods, despite its higher share of undocumented immigrants. Mexicans also experience more scattered spatial integration in White or middle-class neighborhoods. Yet, across both ethnic groups, undocumented families, especially those led by single mothers, face serious housing precariousness and physical and mental health risks, in addition to the stigma and cumulative effects of housing abuse, evictions, and/or the risk of deportation.

This chapter documents for the first time the housing precariousness of undocumented middle-class families. It also documents how group living arrangements and the "encargado system" offer immigrants, the long-term working poor, and retired and elderly families the ability to afford and hold on to their housing in the midst of rapid gentrification. These strategies are often temporary, however, and contingent upon superintendents' or building managers' consent, as often these arrangements violate housing occupancy codes. As my interviews suggest, undocumented immigrants often end up experiencing the worst forms of rental exploitation from unscrupulous landlords, many of whom are *encargados*, and more assimilated coethnics or immigrants with legalized status.

Paradoxically, public housing and rent-stabilized apartments offer immigrant mothers the best form of stable and affordable housing. Unfortunately, the process often requires applicants to wait as long as five to ten years for housing given the long list of applicants and the scarcity of affordable housing. Middle-class immigrants who are naturalized citizens have more access to established networks of support and are more adept at navigating the public housing system to obtain housing, as was the case with Carmen and her family. This explains why fewer Mexican women in this study report never having lived in public housing, and why public housing is a more prevalent strategy for Dominican single mothers given the higher share of Dominicans with legalized status. Public housing increases mothers' economic independence from men or a system of patriarchy, though in exchange they experience class and racial isolation from families and close systems of support, especially during the most critical years of raising their small children. Most important, public housing increases these immigrant families' housing stability and lowers the risks of homelessness and eviction. It also increases school attendance and stability for children enrolled in neighborhood schools. According to Yana Kucheva, public housing should increase poor children's chances for social mobility.[33] But the concentration of public housing in inner-city areas with the highest levels of poverty erodes these possibilities.

5 · AN INTERSECTIONAL VIEW AT SOCIAL MOBILITY, RACE, AND MIGRATION

"My sister-in-law got me this job in the factory where she worked when I first arrived," explained my respondent, a forty-nine-year-old middle-class Dominican woman who was now a home attendant. "I didn't know about any other possible jobs. You know, people always talk [back home] about factory work [in New York City]. Women see these jobs as a way to get their own money and help their families left behind. Here women are more independent. Back in our country, women see other women returning with money and without men. They see them doing well. I truly think there are more jobs here for women than for men." As this respondent emphasized, the decision to migrate combines desperate economic and emotional motives often driven by the hope of a better life, free of debts, but free mostly of troubled men. A general perception shared by this and other respondents is that New York City holds plenty of jobs for women but not for men. This perception is not unfounded, as a low-wage service economy thrives on the imported labor of Black and Brown nannies who increasingly ease the domestic burdens of middle- and upper-class households in advanced capitalistic nations.[1] As an emerging literature reveals, most service functions require the management of emotions, or the "purchase" of intimacy.[2] We lack knowledge, however, about the experiences of educated women who perform domestic or low-wage jobs. This chapter explores the individual and structural inequalities that push and pull women from the Dominican Republic and Mexico to migrate as members of a new, and yet vulnerable, Latin American middle class. In-depth interviews and case stories detail how the simultaneity of gender, class, and racial inequalities women experience, including a legacy of patriarchal and state repression and sexism, has pushed women for generations to lead the migration, including daughters of immigrants who import a higher education.

I organize the analysis into three parts. First, I describe the personal and structural inequalities that lead middle-class women to migrate and the expectations they harbor about life in New York. I distinguish the migration and middle-class mobility of women whose status derives from either their spouses or from their own educational achievements. Next, I explore how migration and a higher education transform the status of women in the family, from homemakers to main breadwinners, and the impact of this transformation on mental health. I then contrast the mobility pathways of immigrant women in low- and high-skilled service jobs, including those positioned in "backstage" functions as domestics or home health attendants, and those in highly visible positions, such as leaders or volunteers in community institutions traditionally controlled by coethnic men.[3] The findings engage an emerging intersectional Latina feminist framework,[4] one that documents the overlapping forms of inequality Chicanas and women of color experience in the United States to compare the experiences of foreign-born Latinas. The last part of the chapter offers an analysis of the different forms of social capital, including racial capital, that increase the access to education and social mobility of Dominican and Mexican women in the sending society and how they mediate the integration as well as new forms of inequalities experienced within an increasingly racialized context of immigrant reception.

ESCAPING VIOLENT STATES AND TROUBLED MEN: WHEN WHITENESS AND POVERTY INTERSECT

"Back then," explained one seventy-six-year-old Dominican female respondent, a retired factory worker, "beautiful young girls of good family, who had a bit of an education, you know, and who also were *blanquitas* [of White appearance] often became prey for the pastime of the dictator or one of his top-ranking officials!" Altagracia, a sixty-year-old professional Dominican woman, shared the following with me:

> In those days, rural girls as young as fourteen often worked as attendants in restaurants or as domestics in middle-class people's homes; but this was a whole different situation! It happened to my own mother—my father's concubine. He was rich, married, and a powerful politician. She escaped and migrated to the capital, where she could not reliably feed herself or send money to her parents, who were left in my care. Finally, she moved in with another older man; but after twenty-eight years, he abandoned her for his chauffeur's much younger wife! At least he left her a small shack on a large piece of an abandoned lot, not too far from the beach.
>
> My mother was a fighter, a survivor: she planted legumes, she sowed and sold small pieces of clothing; she asked young Haitian boys, whom she would feed and mother in exchange for them helping her work the land. After a few years, she became traumatized, for this is not how she had grown up. She was a school-teacher and never had a chance to do her profession, for the men in her life did not want her to work; so she finally emigrated.

These narratives reflect that different and overlapping forms of individual and structural inequalities that since the 1960s have forced Dominican women to leave their homeland for the United States.[5] They also illustrate how most of these women grew up in homes where older sisters, mothers, or even grandmothers had established legacies as migrants. Many of the women from these earlier cohorts immigrated in the company of spouses, but others migrated alone, often to escape the abandonment or repression of men or of the state, as the above narratives reveal. A good number of women from these earlier cohorts were of rural origins, white- or light-skinned, and poor. Almost all of these migrants engaged first in domestic-to-urban migration before crossing international shores, as Ramona Hernández and Nancy López's 1997 study reveals.[6] State repression, manifested mostly through the armed forces, combined with the repression of spouses or conjugal partners to force women into a life of poverty, sexual oppression and indenture, as well as different forms of abandonment. Cecilia Menjívar and Shannon Drysdale Walsh,[7] for example, find that patriarchal and state repression and neglect force many Honduran women to join waves of migrant women and children who leave Central America to seek protection abroad, as the unprecedented and increasing arrival of women and children now seeking refuge at the Mexican-U.S. border reveals.[8] Similarly, the above narratives illustrate that poverty is not always the main reason pushing women to migrate. Rather, a culture of repression leads to intergenerational sexual abuse and the abandonment of women as single mothers who are expected to assume roles as sole providers for their children. As these introductory narratives suggest, a culture of neglect plants in the minds and hearts of impressionable young girls in the Dominican Republic the idea that migration is a silver bullet against poverty, troubled men, and repressive states.

Access to a higher education often leads women like Altagracia to pay a high price for their social mobility, especially if they are White or have light skin in a mulatto nation. Dominican scholars have argued that a European colonization and a legacy of ruling elites educated mainly in Europe have led to the socialization of Dominicans as both "Eurocentric and negrophobic,"[9] in a culture where Whiteness is associated with progress and Blackness with poverty. In this context, generations of light-skinned women have been coveted and also exploited for their racial capital. In the early 1950s the migration of Altagracia's maternal aunts to the United States took place during the latter stage of Trujillo's repressive regime. They were among the first women to migrate unaccompanied by men, exiled as dissidents of the Dominican state. Altagracia's grandfather's refusal to consent to his two teenage daughters attending an evening ball and overnight stay at the dictator's mountain retreat mansion placed the family in jeopardy. The state exiled his daughters and sanctioned his family's land. The residual effects of a culture of repression victimized generations of women considered to possess high forms of body, class, and racial capital—and most coveted by the militarized state's apparatus. Women who were young, virginal, White, and from landowning families became prized as wives or concubines, as Altagracia's family suggests.

Given the legacy of Trujillo's repression and the biological determinism that has valued Whiteness in Latin America since the colonial period,[10] white- and light-skinned Mestizas experienced the worst forms of sexual repression at the hand of the state. This is painstakingly and vividly captured in *In the Time of the Butterflies*, a novel by Dominican American author Julia Alvarez.[11] But unlike the fates of rich or elite Dominican women, whose mobility is often tied to their families' or spouse's fortunes, generations of poor women, irrespective of skin color or phenotype, have paid for their social mobility or their flight from poverty mainly with their bodies. Their rural-to-urban migration, access to higher education, and professional work have often involved accepting some form of sexual oppression, often as the concubines of older, married, rich or politically powerful men. During a focus group I conducted in 2009 in Altagracia's small ancestral town in the Dominican Republic, she and many others proclaimed, "This is exactly what happened to my mother!"

Altagracia was the youngest of a family with declining fortunes, and her great-aunts used to send money to help pay for her mother's education at a Catholic high school in their small—and by then urbanizing—town. Upon graduating, Altagracia's mother became a local elementary school teacher. Her grandfather sought the aid of their family's physician—a highly esteemed man and landed member of the elite as well as an ascending politician. Altagracia's grandfather asked this family practitioner to help find his daughter a teaching job at their local school. Soon, this man, twice her age, began courting Altagracia's mother with gifts and invitations for dining, including beach getaways. To avoid rumors spreading to her family and this older man's wife, Altagracia's mother quit her job and conceded to relocating to a small house outside of town that was procured and paid for by her older admirer. Her parents began receiving bags of rice, beans, flour, and other staples, as well as offers to purchase government-owned land and livestock at prices never before available to the public.

A few years after Altagracia's birth, her biological father's interests in her mother dwindled, and the stigma of single motherhood and unemployment fueled her mother's domestic migration from her small town to a marginalized *vecindario* (neighborhood) on the periphery of Santo Domingo. She left Altagracia behind with her grandparents, as her rich patron offered to pay for Altagracia's care in exchange for silence. In the capital, Altagracia's mother struggled to make ends meet, first working in a cafeteria, then as a babysitter, and later as a math tutor. But with no familial support and in a neighborhood plagued by crime and prostitution, at the abyss of poverty, and with no government aid, she was forced to accept the offer of a second rich man, one twenty years her senior and with an established profession and marriage, who asked her to move into his remote beach house as his new concubine.

A decade later, after Altagracia's mother migrated to New York, Altagracia graduated from a private high school in her ancestral town and followed her mother's rural-to-urban migration to Santo Domingo, moving into the small house her mother inherited from the man with whom she had shared her life as a concubine, intermittently and without the state's or the Catholic Church's consent, for nearly twenty-eight years. In the late 1980s, while Altagracia attended college at a public university, she realized her mother's remittances not only allowed her the privilege of a higher education but also the realization of a second childhood dream of taking English lessons at the most reputable institution in the city. When I asked Altagracia why she was interested in learning English, she shared how the money and gifts her mother and great-aunts would send or bring back planted in her heart a desire for learning English:

> I remember my great-aunts, my grandmother, and then my mother coming back from New York wearing fine clothes and jewelries, smelling really good! They used to bring these tall, blond dolls for their daughters and me, and when you would put your fingers in their belly buttons they would sing in English and move their heads and blue eyes! I used to also watch American movies in English with the Spanish subtitles. And, all of this made me want to learn English! I always wanted to know what the blond dolls' songs said! My mother sent the money from New York so I could study English, first in El Conde and then at the Dominican American Institute—you know, *en dónde van los blanquitos* [where the White kids go].

The wages from a part-time, semiprofessional job and her immigrant mother's cash remittances allowed Altagracia to attend an international language institute. Years later, after landing her first professional job as a certified accountant and auditor for a national bank, thanks to her biological father's political connections, Altagracia and her mother decided to invest in rebuilding the small house in which Altagracia had lived while attending graduate school. The local government's investments in the Carretera de Las Americas (the main highway to and from the international airport) with new paving, lighting, and a mile-long promenade by the ocean side attracted tourists and real estate investors in the early 1980s. During this time, Altagracia contemplated marriage. Yet social isolation decreased her assortative mating chances, or the chances of dating someone with a similar education.[12] Near her small wooden home, amid coconut and palm trees, poor Black children and stray dogs played while Dominican and Haitian peasants, mostly men living in makeshift houses, ventured into the streets for day labor. Altagracia realized how difficult living in this isolated neighborhood made her trajectory to work, study, or even socializing with educated peers: "I remember my great-aunts, my grandmother, and then my mother saying, 'It used to take me an average of three hours, roundtrip, to get to work and then attend evening school. I got home around eight or nine p.m. each day!' Imagine how frightening it is to have to wait for public transport at seven a.m. and then again in the quiet hours of the night, off an isolated highway."

Spatial, class, and racial isolation limited Altagracia's marital options to undereducated men with good intentions or to older, married men searching for distractions. After sharing her office space and profession with her supervisor, a man more than a decade her senior, they engaged in an informal union that lasted fifteen years. After the birth of two small children, Altagracia asked her intermittent conjugal partner and senior colleague never to return, realizing he would never marry her; she dreaded the time when her children would be old enough to do the math and would realize theirs was an "illegitimate" home. A few months after the breakup, Altagracia was told her contract at work could not be renewed for lack of government funding following the election of a new president. She spent five years in search of professional posts, to no avail. With her father's death and her mother's migration, and now no longer able to rely on the patronage of her lover, Altagracia found that her institutional capital and networks had become obsolete. At forty-five years of age, her gendered, feminine capital was also eroded, as her society considered her too old to work or to attract even an older married man.

During a focus group in Santo Domingo, respondents confided with a mix of sadness and contempt as to why many professional women like Altagracia are forced to migrate. One woman who returned to Santo Domingo after spending twenty years in New York declared, "No one is going to offer a forty-year-old woman a job in this small nation!" Similarly, until she lost her secured, professional position at a prestigious national bank, Altagracia had never weighed the precariousness of her vulnerable middle-class status or that of mothers who must raise children without the income or protection of a man or the state. She decided to join her mother and her older daughter, who had immigrated to New York City five years earlier.

WHEN HIGHER-EDUCATED WOMEN MIGRATE

Unlike many of the Black and Brown Dominican migrant women examined in this study, Altagracia had light, honeyed skin and a mix of Iberian and North African phenotypes. She was slightly above five feet tall and had a careful demeanor. She complained about the work as a live-in home attendant, eating other people's bad food, and the lack of sleep that went with caring for an elderly woman who was bedridden and whose care often required her to work 12-hour shifts five days a week, with intermittent overnight work. Altagracia shared how this type of work had caused her to gain weight and also experience poor health but was the only way to earn and save money. The paucity of Altagracia's words revealed a habit of contemplation, of the calibration of words that come with a higher education. Yet the deep frowning marks on her forehead foreshadowed a life of hardship or "of carrying the world alone on her back for too long," as my grandmother would say. Yet, Altagracia's imported professional accreditations and skills, a few years of English training, her racial capital, and her mother's and siblings' networks in New York increased her ability to find work soon after her arrival there. Her mother introduced her to professionals who visited the restaurant where she had cooked for over two decades, including women with home attendant jobs. This increased Altagracia's options. Her mother's address in New Jersey and that of a sibling in a nearby suburb facilitated Altagracia's registering and receiving a certification as a home health care attendant. By 2012, the last time we spoke, Altagracia had worked in the same agency for about ten years. Her income had allowed her to cover the tuition of her daughter's public college education to become a nurse practitioner. Her youngest son was able to complete an associate's degree in business administration and accounting, also from a public college. Both of her young adult children landed full-time, white-collar jobs. Altagracia's group living arrangement in a rented, two-family New Jersey home, shared with her handicapped and retired mother, her two adult children, and the money they derived from the rental of their small home in Santo Domingo allowed Altagracia to invest in her children's higher education.

Altagracia's story illustrates the structural and individual forms of inequalities that combine to push highly educated women to migrate. It also illuminates the contributions that working-class migrant women make to the social mobility of daughters left behind. Mostly, it details how mothers and grandmothers make up for men's deficiencies, particularly those in repressive states. The comparative research of Cinzia Solari reveals that Ukrainian mothers and often grandmothers are the ones forced to migrate in search of work, making up for the neoliberal government's lack of welfare policies with their remittances.[13] My findings document how mothers' and grandmothers' long-term investments contribute to the social mobility of daughters, mostly among Black and Indigenous minorities in Latin America. As the next interview insights reveal, many of these highly educated daughters engage in a second wave of migration in search of better work prospects given the lack of protection their government affords women and the sustenance of their children. They, like their grandmothers, migrate to give their daughters a real chance at economic and gender emancipation.

My findings help define and operationalize three forms of social capital that facilitate the mobility of middle-class women in the Dominican Republic and Mexico. Besides social and biological markers, class, gender, and racial capital include ideological dimensions that affect how members of the new middle class fare in both the sending and receiving communities. Although Altagracia had light skin and a non-Black phenotype, she experienced institutional and social isolation in her community of origin, lacking social ties with members of the mainstream middle class. As an outsider or domestic migrant from a small town to the nation's capital, she had limited networks, and thus she was only able to land a professional job in the public sector, mainly through her mother's connections to the rich man for whom she served as a concubine for almost three decades. Altagracia's spatial and social isolation also limited her chances at marriage. Only half of the women in the Dominican Republic marry men with the same education level.[14] Yet Altagracia was considered White in the Dominican Republic; she was among a minority of light-skinned women who had to pay for their social mobility. Next I illustrate the social mobility and migration experiences of Black and Indigenous women and the role that class (family structure and immigrant status) and race (skin color and phenotype) play in the crossing of geographic and social boundaries in the process of migration.

Black and Indigenous women are often forced to migrate because they lack institutional or family networks among members of the established mainstream middle class who can help them secure jobs. These migrants harbor expectations that a higher education or professional skills will also increase opportunities for their children. As table 5.1 illustrates, 2010 U.S. Census data for foreign-born Latinos in New York City reveals that 49 percent of Mexican women and 30 percent of Dominican women arrive in the United States with less than ten years of schooling. Additionally, twice as many Dominicans (34 percent) as Mexicans (12 percent) import at least a year of college or postsecondary education.

TABLE 5.1   Educational Attainment of Foreign-Born Dominican and Mexican Immigrants in New York City

Education level	Women 17+			Men 17+		
	Born in Dominican Republic	Born in Mexico	All NYC	Born in Dominican Republic	Born in Mexico	All NYC
Population shares						
9 years or less	30%	49%	14%	31%	43%	12%
10–12 years	36%	37%	34%	41%	42%	36%
1 or more years of college	34%	12%	52%	28%	15%	52%
Average years of schooling						
Average education	10.7	9.0	13	10.6	9.6	13

SOURCES: Ruggles et al., 2011; and author's calculation from the U.S. Census 2010 Integrated Public Use Microdata Series–USA and the American Community Survey for 2006 and 2008.

TABLE 5.2   Premigration Work Experience

	Dominicans n = 43 (%)	Mexicans n = 41 (%)	Total Sample (%)
Unemployed	23.3	14.6	19.0
Domestic work	4.7	4.9	4.8
Factory / manual labor	7.0	7.3	7.1
Agriculture	0	29.3	14.3
Skilled work	25.6	12.2	19.0
Self-employed	4.7	9.8	7.1
Professional	12.2	9.3	10.7
Student	25.6	9.8	17.9

SOURCE: Author's interviews, 2000–2003, and follow-up interviews, 2009–10.

Notably, Dominican women are more likely to import a higher education than are their male counterparts, while Mexican women and men import approximately similar levels of education. Table 5.2 illustrates the work and educational levels of women prior to the migration. It illustrates that 38 percent of Dominican and 22 percent of Mexican migrant women import (combined) skilled or professional work experience. Close to 18 percent among both groups were either enrolled in graduate school or imported a college degree. An equal share of Dominican and Mexican women performed factory or domestic work prior to migration. Finally, table 5.2 also shows that more Dominicans than Mexicans were unemployed despite importing higher education and professional skills. Only Mexican women engaged in agricultural work prior to migration.

Upon arrival in New York City, a majority of Dominican and Mexican women who import a higher education but who lack networks with other, more established, or middle-class coethnics tend to concentrate in domestic sectors, as the case of Altagracia reveals. Their new experiences of marginalization, as the case of Berkis in the previous chapters illustrates, alter some of these migrant women's lives irreversibly, leaving lasting scars on their psyches and bodies.

THE MIGRANT EXPERIENCES OF EDUCATED BLACK AND INDIGENOUS LATINAS

As Magdalena, who was introduced in chapter 2, explained tearfully,

> I was a typist in a municipal office in Mexico, but in the New Jersey factory, my typewriter became a sewing machine! I thought that, at least, I would find work with other people like me [i.e., educated] and that things would be the same between me and Orlando [her husband] as they were before he left. When we

reunited, we lived in San Bernardino, California, for a few months to work and pay off the coyote. I came as a *mojada* [one who is undocumented], but the orange groves' chemicals and the heavy load of the fruit boxes made me sick. They were too heavy, and the pay was just three dollars per box. When we came to New York, my husband's cousin helped us get work in the same factory where he worked in New Jersey. I had then three main problems: I lived with a heavy heart because my children remained behind; I went from working five days a week in Mexico to seven days a week; but, mostly, because I now live with domestic violence.

Another respondent, a forty-five-year-old Mexican immigrant and high school graduate now working as a daytime domestic, told me,

I did not want to leave my country, but my husband wanted me to come to New York. He came first. When I married, I was just three weeks away from finishing my first vocational college year. I imagined, at the very least, finishing my degree someday in New York. So I did not think straight and married. I used to work with my mother; she had a small food store. Since girlhood, my mother always ran a business selling typical Mexican foods. I used to do the shopping in the large market for her; I carried heavy sacks filled with onions and potatoes, sometimes weighing twenty-five to fifty kilos, as much as my own weight! Mostly, I used to take care of the clients. I was determined to finish my education in New York!

These narratives reveal that the access to higher education leads women to harbor high expectations about opportunities for work and a middle-class life. Such expectations push some women to lead their migration and others to follow or accompany spouses or conjugal partners. An emerging literature indicates that contemporary cohorts of Latino and other immigrants import higher education or equivalent work skills.[15] This chapter reveals that upon arrival, most higher-educated Dominican and Mexican women tend to concentrate in informal, low-wage, service jobs such as in factories, restaurants, or domestic work.[16] Although eventually many educated women move from informal to more formalized service jobs, such as in home health care or maintenance, the initial integration is in factories (for Mexicans more than Dominicans), in restaurants (for Dominicans more than Mexicans), or in informal cleaning or domestic services. Women importing professional skills or a higher education and with access to transnational network links tend to find work as volunteers for local religious or diasporic institutions, such as Catholic churches or community-based ethnic organizations, as the latter part of this chapter documents. Despite their importing higher education or professional skills, the larger share of my respondents' initial jobs were marginalized. Upon arrival, these women often found work in "backstage" functions and informal settings, such as in restaurants, hair salons, or even food processing plants, where risk to their health or well-being is the norm, as the following case, from a thirty-seven-year-old Dominican migrant, a skilled worker and former nurse-midwife, reveals:

> I came because I did not make enough money as a nurse-midwife in a public hospital in Santo Domingo. I thought I would get a better-paying job in New York. I ended up working for a few years in a discotheque in New Jersey. I used to work the bathroom from four p.m. to closing hours, ranging from two, three, six a.m. I fought and dreaded sleeping on my feet. Officially, I cleaned and stocked toilet paper and hand soap, assisting women with supplies; in reality, I was there to check that people did not smoke *you know what* or have sex in the bathroom, as the young girls working the club as dancers or escorts often used the commodes for their business!

Unlike the light-skinned or White landowner, politically displaced or entrepreneurial, Dominican elite,[17] which arrived among earlier cohorts, contemporary migrant streams include a large share of Black and Indigenous middle-class groups. Many of these ethnoracial minorities owe their mobility to sustained economic growth in Latin America, including initiatives in some nations like Brazil and Mexico to increase the access to higher education for historically excluded minorities.[18] Chapter 2 and this chapter reveal that the remittances of migrant families also have increased Black and Indigenous women's access to higher education. Yet despite their education these new middle-class members migrate due to legacies of institutional exclusion and extreme levels of work instability, as the next case illustrates.

Like other highly educated daughters of immigrants, Eva arrived in the Bronx sponsored by her mother. The loss of employment pushed Eva's husband to migrate first. Eva's parents immigrated in the late 1980s, prompted by the termination of her father's political appointment as the director of a public hospital, following the election of the forty-eighth president of the Dominican Republic, Salvador Jorge Blanco (1982–86). Her family's middle-class status had been contingent until then on access to work in the public sector through political patronage. A decade later, Eva's husband was also forced to migrate when his architectural firm merged with a European company. Eva's husband obtained a visa and joined his in-laws in New York City, importing about US$10,000 in savings—enough, he had been told, to start a small taxi and limousine service.

Although contemporary research on the social mobility of ethnoracial minorities in Latin America concludes that skin color is a key—if not the most important—determinant predicting educational mobility,[19] we lack understanding of how the intersection of race (skin and phenotype), gender, and class (education) mediates the mobility process as well as the viability of Black and

Indigenous skilled workers in different societies. The cases of Berkis and Eva are illustrative in understanding the new forms of intersectional vulnerabilities that push these women to migrate as members of the middle class.

While giggling mischievously, Eva recounted how her mother's family used to frown about the marriage of their daughter to a man with such "strong" Black features: "¡Tan ordinario!" (So ordinary!) her maternal grandmother used to complain during the early stages of her parents' courtship. "But, after Daddy started working as a doctor and moving up the ranks, they all shut up!" Eva had ebony black skin, which she inherited from her father; she also inherited her mother's phenotype, one that demonstrates the mixing of slaves and slaveowners.[20] Eva was tall and had an elegant, staged demeanor. She admired her father's commitment to his medical profession, especially his dedication to helping poor patients. His legacy inspired her, from a young age, to dream of becoming a doctor. Eva recounted how her husband's job loss interrupted her medical school training and hopes of completing her last two years of specialization in dermatology: "I had to stop school, as I could not pay the tuition. My husband came [to New York City] first, to work for a couple of years. I stayed behind, fully in charge of the home. With the help of a live-in babysitter, I went to work full-time. When I arrived, I thought I would find work in a clinic or medical facility, but I immediately realized it was a mistake to leave my career before finishing."

Eva's story and those of other women suggest that educated migrant women arrive with high expectations about their career chances in the United States. About one-half of my highly educated Mexican respondents did not plan to migrate. Generally, the higher their education, the higher the aspiration for achieving a middle-class lifestyle, even if this involved migrating. Yet rising disillusionments and social isolation upon arrival are common because these women lack access to networks with middle-class or professional coethnics. Eva's disillusionment with her work upon arrival affected her marriage and her sense of wellbeing. As she recounted,

> It was a stupid mistake [coming to New York]! All that effort to take away the job of another maid! I thought here I could continue my education or at least find a job in a health or related field, but it has all been a disaster! One day, I came home and told my husband I wanted to study English or earn a certificate in something to find any other job that was not being a maid. I was really suffering from depression and was not even aware of it. I used to cry all the time and hide in the bathroom so my children would not see me. I began studying and got a certificate as a home attendant, working for many years taking care of elderly people.

Migration had transformed Eva's status from a full-time, advanced medical student to a low-wage domestic worker and later a home heath attendant. Both Eva and her mother gradually made headway in service jobs, however, increasing their networks in both ethnic and mainstream institutions. Eva finally moved into the health industry as a trained community health educator.

Middle-Class Migrants' Expectations and Mental Health Vulnerabilities

Paradoxically, middle-class women's perceptions about life in New York are often nurtured by the traveling narratives of lesser-schooled family members who have worked mostly in industrial jobs. Migrant illusions are destroyed by the realities of isolating, low-paying, and often demeaning manual service jobs, an occupational area where most Latino immigrants today concentrate. Many of my middle-class respondents shared the hardship that ex-professional workers experience upon arrival and the toll paid to mental health, as the case of a medical student illustrates:

> In 2000, I decided to return to New York City and live in the house of my ex-babysitter and housekeeper from Santo Domingo. She offered her place and helped me get a job. I worked at a Brooklyn factory, getting up at five a.m. to be there by seven thirty a.m. This was terrible, since I had to drop my child off at a neighbor's house every morning at six a.m. I later worked taking care of an elderly, sick person. I lasted a week. Then, I used to make $160 a week for six days of work through a cleaning agency. I later worked for a Jewish bakery in Lower Manhattan and got another job cleaning homes on weekends. I used to feel awful working these jobs; for example, to get to the factory, I had to ride in a contracted agency van, with all sorts of crazy people at five a.m.! I am presently taking medications for my nerves and emotional problems.

As these narratives illustrate, Dominican and Mexican women face class and gender vulnerabilities that are different in content and form than those faced in communities of origin, where at least they can count on family support and social networks. The case of an unemployed housewife, Ofelia, a forty-five-year-old Dominican mother of three children, reveals how she never worked before the family's immigration to New York City. She is among four of ten middle-class women I interviewed who expected their husbands would continue to be the main breadwinners, despite these women's higher education:

> I came to New York City because of sheer stupidity. My husband and I had a beautiful family with our children. We did not have any economic necessities; but my husband came here dissatisfied with politics at work. He was a public accountant in a government agency. Before this, we used to come to New York City to visit; but, this time, he decided we would stay, try our lives here even after our visas expired. I never used to work in my country; he provided everything. We had service in the home. Here I had to work and face a lot of humiliation. After our divorce, I understood that no one supports a home on a single salary in New York City!

Ofelia blamed her debilitating depression and her family's marginalized conditions on her husband's inability to provide for the family, as he had done before their migration. Financial difficulties and different living arrangements strain the conjugal bond, especially for members of the established Dominican middle class, where men still act as the primary providers. Though Ofelia's husband migrated due to workplace politics, many men migrate because limited opportunities make it impossible for them to meet their families' middle-class expectations. The inability of men to assume positions as primary breadwinners can lead to marital conflict and divorce, creating a greater risk of physical and mental abuse in the family.

Middle-class expectations lead to gender schisms in the family, mostly among men from small towns and rural areas, where a strong culture of men as providers is the norm. Yet, unbeknownst to these men, industrial jobs have nearly disappeared in New York City, thus diminishing their chances of fulfilling their traditional provider role. Mirna, a forty-five-year-old mother, came to an interview with the youngest of her two daughters, who was in college.[21] Mirna wore black cowboy boots and a color-coordinated pantsuit; her daughter wore colorful designer glasses with tortoiseshell rims. Mirna had light brown skin, an oval face, and wavy brown hair. When I asked questions about skin color, her daughter said her mother had a "whitish" kind of look (*guerita*, a term used for White people in Mexican vernacular), adding, "She looks more like our grandmother! Both have the same shape of the face, nose, and even the same hair color and texture! Me, in turn, I am Black, just like my father!" She giggled and shrugged her shoulders.

In the previous five years, Mirna had become the primary breadwinner, contributing the most to the household and sending remittances to family in Mexico. I met her husband, Rodrigo, at their daughter's college graduation two years later. A midsize man in his late forties, he was a dark shade of brown and had sharp, Indigenous (Nahuatl) facial features and hair texture. He had gained a worrisome amount of weight, and there were dark circles under his eyes. During my interview with Mirna, it became clear that Rodrigo's physical and mental health had deteriorated. What affected him the most, Mirna told me, was the fact that his wife and his youngest daughter were now the primary breadwinners in his home. Materially the family was doing well, but emotional schisms threatened the couple's union: "Now, because of his leg problems and diabetes, he can hardly work. Now he tries controlling me; secretly checking my phone's calendar to see if I have appointments to clean homes or babysit. He wants to know my clients' names—who they are—but most important, how much they pay me! I just try not to be home too much."

Rodrigo's illness, loss of control, and social isolation made him difficult and oppressive. He blamed Mirna for never being home to take care of their youngest daughter, who still lived at home and had no secure job after graduation;

instead, she had opted to work with her mother until she made up her mind about graduate school (she was interested in becoming an immigration lawyer). Rodrigo also blamed Mirna for their oldest daughter eloping with her boyfriend and moving to another state. As Mirna noted, "When I arrived, I could not work because he did not want to leave the girls with anyone. When they started school, I started cleaning houses. Today I make the most money, as his health has declined. This makes him jealous. He is getting very difficult. He still insists on waiting for me to be home to have dinner, as if the dining table or kitchen was attached to my hips!" She continued, "I did not want to migrate, but I wanted work. I was tired of always having to ask my husband for money. Now, I make my own money and he keeps track of my clients and income!" Her daughter then added, "He also wants to see whose house she is cleaning, making sure she is not cleaning the houses of single men!" Detecting some form of domestic abuse, I offered to locate counseling services. Mirna was already working with a lawyer with whom her daughter interned to use domestic abuse laws to change her undocumented status to that of a legal resident.

Other stories in previous chapters of this book reinforce the findings presented in this chapter about mental health concerns for migrants. Berkis, for example—a highly educated accountant from the Dominican Republic—found work first as a maid, cleaning, cooking, doing laundry, and shopping for elderly patients, and then as a health care attendant in the home of a Cuban man in his early seventies who had Alzheimer's disease. His wife usually praised Berkis for not acting like other Dominican women they had had as home attendants, who had not met the minimum expectations of the man and his wife. Berkis paid no mind to the wife's racist innuendos, but, five months into the job, the woman was hospitalized with a hip injury and the man began to sexually harass Berkis. "Look, to avoid problems, I decided to quit my job!" Berkis told me. "He began accosting me sexually, asking me to show him my breasts, offering money, and even suggesting I would be his ideal wife if he had a chance again. I took it he wished his wife would not come back! When I tried to pay him no mind, he would get upset and call me racial slurs, like 'stupid Black bitch!' I decided to protect my sanity and avoid problems; it was best to leave." Already depressed about her prospects, a divorce, and poverty, Berkis had a complete mental collapse, which Catholic services helped her through, as Berkis said, "for the sake of my children."

The Crossing of Spatial, Class, and Racial Boundaries and Mental Health

Despite economic or educational gains, the migration experience invariably—and especially for the undocumented—introduces risks and vulnerabilities, some with long-term impacts on mental health. Mirna's narrative vividly illustrates the trauma of crossing the border with her children as an undocumented migrant a decade earlier:

I went back to Mexico to pick up my daughters because my husband's boss decided to support his legalization process through the 245 law.[22] To qualify, undocumented workers needed a sponsor, preferably an employer who could offer a work affidavit. We told his boss our daughters lived with us; but they were still in Mexico. So, since my husband had to work, getting them became up to me. This was a tougher trip than the one I did alone a few years earlier. We took a different route, leading to a week of walking along the river, swimming, floating, crawling among branches and mud, along its bank. We even crossed a sewage tunnel with black waters filled with feces, with each one of my daughters on the back of two men. In the river we witnessed bodies of dead men floating, blown out of proportion. It was shocking for life! My eight-year-old still remembers!

After nearly five years of separation from her two small daughters, Mirna risked arrest, even death, as she crossed the border. She was lucky she was not physically abused. Women with fewer resources are not so fortunate. One of my respondents, a thirty-six-year-old Mexican high school graduate and entrepreneur, described the sexual abuse she endured while crossing the border: "I arranged the crossover with a coyote my family knew. The man demanded we give him all the money ahead of time. He said he would share half with a second coyote who would take me to the final destination in California, [but] this second coyote kept harassing me for more money. When I told him I did not have any and that I had given the other man all the money, he looked at me with morbid eyes and said he knew how I could pay."

This second guide threatened to leave my respondent in the desert at night if she did not comply. He knew the trail and controlled the flashlight, water, and food, so she had no choice: "The rest of the trip, which lasted another week, I had to let this fat and disgusting old man rape me whenever he pleased. I remember crying and wanting to wash and rid my skin of his hideous smell! When I got to New York, the Latina woman for whom I first worked as a live-in nanny noticed I looked and smelled sickly. She took me to the doctor right away. I was very depressed and would cry all the time. I had recurrent nightmares about that horrible man!"

Shortly after arriving, my respondent found out she had a virulent sexually transmitted disease; it scarred her reproductive organs and diminished her ability to mother children in the future. The migrant experience left her scarred for life, especially as she had migrated with a heart already broken by the domestic abuses that led to her marriage's dissolution and the pain of first being separated from her children. Such experiences of physical and sexual abuse scar the body, but most notably the psyche, of migrant women. My interview insights reveal that six of ten respondents experienced abuse at the hands of unscrupulous smugglers, landlords, employers, or their spouses. The scars on her body, this respondent told me, holding back tears, were not as painful as the memory she carried of the experience. To make matters worse, a few years after her arrival in the United States, her fifteen-year-old son was killed by a gang.

The above narratives capture some of the new forms of gender, class, and civic inequality that women confront when spouses or conjugal partners lead the migration. High rates of marital vulnerability, and also of households headed by women, led many of my migrant respondents to become even more resolute about furthering their education. About half of my Mexican respondents had not originally planned to migrate, but they knew that the higher their education, the higher their chances were of attaining a middle-class lifestyle. The higher the women's education was, the higher their chances were of migration.[23]

Beyond the perilous migration trek, upon arrival many of my respondents experienced new strains in their marriages, something that is well documented in the literature.[24] The residual effects of long separations strain conjugal bonds and the bonds between mothers and children. My interview insights reveal that most women who lead their migration leave their children behind, while women who migrate with spouses tend to reunite with children sooner. Despite migration, marriage, and labor market barriers, some of which had a long-lasting, piercing impact on my respondents' mental health, I find that some service jobs do, at least, increase migrant women's chances to escape economic and marital oppression and, at best, offer them chances of social mobility and integration in host societies. I also find, however, that importing some education level increased most of my middle-class respondents' mobility. Women who utilize human and racial capital tend to experience higher chances of work mobility in both mainstream and ethnic establishments.

THE MOBILITY PATHWAYS OF UNDOCUMENTED MIGRANTS

We return to Mirna, the forty-five-year-old mother introduced earlier. Before our interview, I heard mother and daughter plan to have dinner afterward at a favorite eatery in Lower Manhattan. They shared the news with unabashed complicity and giggles that they preferred to eat away from home. Mirna's daughter took the lead in sharing the source of their amusement: "Preferimos comer solas, sin mi Papa!" (We prefer to eat alone, without my father!) The plan was to eat in SoHo, where Mirna has cleaned a few apartments for over twenty years. Both women are familiar with Soho and the West Village. Mirna's daughter attended high school nearby, something that had been facilitated in part by Lisa, one of Mirna's long-term domestic employers, who would become a proxy family member until her death.

As the one in her marriage with the higher education, Mirna harbored loftier expectations for herself, and especially for her daughters, than those her husband had for them. Upon her arrival, Mirna found a job as a daytime babysitter and housekeeper for an Argentinian Jewish family in Brooklyn. For $250 a week she was asked to clean the house; take care of three small girls, ages two, six, and nine; do the family's laundry, fold it, and put it away; prepare three meals; and run errands, like dropping off clothes at the local cleaners or taking the girls for snacks after school. She was also asked to arrive at 7:00 a.m. to walk the two older girls to school and care for the toddler at home or in the park until 3:00 p.m., when she was to return to the school to pick up the girls. Before finishing her day, at 6:00 p.m., she was also asked, invariably, to walk the dog. One day, when Mirna was walking the dog with the three small girls, the dog got into a fight with another dog and bit Mirna on the back of the leg as she tried to separate them. Upon returning to the family's home, she nervously complained to the owner. Rather than making an offer to take her to the nearest doctor, her employer scolded her: "I don't care what happens to you or my wife with the dog! Just make sure it never hurts my daughters; if it does, you don't know what could happen to you!" Mirna then called her husband, Rodrigo, to say she wanted to go to the hospital and was going to quit her job. Rodrigo insisted that she hold off, as she was undocumented, and instructed her to come home, where he would take care of her wound. He reminded her that another employer might treat her worse: "Better with a bad one you know than a good one you don't know," he said, attempting to de-escalate the situation with humor. Mirna told me she had felt trapped and utterly disappointed, as these were not the responses she expected from either her employer or her husband; this was certainly not the life she had expected in New York City.

A few years later, when the girls were brought from Mexico, Mirna's husband insisted she stay home and care for them. Besides, he said, the money they earned from a small bakery (which the husband had purchased with a cousin) was enough to make ends meet. When a second cousin arrived they decide to rent a small house down the street from where they lived and become *encargados*, renting rooms to other people—coethnics at first and, later, college students. Once the girls started middle school, Mirna enrolled in English lessons offered to parents in the same school her daughters attended. Then, like magic, her work and life opportunities (as well as her expectations) expanded. She made friends with an Argentinian woman, a newly hired Spanish-speaking teacher at the school, who referred her to a few day jobs as a babysitter and later as a housekeeper in the home of upper-class professionals in Manhattan.

In the past five years Mirna had assumed the role as the head of household, the breadwinner. Rodrigo's business failed, and his poor health limited the time he could work if a job required standing on his feet all day. Mirna was obligated to clean more houses and to take babysitting jobs on weekends and in the evenings. As Rodrigo became increasingly confined to home, Mirna expanded her life in the public sphere through her work, and she learned about what women do with education. Years later, her savings, the money rescued from her husband's

business, and the input from her employers allowed Mirna to get insights as to
how to apply for specific loans as a first-time minority homeowner. She and
Rodrigo purchased the small two-story house where they had lived as tenants.
Loans also allowed them to improve their home, to renovate the attic and the
basement to increase the number of rooms they could rent out. The money they
could save as new *encargados*, and the connections Mirna made working her day
jobs, led her to explore specialized charter schools for her daughters. Her long-
standing client Lisa, a top journalist for a leading newspaper, became Mirna and
her daughter's advocate and mentor. She steered Mirna toward registering her
daughters in a specialized public middle school in Lower Manhattan; later she
helped Mirna's older daughter enter one of the City University of New York col-
leges and helped her younger daughter obtain a scholarship and admission to a
private Catholic university.

The Bonds of Migrant Women and Their Female Employers

Unlike the average Mexican manual worker, whose immigration to and initial settlement in New York City is facilitated mainly by spouses or conjugal partners'
links,[25] middle-class women rely on a combination of local and transnational links
among families and friends, but mainly among employers and coworkers. Close
relations with employers increase opportunities for migrant women and their
children, as employers can help workers with information about how to seek services or escape the abuse of spouses or others. This is the case for women whose
functions as domestics or proxy family members for employers allow them to form
bonds not only of intimacy but also of reciprocity. As Mirna recounted,

> Lisa was never married and did not have a family, save for a distant sister in Colo-
> rado; so we grew closer. I worked for her for seventeen years until she died. When
> she was diagnosed with cancer and weakened, she asked me to help her go to the
> hospital for chemotherapy, or to come to her apartment to help clean her wounds,
> give her medicines, and make her meals. She preferred this, as she could not
> afford to pay a visiting nurse. She showed me how to care for her, and I wanted to
> do it. I did not want to leave her alone on days when she was very sick. I would
> cancel my cleaning jobs or have my cousin cook for my girls, after school, so I
> could stay and sleep over. My daughters were already teenagers.
>
> A few times my husband and I drove Lisa to the hospital for her chemotherapy
> because she was too weak. On the day of her death, I never left her bedside; she
> kept staring and smiling at me the same way she did when she was at her desk,
> typing away, and I passed by to quietly clean her office or bring her a cup of tea. I
> stayed in the hospital with her that week, sleeping in chairs. My oldest daughter
> and I took turns, so I could eat. The day before she died, her only sister called
> me and told me to come clean Lisa's apartment; she said, "Mirna, make sure you
> take anything you want and throw all the other junk away!" I could not believe

she felt that way about her sister's belongings. As it was nearly Christmas, my daughters and I set up Lisa's Christmas tree in her small living room. Even though she grew up Jewish, she often celebrated different holidays, especially Christmas with my girls and my family. I knew she was not coming back home, but I wanted to set up her tree just in case her spirit did. As my mother would say, "The dying always return to say goodbye to loved ones." I was surprised her sister never came to see her at the hospital; she only came to arrange the burial and handle the details of her apartment's expenses. My daughter and I still have her picture in our living room, and the small bag she used for her books and notepads to go to work every day. We still cry during Christmas when we always remember her leaving us.

Some scholarship has shown the exploitative, sometimes alienating conditions domestic workers experience behind closed doors.[26] But not much is known about how both employers and workers can benefit from the emotional and compassionate ties that bind them. Mirna's story captures how she and her daughters relied on Lisa to learn about opportunities for Mirna's and her daughters' education and how to apply for scholarships,[27] as well as learning how to apply for a bank loan as a first-time minority homeowner. After seventeen years of working for this employer, Mirna, her husband, and her two daughters volunteered to care for her until she died, estranged from the only sister or blood relative she had. As Mirna recalled of an earlier interaction with Lisa,

> Upon my daughters' arrival, Lisa told me to bring them with me whenever I needed. She was even kind enough to help me register them for English lessons that summer, near her neighborhood in the West Village. She used her address so my daughters could attend better schools. Every morning, after dropping my daughters off at school, Lisa recommended I take the English lessons they offer to parents. For over five years, I cleaned Lisa's house on weekends. When my daughters came, she changed my schedule to bring them with me. While I cleaned, she would take my girls to buy sweets and treats, or to the museum or bookstores. She bought them books, taught them words in English, and gave them homework—a list of words to learn. She would ask my older daughter to give her a list of Spanish words, for her to learn them as well! Gradually she became like a family member and my daughters, five and nine years old, like her adopted nieces, her family!

Sociologist Mary Romero documents how service jobs sometimes increase domestic workers' children's life chances in the host society.[28] Yet we lack insights into the bond that domestics and their employers develop, or how domestic workers and their children contribute to these upper-class employers' lives. Mirna and her daughters kept Lisa company during the holidays, inviting her to their home in Brooklyn. She became part of their family and adopted some of their cultural practices, rather than Mirna, who worked for Lisa, only adopting Lisa's cultural practices. Similarly, the gradual mobility and integration of Eva, the professional woman I introduced earlier, was facilitated by one of her employer's family members.

The Networks of Educated Immigrants

These insights into Mirna's and other women's work experiences in service jobs led me to further explore the mobility pathways of middle-class Black and Brown Latinas in low-wage and skilled service jobs. As Eva, the fifty-eight-year-old respondent introduced earlier, recounted, women who import a higher education or professional skills experience greater disillusion than their lower-educated coethnics, as they harbor higher expectations about their careers and a middle-class lifestyle. Eva explained,

> It was a stupid mistake [coming to New York]! First cleaning houses, later in a pocketbook, wholesale store; then as a home attendant. I arrived at eight p.m. to do the same routine: cook dinner for my family, prepare the clothes for work and for my children's school for the next day. I used to cry all the time and hide in the bathroom so my children would not see me. I confessed to my husband that if not for my father's illness, I would go back to Santo Domingo, even on my own. But, I thought later about my children's future and my husband's taxicab business was thriving. Then, a lawyer I met at an NGO [nongovernmental organization] referred me to a home attendant agency. I completed a certificate as a home attendant. I worked for many years taking care of elderly people; later, another colleague who volunteered at an organization invited me to join a class. A year later I was a trained health care educator.

Gradually, as both Eva and her mother slowly made headway in service jobs, they broadened their networks. As her narrative illustrates, middle-class women tend to build networks in both ethnic and mainstream institutions, unlike male counterparts, who tend to concentrate in service and maintenance jobs mostly among coethnics.[29]

Dina's story illustrates the mobility pathway from housewife or homemaker to breadwinner and small entrepreneur. It is clear from Dina's story (and those of others in this chapter) that the higher the education women import, the more they are able to increase their access to networks among both ethnic and mainstream institutions, as figure 4.1 demonstrates. At age twenty-six, after five years of marriage, Dina became a widow. For a few years before her husband's death, a sales job kept him away from the home frequently, causing the couple's marriage to deteriorate. The birth of their first child, followed by a second three years later, created new forms of financial strains and schisms between the couple rather than sealing their marriage bond. Dina was tall, with a full and attractive figure. A few shades darker than her mother's and grandmother's white skin, she looked more like her father's family, with caramel-colored skin, tight curly dark hair, and full lips, which upon showing me pictures of her children, only her son had inherited: "Ese no puede negar a su abuelito" (He cannot deny his paternal grandfather [implying her son had darker skin and facial features like his grandfather's]). Within the small, yet sprawling, urban commercial center of town, Dina's maternal family members, and especially her mother, were known as "serious" businesspeople. A few years before her husband's death, Dina had asked him to leave the home after learning about his infidelity. She had already made up her mind about migrating to New York. Her mother petitioned her family, with her husband included, but Dina decided not to include him. When I asked her about the reasons for her mother's migration, she shared similar painful memories about her mother's, and her own, legacy as the breadwinner:

> My father left us when my youngest sister was only two weeks old. My mother says he left her with one wooden bed, two rocking chairs, four small kids, and thirty-three cents in her purse! But her grandparents owned land and helped her recover. My mother opened a small business. She started a small *mercadito* [kiosk] to sell mostly fruits and juices, and then she bought a small *colmado* [delicatessen]. She owned eight cows, too, and rented land to feed them. We used to sell milk in the store, but mainly food staples on a small scale. A few years later, she bought the house next door, expanded and converted her business, becoming a large supplier, an *almacén*. She became a wholesaler of sacks of grains and other food supplies, and oils.

Dina's mother contemplated migration, as the cost of private education for her daughters was too high and her business was dwindling. As a business owner with landowning parents, Dina's mother qualified for a visa to visit her aunt in New York City in the 1980s. Dina and her sister remained behind with their grandmother. After her mother left, "I was mainly in charge! I was thirteen and caring for myself and helping with my sister's education. All the time, she [Dina's mother] sent us money to pay for our private schools and my university." A year later, when her husband died, Dina followed her mother's trajectory, leaving her children behind, planning to work, to save money and then return for them. She reunited with her mother in Mount Pleasantville, an expanding suburban city at the periphery of northern Manhattan and the East Bronx, a new destination for Latino families since the mid-1990s. Ten years after her arrival, Dina opened a small takeout café in the marginalized area of southwest Mount Pleasantville historically settled by the latest newcomers and immigrants.

Until the 1990s, the downtown area of Mount Pleasantville was a traditional destination for eastern and southern Europeans, and its local government the bastion of Irish and Italian gatekeepers and politicians. By the time Dina arrived, Dominicans, Mexicans, and growing shares of Central Americans had become the life and soul of the older, industrial part of town, now on the first stages of gentrification by a Brown and foreign-born gentry. Dina's small business thrived, first as a takeout, then as a restaurant with an added lounge, and with music and entertainment provided on the weekends. One day she realized that her pro-longed business hours and absences from her home led her teenage son to play too much pool and smoke too much marijuana. Her daughter spent most days alone in their home, failing in school, distracted by boys. Dina decided this was not the life she wanted for her or her children. She leased the business and then sold it, using the money to take a long trip back to her ancestral town in the Dominican Republic, where she invested in land and livestock. She returned to New York and took a certificate course as a home health attendant, following in her mother's footsteps. By the time we met, she had worked in this business for about ten years and was planning to retire in five years. Dina's service jobs expanded her networks to women who were also educated and worked as home attendants. Her networks led her to volunteer at a local church where she soon began to lead prayer groups for church festivities and also participated in retreat groups with other parishioners. Her service job as a home attendant and many of her employers and peers helped Dina and her daughter to find part-time jobs while attending college. Dina's daughter became engaged to a young Italian man whom she planned to marry. Dina said her daughter and the fiancé both had great ambitions, but that he had less of an education than her daughter did. Dina's son still lived at home and worked while completing a four-year college degree in computing.

Dina's story represents the experience of women who import a higher educa-tion and whose family's migration is led by women. It was clear for Dina and other women like Mirna that divorce or migration forces many to assume new roles as main providers. Women like Eva and Ofelia, unlike Dina, expected their husbands would continue as the primary breadwinners or providers for their families, the way they had been prior to migration. Paradoxically, these women experience greater disillusionment upon migrating, which often fragments the marital union and can have serious consequences on their mental health, as the case of Eva suggests.

While Eva, Mirna, and many other respondents increased their networks' reach within ethnic and mainstream institutions, their husbands' jobs centered mostly on coethnics or immigrant-based institutions. My interview insights reveal that more Dominican women (46 percent) than Mexican women (12 percent) rely on women-based networks for help with immigration and the initial work integra-tion.[30] Migrant women who lead their migration have more diversified and far-flung networks than those who migrate to reunite with or accompany spouses. Next, I illustrate the mobility trajectories of immigrant women in skilled service jobs and the networks that facilitate their mobility chances.

From Hidden to Public Figures: Class, Gender, and Racial Capital

In the past decades, Latinos have carved out new political, economic, and geographical spaces in New York City.[31] This larger restructuring, in turn, has reconfigured the spatial distribution of Dominican and Mexican immigrants in the five boroughs of the city, with Dominicans more concentrated in poorer sections of the Bronx and Manhattan. As chapter 3 illustrates, this spatial redistribution has taken place amid the enactment of anti-immigration laws[32] targeting the apprehension and deportation of foreign-born Latino men.[33] This new form of racialization has also paralleled the increasing visibility of Latina women as leaders in the public sector. The election of Alexandria Ocasio-Cortez in 2019 as the youngest woman to serve in the U.S. Congress, and of Julissa Ferreras-Copeland, a second-generation Dominican American, the first Latina and woman to chair the New York City Council's Finance Committee, illustrates the rising of Black and Brown Latina leaders. The mobility pathways of a handful of Dominican and Mexican women in leadership roles within ethnic organizations attest to this growing gendered mobility trend in the face of increasing racialization.

Eva explained her mobility pathway from her low-skilled service job as a home attendant to working as a volunteer and then to working as an educator for a migrant organization as follows:

> One day, the daughter of a Latina woman for whom I worked as a home attendant realized my medical background and desire to find work in a relevant field. She invited me to a group meeting at a community center where she volunteers. She recommended training as a community health education promoter at an immigrant agency funded by the Mexican Consulate's Ventanillas de Salud, or preventive community health education program. A few of my trainers included Latinas, but also non-Latina professionals in several bureaucracies of the city, one of them a medical doctor. My professional network expanded as I committed to working on immigrants' behalf as a health educator in the Bronx. I conducted workshops on diabetes and mental health. This job led to a position as codirector of a health education program for a smaller organization in the Bronx.

Similarly, Laura, a forty-two-year-old woman with an advanced degree and professional experience from a top Mexican university, found work in a migrant organization serving Latino immigrants in Manhattan. Her demeanor was surprisingly down-to-earth for someone with many years' experience as a human rights attorney in Mexico. Laura was the middle sibling of three sisters and the one with the highest education, the first woman professional in a long line of male providers in her family. Laura was once married in New York to an equally educated "1.5 generation" Latino professional. After less than five years, the marriage dissolved. Laura said she had "remarried" her career, not taking men too seriously. Having to carve her way into a secured profession in a new land, learning a new language and a new culture, and living away from her family was a challenging yet empowering experience thanks to the support of local and transnational religious ties. Among these networks, her academic mentor and friend, a powerful academic and political strategist at an elite university in Mexico, was a main sponsor, giving Laura small projects as an independent contractor.

Since arriving in 2005, Laura worked in different capacities at several community agencies. Through her transnational ties with a Jesuit mentor, she established connections with Catholic institutions in Manhattan. She was referred to two community agencies where she took English lessons. Soon she began to volunteer in a church, running workshops about immigration rights for parishioners; then she found work as a part-time program director for an agency affiliated with the church; and then she worked as full-time administrator and coleader of the New Mexican Alliance (NMA),[34] an immigrant organization in the city. Using her imported human capital and experience as a lawyer and educator, Laura also designed legal advocacy and education programs at the NMA. Among her key roles were writing grants, organizing fundraisers, and organizing public forums, including conferences. In less than five years of service, she had linked the NMA to local and transnational organizations in New York City, Mexico, and a few nations in Latin America. Her main accomplishment was linking the NMA with ethnic and mainstream institutions with the know-how to procure funding, such as the New York City Human Resource Administration and the City Council's office. She worked as a consultant and established strong relations with Latina leaders. Yet despite Laura's imported human capital and contributions to the NMA, most of her work remained "backstage." For example, in 2015, the NMA's first major conference at the Columbia University School of Social Work was widely publicized, and the event included academics from Latin America and the United States, but on the NMA's social media page and in other news reports covering the event her name was absent. Women's work at small community-based organizations (CBOs) affiliated with or financially supported by religious institutions or diasporic bureaucracies are often "backstage" positions, in contrast to the more visible roles of Latino male leaders in these institutions.

My ethnographic observations at two community organizations suggest that a transnational education and public and private institutional links fuel the ascendancy to power of Black and Brown leaders. But the networks of highly educated Latina leaders stretch beyond the boundaries of the local church or small migrant institutions, where males predominate, and lie more within mainstream, nondiasporic institutional spaces, as the case of a few women-led CBOs will illustrate. This may explain why Laura's role remains a "backstage" one without much publicity in the NMA, a small immigrant organization supported by a church and transnational, diasporic institutions.

Beyond the diversity of networks, gender and racial capital become exceedingly important in the rising mobility of Dominican and Mexican women as public leaders in migrant organizations. When asked what has helped her professionally, a forty-year-old Dominican leader candidly spoke about her family and her local community outside the city:

> I've straddled both the immigrant and the nonimmigrant world seamlessly. I grew up in a low-middle class community in NJ [New Jersey]. My parents had Peruvians, Dominicans, PR [Puerto Ricans], Spaniards [as friends]; an incredible mix of friends, including a group of Dominicans who were politically aware, very sophisticated, and worked as activists here and back in DR [the Dominican Republic]! My parents were very political. I inherited this consciousness—from my parents and from working with a congressman when I was a college activist. My parents' community also included Irish, Italian, working-class Whites. My parents made a list each month with invitations for our parties. It included both Latinos and White neighbors.

This leader's narrative reveals the influence of her family and of her local Latino and White community in her professional socialization. Growing up in a middle-class home and a mixed-race community outside of New York, the family had friends in majority and minority groups, and access to her parents' diasporic political networks helped this young Latina leader foster an early consciousness about the needs of the Latino community. Her education at an elite university in New York City, her gender, and her white skin and European phenotype, or racial capital, may also help explain her ability to "straddle" (as she put it) both ethnic and mainstream communities. This may have also helped her form institutional alliances with Latino and White mentors and leaders, increasing her ability to tap into resources for her immigrant CBO in the heart of the traditional Dominican community in Upper Manhattan.

Earlier studies show that input of the family and of the local community explains the exceptional educational mobility of immigrant youth in the United States.[35] My analysis of the mobility pathways of Dominican and Mexican immigrant women shows that the leadership of Black and Indigenous women in New York City has been fueled by the collective input of families, educational mentors, and employers in local and transnational communities.

Beyond the investments of families and local institutions, the mobility of elite Latinas is also fueled by transnational networks and institutions, as the cases of Laura and the leader introduced above reveal. Yet the ascendancy of Dominican and Mexican women as public leaders takes place in New York City increasingly in communities with long legacies of poverty and racialization and among women with established experience serving their communities. For example, before becoming directors of two Latino immigrant organizations in New York City, two Mexican female leaders participating in this study had already worked in elite financial institutions and benefited from the resources of transnational families and institutions. One of these women had been socialized in Mexico and New York and benefited from the input and resources of her transnational, entrepreneurial family with businesses serving the Mexican community in both places. Participation in community and academic projects in New York City exposed this young CEO to the economic, educational, and political needs of the emerging Mexican community. The socialization of a second female CEO, a Dominican community leader, also took place in an upper-middle-class family with strong local and transnational political ties. A transnational socialization, I find, increases these and other leaders' mobility as well as unique contributions to their ethnic CBOs.

Lastly, longitudinal observations within two Dominican CBOs (hereafter labeled DomOrg1 and DomOrg2, to preserve anonymity) reveal how the combination of gender, class, and racial capital mediates the mobility pathways and successful tenure of Latina immigrants as public leaders. This is the case of the White Dominican woman who is the CEO of DomOrg1: the access to networks in both Latino and mainstream White institutions allows her to draw resources from both communities as she has led the largest immigration organization serving Dominicans in the city for over twenty years. Similarly, the leader of DomOrg2, a Black Dominican member of the "1.5 generation," has also been in her position for close to thirty years. I argue that her ability to establish grassroots linkages and collaborations in NGOs and governmental bureaucracies within the Black and the Latino community has allowed her to expand her services in both the Dominican and Black community. In 2016, a fundraiser at a church in Harlem was attended mostly by African American women parishioners in their sixties and seventies. Wearing long dreadlocks and Afro-Caribbean jewelry and clothing, the Black Latina leader of DomOrg2 greeted the church's well-known African American pastor with an embrace. She then delivered a salutation to the audience and made a pitch—in English, then in Spanish—on behalf of her CBO. In past years she had worked with a prominent African American female scholar to help cowrite a few grants to establish public health education programs in Harlem. This and other strategies allowed this leader and others to expand their reach in the growing Latino (mostly Dominican) community of West Harlem and the (mostly African American) community of East Harlem (though the demographics of both communities are rapidly changing due to gentrification). I find that the distinctive racial capital of Black, Brown, and White Latina leaders in two communities that share and value their racial, gender, and class capital has ensured Dominican and Mexican women's leadership on behalf of immigrants and racialized minorities. Further research is needed to explore the conditions that lead to valuation about the racial or gender characteristics of leaders, and when race becomes an asset or a liability not only in migration but also in the mobility prospects of migrants.

CHAPTER SUMMARY

The crossing of geographic boundaries also entails the crossing of cultural, class, and racial boundaries that have bearing on the lives of migrants. For women this often involves the transformation of their status and authority positions in the home, the workplace, and the larger community. When Altagracia was an adolescent, the migration of two great-aunts set them free from the economy and sexual oppression of a repressive dictatorship; her mother also migrated to escape political and economic oppression. Altagracia's migration, unlike that of her ancestors, symbolized intersections at different levels of gendered exclusion as she lost her gendered capital (marriage prospects) and became a single mother. She realized that without the sponsorship of a male patron or lover, or even that of the government, women cannot find work or gain economic independence. As López and Hernández's earlier research reveals, many women, often from rural communities and with low literacy, migrate due to the abandonment of men or the state.[36] Altagracia and many other Dominican and Mexican respondents migrated not only because they were not able to find professional work but also because men in their lives were abusive or could not provide financial support for their families, and the state acted as an accomplice by not providing women with public aid or welfare on behalf of their children. This is a very different migration from the one conceptualized by classic and neo-macroeconomic theories of labor migration, which conceive migrating individuals to be pushed solely by a desire to improve their and their families' economic situation.[37] These approaches, often based on migrations led mostly by men, leave out explanations about the intersectional forms of inequalities that push sexual, racial, and class minorities to migrate despite their higher education.

Overall, whereas higher education decreases the odds of male migration, for women, the likelihood of migration increases with education.[38] Since the 1990s, the share of households joining the middle class in the Dominican Republic and Mexico has surpassed many other Latin American nations.[39] Paradoxically, the restructuring of the Mexican economy following the passing of the North American Free Trade Agreement in 1994 and the subsequent integration of neoliberal economic initiatives have increased the migration of highly educated Mexican women professionals to the United States.[40] While the migration of educated women in Mexico is often fueled by the earlier or simultaneous migration of spouses to seek better professional opportunities in the United States, among Dominican women the tendency has been to lead their own migration, often leaving husbands or partners behind.

Nancy Foner's historical research documents the immigration of Black women from the Anglophone Caribbean to Canada, England, and the United States, most of whom were destined for low-skilled service jobs such as home care attendants or health aides.[41] The nature of the U.S. health care system, Foner argues, forces many migrant women to stay in low-wage service jobs to provide health insurance for their families. Yet only those with a legal status and who can speak English qualify for these jobs, increasing the selective immigration of college-educated women. Anthropologists and sociologists also document the migrant experiences of middle-class women from Central America, Mexico, and Cuba in the United States.[42] This chapter documents the experiences of women who lead their migration. Unlike their leading role as main providers, middle-class women who follow spouses or conjugal partners share more conservative views; they tend to see men as primary providers, as many derive their status from their husband's or their own family's social class position. These women often experience the harshest challenges adjusting to life in New York City. Upon arrival, their spouses often find meager wages and work opportunities; this in turn lowers their families' quality of life and their own well-being, and it can ultimately lead to the erosion of a marriage. Scholars have documented the challenges confronted by middle-class Indian, Latina, and West Indian women when they migrate first, becoming the primary breadwinners.[43] Research by Sheba George reveals that when men are forced to rely on their wives' finances, during the initial stages of their adjustment (and in most cases, permanently) these men often experience great mental and emotional afflictions.[44]

My interviews inspire reflection about the growing significance of migrant women's remittances in filling the needs neglected by the Dominican and Mexican states, as well as about the mental health afflictions Latino men suffer when they are unable to provide for their families and/or are no longer the ones in control, as George's research has shown.[45] Unlike Indian men, who after a while tend to recover their patriarchal status as heads of families with the help of their own ethnic and religious diasporic organizations and through community programs and education, Dominican men (more than Mexicans) experience racialization and exclusion. The increased backlash, which has in recent decades targeted Black and Brown men for detention and deportation,[46] has increased poverty and forced women to assume new roles as primary providers. As members of the largest and fastest-growing Afro-Latino group in New York and on the East Coast, Dominican women continue to face the highest incidence of being single heads of households.[47] I argue that intersectional inequalities based on family structures, race, class, and immigrant status adversely affect opportunities for Dominican immigrants in New York City, despite their imported human capital and their growing visibility in leadership positions in the public sector. Substantiating the cogent insights by sociologists Nancy López and Vivian Gadsden, as well as other scholars,[48] with a focus on the institutional and personal inequalities that Latinas and women of color experience in the United States, this chapter documents the most precarious forms of gendered and racialized inequality and mobility that Dominican and Mexican women experience before and after migration.

Finally, the findings in this chapter extend Cinzia Solari's argument in *On the Shoulders of Grandmothers* that the migration of family women benefits both the sending and the receiving communities. Solari finds that as a new recovering republic, Ukraine cannot afford to provide jobs to all its citizens, forcing many to retire early, including professional or highly educated women. Many of these skilled women tend to migrate to find jobs in California or Italy. The remittances they send back to their families, often to adult married children, help the families meet the cost of babysitters or supplement the income of mothers so that they can stay home to care for their children. Solari argues that these migrant women are filling in the services that the state cannot provide.[49] Similarly, I find that many of my women respondents grew up in homes with migration legacies. The educational and social mobility of family women left behind is only possible through the remittances migrant mothers and grandmothers sent to families, as the cases of Altagracia, Dina, Eva, Ofelia, and many others reveal. Without these women's remittances, Black and Indigenous minorities would lack the resources to pay for their higher education.

Migration, especially for the undocumented, often entails the transformation of women's lives as regards to their status not only in the family but also in the larger society, often with a long-term impact on their mental health. The experience also transforms women's relations with institutions and family or diasporic bureaucracies, such as the Catholic Church and migrant organizations, all traditionally organized around men. The mobility pathways of Dominican and Mexican women show that these women's leadership is fueled by the collective input of families, educational mentors, and networks in the local and transnational communities. Yet the public leadership of Dominican and Mexican women emerges in New York City mostly in communities with legacies of poverty and racialization, and among women with sustained experiences serving the poor.

6 · "¡Y ELLOS PENSABAN QUE YO ERA BLANCA!"
Racial Capital and Ambiguous Identities

In chapter 5, Mirna's story suggested that domestic work increases the likelihood of immigrant women forming intimate bonds with female employers and, in turn, improving their own and their children's opportunities. Yet Mirna also confronted oppression and exploitation as a domestic: a previous employer threatened to report her undocumented status if she did not meet his multiple expectations. This chapter further explores the work experiences of immigrant women in neighborhoods undergoing gentrification and the role of skin color and racial capital in their work mobility and in racialization processes. I analyze how service jobs in the beauty industry demand of women workers the management of gendered and racialized Latina identities and of emotions implicit in the act of servitude.[1] Most significantly, the findings contribute to a new understanding of skin color and racial capital in the work stratification of Latino workers in old and new immigrant destination areas undergoing gentrification. The conclusions engage a discussion about the underpinning of a new theoretical framework on the social construction of race as depicted in the experiences of mobility, as well as the discrimination experience of immigrant workers with ambiguous, or "in-between," racial identities.

I start my analysis with a couple of caveats. First, unlike the clear divide that shapes the valuation or commodification of a Black or White identity in the workplace,[2] I assume that people with in-between or mixed-race identities,[3] such as Latinos, will experience different valuations or interstitial identities as either White or Black depending on the racial composition of the context of reception—in this case, the workplace. Second, as research documents that lighter-skinned African Americans and Latinos have access to higher wages in the United States,[4] and that lighter-skinned Afro-descendants and Indigenous minorities in Latin America gain greater social mobility, or higher education and white-collar jobs,[5] I further explore how skin color and education affect the stratification of immigrant women in service sector jobs in New York City. Draw-ing on ethnography and in-depth interviews gathered in a handful of hair salons at old and new immigrant destinations in New York City, I also analyze the role of skin color and phenotype on the functions, status, and mobility prospects of Dominican and Mexican women. In addition to race and other social character-istics, I explore how the ecology of the workplace and the changing demograph-ics of neighborhoods affect the work prospects and conditions of immigrant women in low-skilled service jobs. Finally, I examine how racial capital (the positive valuation of an immigrant's racial identity) and racial capitalism (the commodification of a non-White or White identity) mediate social mobility and new forms of racialization in service-sector jobs.

THE ECOLOGY OF RACE AND SERVICE WORK IN NEW IMMIGRANT DESTINATIONS

Silvia's hair salon has five booths attended by five White women, including Angela, a Dominican immigrant in her early forties. Daniella, a sixth worker, is the most senior in age and work tenure other than Silvia, the owner. Three other hairstylists and two floor attendants are all Gen Xers, in their early thirties and forties. Daniella is the only one who does not handle hair; her duties as a mani-curist take place in a small corner workspace near the two hair washing stations at the back of the store. Daniella is also the only one who works from a chair; the others must earn a living on their feet. The shampoo girls work three to five shifts a week, usually from 9:00 a.m. to 7:00 p.m., but often till 9:00 p.m. Next to Dani-ella's table and the washing stations, Angela's booth is a mere five or six steps from the back room, a supply space and kitchenette that is about four and a half feet wide and five feet long. A small countertop allows the women a "backstage" space for quick meals, away from the views of clients. On weekends or holidays and on days when she does the late shifts, Angela treats herself and her clients to occasional ice-chilled beers or vodka drinks.

On a good workday, or when she attends at least six to eight clients per day, Angela brings home between $650 and $800 in cash, not including $150–200 in tips. This is two to three times more than the monthly disability check her hus-band receives. On average, the national yearly salary for hairstylists oscillates between $23,166 and $34,258. The highest pay is in New York and California.[6] At Silvia's, Angela is the second top colorist, hair designer, and wage earner after Silvia, the owner. Angela asserts these are the highest earnings she has ever received in her twenty years in the beauty industry. In most other jobs, especially her last one, Angela paid the owner, a White ethnic man in his early sixties, half of her earnings for the right to rent a booth and the use of hair products. At her present job, she pays less than a third, or a fixed monthly fee of $1,200, for the rental of a work booth and use of hair products. Beauty salon employers are responsible for marketing, recruiting, and maintaining a clientele, but Angela's hiring entailed a proviso that she would help build a clientele for Silvia's beauty salon in exchange for a commission.[7] In 2015, during the last stage of my research, the wages of floor assistants or "shampoo girls" at Silvia's ranged between ten and twelve dollars per hour, which is at least five dollars more per hour than what undocumented Mexican floor assistants received at Angela's previous job, another hair salon less than a mile north of Silvia's, which I describe later.

Daniella, the manicurist, and Silvia have worked together for over fifteen years, since Silvia first opened the salon in the southwestern part of Mount Pleasantville, one of the oldest and largest cities on New York City's periphery. Silvia's first salon was within walking distance of the now gentrifying area that once was an industrial park in the downtown area with a mostly African American, Latino, and ethnic White community. Old brick-and-mortar buildings once housed Clairol, General Motors, Otis Elevator, and many other factories that in the early twentieth century attracted African Americans fleeing the Jim Crow South as part of the Great Migration. Eastern European immigrants followed and, in the 1950s, Puerto Ricans; in the early 1970s, Dominicans and small shares of Cubans, Middle Easterners, and South Americans filled the housing and work slots left by retiring or dying ethnic Whites. Today older tenements and factories, converted into modern highrises and commercial strips, are coveted by new waves of young professionals who grew up in Mount Pleasantville but were born or have families with origins in eastern Europe, such as Albanians and Ukrainians, and members of an emerging Black and Brown Latino middle class, most of whom owe their ascendancy to jobs in the information technology industry.

Almost ten years ago, after a painful divorce, Silvia relocated her young daughter, home, and thriving small business to a more economically stable and Whiter neighborhood in the northeastern part of Mount Pleasantville. One of her clients, a real estate agent, told her about the rental of a corner store in a two-tiered shopping mall. Nested within a 1.5-mile commercial throughway, a growing strip of shopping malls near Silvia's caters to the consumption needs of a new middle class. Retail stores specializing in wholesale household goods sell mattresses, appliances, furniture, and secondhand automobiles. In later years a horde of new entrepreneurs affiliated with the hospitals in New York City opened urgent care satellite clinics. The chiropractic, physical, occupational, and renal therapy services target an aging and diminishing White lower middle class and working class whose socioeconomic mobility has taken a big toll on their bodies. Alcohol and drug rehabilitation centers were the first to open in Mount Pleasantville's downtown areas during the early stages of gentrification with the arrival of a White middle class. These first developments assured prospective home buyers or business investors of the healing and imminent hygiene of poor, inner-city communities, and especially of their low-income residents (who experienced forced displacement, as chapter 3 illustrates).

Behind Silvia's salon, manicured shrubs and lawns frame ascending slopes. They hide the modest brick houses of the established yet middle class of Irish, Italian, and, increasingly, shares of light-skinned Middle Easterners, West Asians, and Indian families. Now a new emerging middle class composed of Africans, Black and Brown Latinos, Chinese, Filipinos, and West Indians with roots in the Bronx or Queens have joined this part of the neighborhood. White picket fences, American flags high on steel poles, white lions, and shrines encasing the Virgin Mary draw symbolic boundaries between the old ethnic White, of a not-too-distant immigrant stock, and the new non-White and more educated middle class.

Not far from the mall that houses Silvia's salon, a South Asian community of Bangladeshis, Keralanis, and Punjabis, including many small entrepreneurs, encompasses about five blocks of rent-controlled duplex housing. Two blocks southeast, low-income and poor families, mostly African Americans, Dominicans, Puerto Ricans, and West Indians, reside in scattered single-unit public housing. In the early 1990s, the federal government sanctioned the city to build public housing on this side of town. The development of public housing in this middle-class neighborhood led to the rapid exodus of White families, which I argue vacated homes for an emerging middle class of White ethnics and racialized, middle-class minorities. The change in the demographics of the neighborhood has contributed to business development, catering to new residents' needs for swimming pools, plumbing, hardware, furniture, cars, electronics, and discounted travel, home, and car insurance packages to meet the needs of a middle class in the process of reinvention. Establishments that tout tarot card and palm readings, tattoos, hair threading, hair replacement, and foot reflexology, as well as spas and nail salons, attract the young and upwardly mobile second-generation youth, many of whom are in the newly minted middle class but also come from striving and hardworking families in affordable public housing.

On the floor above Silvia's, a law office sign reads "Divorce for $400." A block south, above the small offices of a commercial bank, a big sign reads "Private Investigations, Virtual and Personal Detectives." Just across the street, a Middle Eastern family sells and rents wedding gowns, tuxedos, limousines, and DJ packages. In the same block, a lingerie store bears a sign that reads "Bathrobes, Barbie Dolls, Erotic Toys and Videos." A firehouse and two commercial banks face each other, alerting locals as to where the south and the north, or the affluent and less fortunate, merge. At this intersection, several overhead traffic cameras take pictures of car license plates and pedestrians—mostly the faces of patrons at fast-food eateries such as Dunkin' Donuts, Taco Bell, and Wendy's and those at a large H Mart owned by Koreans and staffed mostly by South Asian women, Dominicans, and Mexicans.

In the late 1990s, owing to his far-flung immigrant connections, Angela's husband secured a place to live in northwest Mount Pleasantville, a half-hour drive from his Upper Manhattan community. He had found work as a night guard for a well-respected retail store in a newly built upscale shopping mall. After selling his used jewelry store and pawn shop in Manhattan, he relocated his young and pregnant wife to an ethnic White working-class neighborhood with better schools. Ten years later, Angela joined Silvia's team. She had heard about the search for a top colorist and hairstylist from one of her steady clients, a Jewish lawyer with a chip on her shoulder, described as "un dolor en el——, pero la mejor entre todas mis clientas" (a royal pain in the——, but the kindest of all my clients). Within a few weeks, Angela decided to leave her job of over ten years to join Silvia, but not before calling her most important clients, including me, to let them know about her new work location.

An emerging scholarship rooted in Marxist theories of inequality has argued that White employers benefit from diversity, or the growing integration of non-White workers, especially given the suites of civil rights laws put in place to increase diversity since 1967.[8] Yet an emphasis on diversity has led to the commodification of non-White identities and to new forms of racial capitalism, which, according to this scholarship, benefits mainly White employers. The emphasis on diversity, Nancy Leong's seminal work has argued, diminishes erosion of the root causes of racial inequality or the systemic and institutional practices that exclude and marginalize non-White minorities.[9] Drawing on this literature, I explore the stratification of Latino workers in service sector jobs and the role that skin color, phenotype, and education play in the positions and functions that Dominican and Mexican immigrant women occupy in different contexts of reception and implications for the reproduction of new forms of racialization and racial capitalism.

Interstitial Spaces of Mobility and Racialization in Service Jobs: Angela, a White Dominican

I met Angela during the first stage of my field research in 2003 at her previous salon, Eden's Paradise, not far from Silvia's. Her boss, a middle-aged man with working-class origins and an affected middle-class demeanor, used to do my hair. One day as I walked into his salon, Carolina, the Mexican receptionist, stared at my hair and then at my face, as most salon workers would upon meeting a prospective client in the beauty industry as they try to discern the client's needs. She lowered her voice and, with a smile and affected concern, greeted me: "¿Usted esta aqui para ver a Marcelo, no?" (You are here for Marcelo, no?) Before I could answer, she interjected, "Sabe q' tenemos una chica nueva. Ella es dominicana. ¡Pero muy buena en su trabajo, casi o mejor que el dueño!" (You know, we have a new girl who is a stylist. She is Dominican. But great at her job, as good or better than the owner!) Soon, I preferred that only Angela do my hair. A few months later I found out that, despite attracting the most clientele, Angela was unhappy at the salon.[10] Her boss praised her with sweet talk but treated her only a bit above the "shampoo girls." She felt he exploited her in the same way, though with "gentler gloves." As an incentive for bringing in new clients, Angela's boss promised her an increased commission, but he broke that promise, camouflaging it with intermittent reduced payments not near the 20 percent he had offered her. Angela also felt he stole her White, non-Latino clients, as Carolina and another receptionist had begun to schedule her clients on days when she was off or would tell them that Angela's schedule was already booked. Mostly, Angela resented her lack of control over her schedule, and even over the supervision and duties of her floor assistants.

A feminist literature documents that despite the gains women have made in education and entry into the labor force, most tend to concentrate in work sectors with other women. In addition, when women enter sectors traditionally dominated by males, they often lack authority. In this salon, the majority of workers were women, which is typical in the beauty industry; yet, according to reports from her clients, Angela's skills ranked above those of her boss and even higher than another male hairstylist, a southern European man in his early fifties. As the only non-European hairstylist she felt excluded and denied professional status or wages the other stylists enjoyed.

Angela felt increasingly mistreated as she noticed her employer and the receptionist would assign her the few Black and Latino clients and a growing number of Albanians who did not speak English and whose humble origins meant they adhered to traditional long hairstyles, which took longer to do and were more work. Occasionally her schedule would include older, ethnic White seniors with limited budgets who came as "walk-ins" for specials on haircuts or coloring that did not include drying or styling. She was also the only stylist assigned to do family groups, mostly for Black and Latino families' sweet sixteen parties or weddings. "They think that because I am Dominican, I am the only one who knows how to or wants to handle coarse or Black hair," she told me. What upset Angela was that she felt the Mexican floor assistants, including the receptionist, would not back her up and talked behind her back. "I understand that their situation is difficult because of their papers' situation," she explained. "But that's even a better reason they should work tightly with me, the only other Latina in the shop who can advocate for them. But they kiss his White——!"

Angela understood and sympathized with the Mexican women's vulnerable position, but Alma, the youngest and most vocal of the three assistants, felt that Angela did not understand what it meant to work for a long time with an employer who risked his business by employing undocumented workers. Alma also confided that Angela was demanding and had a chip on her shoulder. Alma explained her feelings, clearing her throat to manage her conflicted emotions, always checking my eyes for empathy: "Angela doesn't understand—and probably never will—what it is to live and work in a constant state of fear—of being deported; of leaving your children one day behind, alone, in this country!"

One day Angela took a big blow from her boss after he asked one of the floor attendants to change the Latin music Angela had chosen. She did not complain, to avoid problems, "pa' evitar no tener que decirle a ese hombre que se vaya pa'la misma——" (to avoid not having to tell that man to go to——), as she explained when we spoke about her working conditions. Looking down at my hair, blowing dry the last wet section she had put in a *moñito* (bun), Angela explained that her boss exhibited these macroaggressions only when White clients or his other European hairstylists were around, not when the two of them were alone or worked side by side. She avoided talking about the radio incident because tensions with her boss were rising. The day before he had asked the older White South American worker, Divina, who alternated as a shampoo girl and manicurist, to lower her voice when speaking Spanish with one of Angela's Dominican clients.

Alma and the others began to speak to me in Spanish after Angela left— always cautious, lowering their voices, even when the boss or his clients were not around. They were convinced the two security video cameras recorded conversations, as her boss had claimed. Each of the women also addressed me in the formal word for "you," *Usted*, a traditional way of conferring respect to older or higher-status persons in Latin America.

One day while washing my hair and untangling the ends, Nadia, the oldest of the three Mexican women, in her mid-fifties, lowered her voice and asked if she could ask me a question. I nodded. "Do you know how someone who works in a beauty salon can find out how to apply for retirement benefits?" she asked. I felt moved by rare emotions, glad that Nadia finally trusted me enough to ask this question. Even if it was said using the third person, it still suggested that it was Nadia herself who might no longer be undocumented. I was glad that the class boundary that at first kept her and her peers at a distance from me was blurring, as they had been offering me food and drinks they ordered for themselves. "It depends on how long that person has worked and how the employer has paid them wages," I replied. Nadia kept silent for a while, weighed everything carefully before speaking. Finally she said, "Mi amiga ha trabajado por casi veinte años, pero solo en los ultimos años le han pagado con cheques" (My friend has worked for over twenty years, but only in recent years has she been paid with checks). I gave her the phone number of a Latino lawyer with whom I volunteer at a community center and suggested she mention my name. Carolina, the receptionist, later confirmed that almost all of the floor assistants were paid in cash. Only one of them was paid by check, but Carolina did not know for certain if the boss reported the taxes he deducted.

"Mexico Is Racist!": Carolina, a White Mestiza

Carolina, the Mexican receptionist, smiled with joy as she told me that her daughter, a second-generation woman of twenty-one with an Indigenous Mestizo phenotype and light, honeyed skin, was to marry a Dominican man. She burst into laughter when I asked if he was darker than her daughter. She was afraid to say yes, but her mocking eyes betrayed her. She explained that the lower valuation of an Indigenous identity in Mexico, especially in her native Puebla, had permeated social relations, leading almost always to the selection of lighter-skinned people as spouses for as long as she could remember. Another worker, a darker-skinned Mexican with a strong Indigenous phenotype, corroborated Carolina's story. She said her husband was a light-skinned Mestizo, a coethnic from her town in Puebla, and then related—keeping her eyes fixed on her recently manicured nails—how Mexican people always frown at the marriage of a Mestizo (the progeny of an Indigenous person and a White person) with an Indigenous woman (a Native American of Mesoamerican descent): "¡Mestiza si, pero India no! ¡Se ve mal que un hombre güero[11] se case con una India, la gente siempre dice algo!" (Mestiza, yes, but not Indian! It looks bad for a light-skinned man to marry an Indian woman; people always talk!)

Carolina and I joked that her daughter's choice of a dark-skinned husband is retribution for the pernicious history of discrimination in Mexico and the United States. Yet Carolina makes a caveat: ¡"Pero él es un muchacho muy bueno, y creo que los niños saldrán muy bonitos!" (But he is a very good person, and I think their children will be really cute!) Herbert Gans has argued that people often reproduce racialization or stereotypes about successful African Americans as being "exceptional," or more "deserving minorities," than other members of their group.[12] In Latin America, scholars attribute higher status or success to lighter skin or Whiteness.[13] Christina Sue's Land of the Cosmic Race documents that even in Mexico's Veracruz, a state that served as the major entry port for the importation and sale of African slaves, most people still associate a lighter skin with a higher social status.[14] This is due to the legacy of the racial and class stratification imposed by colonizing Europeans through the Casta System,[15] but also to the strategies of Mexican ruling elites, after independence, who sought to assimilate Indigenous minorities as members of a new nation into a stronger hybrid race known as Mestizos.

In the mid-1990s, Carolina arrived in Mount Pleasantville with one year of postsecondary education. She tried her luck in a factory in New Jersey, but transportation problems proved disastrous, as her children were still small. She then found a job as a shampoo girl at Eden's Paradise. Her uncle's wife, who cleaned a bank next door to the salon, had learned about the job from Divina, the salon's White South American manicurist. Carolina and the two other Mexican shampoo girls, Alma and Nadia, had Mestizo phenotypes with hardly discernible Indigenous traits; Carolina, the lightest skinned, always wore her hair colored in a golden blond shade, with ash-blond highlights framing her face. Her boss, who took care of most of the women's hair on his crew, said she needed to brighten her face; he changed her natural brown hair color first to an amber and then to this golden- and ash-blond combination. Carolina had worked at Eden's Paradise since her daughter started kindergarten; she appreciated that her boss often accommodated her work schedule around her children's school hours.

Alma, the youngest, wore her hair the shortest, with a blunt punkish cut and a dark brown base with an auburn-purplish Ambrose (a style where only one to two inches of the tips are colored in sharp contrasting highlights). All of the women were petite and dressed in dark slacks and comfortable walking shoes, save for Carolina, who always wore high-heeled boots or stilettos, jewelry, and low-cut shirts, for which Divina, the oldest of the floor assistants, often teased her. One day I noticed that all the Latina workers, including Angela, the White Dominican hairstylist, had ambiguous ethnoracial identities: they could pass for ethnic Whites from North Africa (i.e., Algiers, Egypt, Morocco, or Tunisia) or for honeyed- or light-brown-skinned people from southern Europe or the Middle East. I also concluded that all the women, except for Divina (the oldest South American), had imported at least a year of college, with Angela possessing the highest accreditations.

THE WORK FUNCTIONS OF EDUCATED, UNDOCUMENTED WOMEN

As the one with the best English, the longest tenure, and the lightest shade of honeyed skin among her Mexican coworkers, Carolina worked in a "front-stage" position, mainly as the receptionist and a cashier. She was the only one not to do errands outside the store or wash or do any manual labor. She answered the phone; managed clients; reminded her boss of personal tasks for private clients; dealt with vendors and accountants; and also managed the owner's, his wife's, and his children's personal schedules. Yet despite having the most authority, a higher wage, and more flexible hours among the three Mexican employees, Carolina felt the most exploited, due to her gender and her undocumented status.

Besides being attentive to the facial clues and callings of hairstylists as to which client was next in the wash or styling queues, the other Mexican floor assistants had many other tasks. Beyond shampooing off the heavy residuals of color jobs and the chemicals from highlights and relaxers, they were always on high alert, expected to rush to buy food or make coffee; sanitize brushes; launder, dry, and fold towels and the black smocks worn by clients and staff; empty garbage cans; clean toilets; and sweep hair from and mop floors. They also had to go to nearby stores to buy soft drinks or meals for clients. They had to water the boss's plants, supervise deliveries, and conduct inventories. Alma and Carolina, the youngest, also placed telephone orders, called clients to remind them of appointments, and printed daily appointment lists. At the end of the workday they bagged up and put out the garbage, turned on the alarm, turned off the lights, lowered the heavy security gates, and put padlocks on the front and back doors, in addition to taking turns helping the owner count the money at closing time.

Carolina and a light-brown-skinned West Indian woman, also in her early forties, and with an affected middle-class, White Connecticut manner of speaking,
took turns acting as cashier. They answered the phone, scheduled and confirmed
appointments, handled walk-ins, walked to the nearest bank to get change or
make deposits, managed the cash registers and cash flow, loaded the printers
with paper, printed receipts, and kept spreadsheets of clients' hair color formulas
and payment histories. They ordered supplies and dealt with vendors or insistent
or dissatisfied clients. At closing time, Carolina helped the owner count the
money and double-checked the balances for accounts payable and receivable,
using an accounting program that he was having trouble mastering.

The fourth assistant, Divina, in her mid-sixties, was an exception: a White
Latina from South America with a little bit of a chip on her shoulder, as she was
the only one with a documented immigrant status and able to speak English
moderately. She boasted that her White skin was from Portuguese ancestors
who settled in Brazil without ever "interbreeding" with *Prietos*, or Blacks. She
had arrived at the salon in her forties bearing only a high school diploma. Her
job at Eden's Paradise was her first and would be her last; she had never worked
outside the home until her husband died. Besides washing hair and helping with
the laundry, she did occasional manicures. According to Angela and Alma, Divina kept the shortest hours yet made the highest wages. When I asked Divina
why she worked so few days, she retorted, "My boss has been cutting my hours
and my days, trying to push me out, hoping I go. But I am waiting for him to fire
me. We will see!"

Since the early 1990s, a psychedelic motif on the front sign advertised Eden's
Paradise as a "unisex" salon. The hairstyling crew, all foreign-born Europeans,
were in their mid- to late fifties: one woman with a northern European accent, two
men with dark skin and Mediterranean accents, and a West Asian woman, with
the thickest accent and the lightest skin of them all. Angela was the exception,
coming from the Dominican Republic in the Spanish Caribbean. In addition to
her pearly white skin and eastern European phenotype or racial capital, she had
the highest education level. A year after Angela joined, her boss had hired the
West Asian woman in an attempt to attract clients from the rapidly changing
demographics of his neighborhood.

The most recent hire wore her hair in long, platinum- and ash-blond tresses
that brought out the porcelain quality of her white skin. Her presence made
more visible the material and social inequalities that divided the fates of European and Latino workers at Eden's Paradise. This divide was most noticeable in
the wages Angela and the new hire were offered, and also in the location of their
work spaces: Angela's work booth was in the back, next to the bathroom and the
back storage room, while the new hire's booth was close to the receptionist's
booth and the boss's station, in the front of the salon. Angela heard that the new
hire was offered a salary similar to hers and the promise of a commission, despite

not being a colorist and her boss's complaints about lower revenues and an inability to pay Angela her overdue commission. She felt that this was "the straw that broke the camel's back" and she soon quit.

RACIAL CAPITAL, AMBIGUOUS IDENTITIES, AND SOCIAL MOBILITY

Angela's new job was not far from her previous one at Eden's Paradise. Her new boss benefited from Angela's ambiguous racial capital; her hybrid Latina and White identity, as well as her skills and education, helped Angela land higher pay and more authority at Silvia's. In turn, it helped her new boss attract and accommodate a dwindling older, ethnic White, clientele while slowly growing a non-White, middle-class clientele. In fact, some new clients confused Angela with Silvia, her boss. Silvia's honeyed-brown skin, dark eyes, long and thick wavy brown hair, and slightly full figure often led new clients to assume she was the Latina and Angela was the European. Angela laughed one day after we had shared a few beers and tostones while my hair dye settled in: "¡Y ellos pensaban que yo era la blanca y que Silvia era la negra!" (And they [the clients] thought I was the White one and Silvia was the Black one!) Angela's golden white skin and her phenotype (with a small nose and lips and a broad jaw and forehead), which caused her to resemble people from the southeastern Caucasus, such as Armenia or Georgia, added to this confusion. Invariably she kept her hair in a blunt, modern cut, sometimes shaved at the bottom of the nape or above the sideburns, and other times spiked, dyed in varying shades of platinum or golden-ash blond. Her designer jeans and modern stilettos, the small tattoos at the back of her neck, the jeweled studs in her belly button and earlobes, and her Apple Watch on a pink leather strap were icebreakers for both older and younger, White and non-White clients.

At one point Angela began to mention plans for a tummy tuck and Botox injections. She would often say to Nena, her coethnic floor assistant, "Look at the business I am in. Who's going to hire an old or ugly hairstylist? Besides, I will be on the market soon." This last comment presaged her decision to end her long-term, moribund marriage with a man twenty-five years her senior. I concluded that in her previous job, Angela's ambiguous identity was valued more for her ethnicity than for her race; at Silvia's, however, Angela was valued for her racial and ethnic capital, as this hybrid identity had increased Silvia's local and more distant clientele, including Latinos from the Bronx and Manhattan. Silvia, a single mother, admired Angela's skills but also her feistiness and independence from men. As Angela was the primary breadwinner in her house, Silvia thought she "called the shots." Angela always joked, "My husband does not give me a hard time, does not control me or meddle in my business. He knows better than that!"

The Racialization of Middle-Class Latinas

Nancy Leong has argued that a non-White identity is valued or commodified by employers depending on the context of reception and historical time.[16] I argue that this valuation is different or much more complicated in the case of mixed-race people and based mostly on the context of the history of racialization and who is doing the valuation. For example, Angela's ambiguous racial identity was both valued and devalued in ethnic White hair salons staffed by less-educated ethnic employers in Mount Pleasantville, a community with a pernicious history of institutional racial and class segregation. This history, I argue, places greater psychological stress on mixed-race workers to manage their racialized identities, especially in service jobs, as these require high levels of interaction with both employers and clients.[17]

While Angela's and Carolina's ambiguous identities as *blancas*, or light-skinned Mestizas, increased receptivity among their White employers in Mount Pleasantville, a Latino immigrant destination, the absence of a powerful Latino community could increase new middle-class immigrants' psychological pressure to repress their ethnic identities as Latinas. At Eden's Paradise, Angela and the Mexican assistants were ostracized for speaking Spanish or listening to Spanish music in front of clients, and Angela was assigned mostly non-White clients. Even so, Angela mostly complained about her Mexican peers and her middle-class Latino clients, whom she felt had "attitudes": "These people always want me to take care of them when they call without appointments; yet they are the first to complaint about their hair, never satisfied. They think they are more important than anybody else, just because they have money!" I knew Angela included me among these clients, as I complained or fussed about the colors or styles recommended for my hair. "¡Tu eres una aburria!" she would say, laughing. "¡Una vieja, una *blanca*!" (You are a bore! An old woman, a *Whitie*!) The latter was meant to be the bigger insult because I was a race scholar. She would often complain about my hair color choices or the way I dressed as too White or too plain or boring for a Latina. I believe that my ambiguous "in-between" identity, and mostly my demeanor, upset Angela—and even her employer, who thought of me as "not Latina enough!" Even my adolescent daughter complained, "You are a fake Latina, mom! You don't wear hoops or red lipstick or go to the nail or hair salon!" Angela's and my daughter's comments, but also those of other people, including my academic peers, have made me reflect on the price that racialized minorities must pay for their social mobility, especially in new immigrant destinations, where a non-White middle class emerges without positive referents or public role models.

As a new junior faculty member at Fordham University's campus in the Bronx, I had my first red flag about the price that racialized minorities pay for their social mobility when students, visiting parents, or even faculty from other departments would often confuse me with the support or custodial staff. Upon seeing me dress casually on a holiday weekend, one male Latino junior faculty in my department, also foreign-born, asked, "Why don't you always dress like this? These clothes"—he pointed to my jeans, boots, and gold hoop earrings—"make you look more hip, modern, cool!" A few years later, the chair of my department, a White forensic anthropologist, noted the opposite: "A student came looking for you and she did not remember your name, but said she was looking for a pretty professor who dresses very nicely. Then I knew who it was! I suggest you start dressing a bit frumpier, for I hear you are making the other female faculty jealous."

INTERSECTIONAL VULNERABILITIES OF GENDER, RACE, AND IMMIGRANT STATUS

Carolina Gets Her Papers

One day, a week before Thanksgiving, Carolina, the receptionist at Eden's Paradise, was in a festive mood that her eyes could not contain. She was traveling the next day to Mexico. She did not know which news made her happier: getting her green card or going back to her homeland after twenty-five years. Standing behind the cashier's booth, Carolina smiled, her wide, amber-colored eyes illuminated by the blondish caramel highlights that framed her small face. She exuberantly related the news, detailing the hour of her flight, the length of her stay, and the family reunion plans, while carefully lowering her voice because clients were nearby. She fretted about having to stay to help the owner close the salon that evening, as she did four straight days a week, for her flight was at 7:30 a.m. When I asked if her husband or her college graduate of a daughter would also go, she giggled with malice, "Nope! Just me!" I asked Carolina where she would go upon arrival, and she answered, "God only knows! I don't even know what my old neighborhood looks like or how to get to the home where I grew up, after all these years!"

We were gathered facing Carolina's reception stand atop a wooden platform that made it almost impossible for people my height to sign credit cards without standing on the tips of their toes. Alma pretended to be busy fixing hair products behind two large wooden shelves. Divina and Nadia stood by. We looked at each other, laughed and sighed, reminding Carolina to pack tissues in her purse because she would cry her eyeballs out, the way I did when I flew back to my country after ten years' absence. Carolina's eyes closed halfway, as if holding back tears, and I quickly changed the subject: "¿Y, en serio, cuantas maletas tu llevas?" (And, seriously, how many suitcases will you take?) The joy in Carolina's eyes returned, and her coworkers joined in with more questions and laughter.

I waited for the right moment to ask the question I had weighed for quite a while. I asked Carolina if she would look for another job now that she had a legal immigrant status. A long silence ensued. I heard one client in the back complaining to Nadia that the water in the hair washing station was too hot. A young, Brown Latino man came to the front door to drop off a few brown bags with beers and the pizza that Alma ordered to celebrate Carolina's farewell. I gave Alma, now my closest ally after Angela had left the salon, the money to pay for the goodies. Alma spoke with smiling and complicit eyes, asking each one of us to choose one brown bag and a slice. Carolina took a sip and hid her bag hastily beneath the counter. The others placed theirs behind the tall shelves that held hair products. I took a few sips and repeated my question: "So, Carolina, will you look for another job, or stay?" The women took another sip. Alma giggled nervously, covering her mouth with her hand, eyes affixed on Carolina's, with complicity and anticipation. "Oops," Alma said, still holding her hand over her lips, "let's not make much noise!" Everyone stared at Carolina, expecting a response. Carolina sighed and smiled but with a serious look in her eyes, much as she would do when staring at a clients' hair to divine the type of treatment she would recommend; but this time, she had a very different possession in her eyes. "I am leaving!" She said it as if disclosing a long-held secret about the betrayal of a spouse. She looked at me, knowing that I was interested in the work conditions of women like her, but never ever before dared to ask, as I did today. "I am leaving because I have not had a salary increase in twenty-five years." The other women nodded in agreement, their smiles long gone, eyes cast down. Alma looked into my eyes. I am stunned, and something quivers in a deep part of my essence, making me quieter than I had intended. The oldest of the three women, Divina, kept her head down, shaking it from side to side. I ask her, "How about you? Has he ever increased your pay"? The Mexican women exchanged complicit looks, as if they had pondered this same question for years. Divina looked at me with gleaning eyes, making sure her Portuguese accent was ever the more resonant, "He knows not to f——with me because I have my papers and I will f——g report his f——a——!" There was laughter all around.

CROSSING CLASS AND RACIAL BOUNDARIES IN OLD AND NEW DESTINATIONS

When the East and the West Merge in an Indian and Dominican Hair Salon

About a mile south of Silvia's, an Indian hair styling and threading salon sits next door to a Latino bakery owned by a Puerto Rican couple, a foot massage and reflexology salon owned by Malaysians, and an upholstery store—the oldest business on the block—owned by a working-class Italian man in his seventies. The latter is a remnant of a distant past when Italians owned small family shops, the Irish owned the pubs and held municipal posts, the Polish owned the funeral homes, and the German Jews owned most real estate lots in Mount Pleasantville. In 2010 the city's population was nearly 200,000, but by 2019 it had increased to 400,370. Of this population, Whites were a declining majority, changing from 90 percent in 1970 to 54 percent in 2010. Meanwhile, the numbers of non-White groups, such as Asians, Blacks, and Latinos, continued to rise. As the second-largest group in the city, the Latino population increased from a mere 3.5 percent to 37.5 percent in the same period. Dominicans and Mexicans made up the largest foreign-born Latino group in Mount Pleasantville[18] (as well as in New York City).

An Indian family, a husband, wife, and her sister from the Punjab, owned and managed the beauty salon down the road from Silvia's. Two Dominican women worked in the back of the store. Two young Indian women, with dark brown skin and of small stature, did the hair threading, also in the back of the store. Two lighter-skinned, older women in their fifties worked in the two front chairs; they also shared the role of receptionist and cashier. The husband, a medium-brown man of small stature, in his early fifties and with a congenial, if staged, demeanor, mostly greeted clients and worked as cashier. While he was in charge of smiles and cheerful greetings, the Indian women did the work, using their lips to hold a long piece of thread tightly folded in two, wrapped around the thumb and index finger of each hand. The work calls for much orchestration and highly concentrated coordination, pulling with precision the roots of small soft hair from the eyebrows, lips, facial contours, and even the arms of female—and occasionally male—clients.

The small waiting room has two vinyl seats. Indian soap operas or Bollywood musicals play on a small TV mounted on the wall. The man pays attention behind the cashier's counter, coordinating which worker is available, and which client is next or has made a special request. While he is seated, the working women are on their feet all day. Besides his gesturing with his hands, lips, or the movement of his head as to which client is next, and the Indian women bowing their heads to point clients in their directions, there is no real communication between workers and clients. The women's lips are tightly closed, holding threads.

My two youngest daughters, in their late teens, have had their eyebrows done here for a few years. One day, while dropping off my youngest, who aspires to someday be an anthropologist, I heard her exclaim, "Mom, I hear bachata music in the back!" For a moment I thought the sound was coming from the TV. In the end, both my daughter and I confirmed that Dominican women do hair in the back of the Indian salon.

The back of the salon was frequented mostly by Black and Latina women—chiefly Dominicans and West Indians. Their second-generation daughters were mostly hair-threading clients. I was among a minority of middle-class Black and Brown women served at both the front and back of the salon. After listening to the lead

Dominican hairstylist speak Spanish with a client, while the wife of the Indian man tugged at my eyebrows, I asked, "Would they do my hair in the back, you think? Would I need an appointment?" The woman answered both of my questions silently, first nodding in the affirmative and then shaking her head to the contrary to indicate "no"; then, with a gesture of her head, she signaled to her husband to speak with me.

The Indian man smiled and so did his eyes, signaling with his hands that I should walk to the back of the store. I approached slowly and sat in the only space I found empty, under an old-fashioned and beat-up hair dryer with a big see-through head bonnet. The only Latina woman in sight stood about four feet from me; she immediately made eye contact, smiled, and nodded her head, as speaking would be useless given the background noise. She signaled to indicate that it was okay for me to sit there. She was drying the hair of a middle-aged Latina, and while she did so she took a good look at my hair from afar. She asked if I wanted coloring, cutting, or just washing and setting. I noticed she said "setting," which connotes rollers and drying under the old hair dryer. "I would like a blow dry, if you have the time," I explained. She smiled and nodded in the affirmative, as the noise of the blow dryer muffled most sound. She informed me that she had another client coming for a color job. "It will take only thirty-five minutes to set her, and then I'll do you," she said with an affected smile. While waiting, I noted the restricted space of her workstation, the loud sound of the blow dryer, and bachata music playing in the background from a small radio on the floor. The news on the TV was in an Indian language, which I later confirmed was actually two languages—Hindi and Punjabi. My sociologist's mind wondered if the Indian women had ever had their hair done by the Dominicans and if the Dominican women had ever had hair threading done by the Indians. But mostly I wondered how this intra-ethnic business venture happened, and if higher education, gender, or gentrification was a main determinant or mediating variable.

From my chair I noticed the careful movement of the Indian women's bodies, hunched over while working on clients' faces, the latter stretched out on black vinyl chairs, eyes closed. Six women, different shades of brown, from different families, educational backgrounds, and cultures, earn a living from 10:00 a.m. to 7:00 p.m. standing on their feet. The unusual silence that engulfed the Indian women's labor contrasted with the loud sound of bachatas and the Dominican women's gregarious voices, "backstage," as their work demanded lots of interaction with clients. The Indian women's labor restricted them from speaking; the act demanded their undivided attention as they pulled thread in a mechanical movement, orchestrated with the neck and both hands. Their bodies were motionless, transfixed on the precision of their work while adjusting long strands of thread wrapped around the index finger and the thumb and pulled by their sealed lips.

I noticed other paradoxes: while the Indian soap operas or movies on the TV depicted Indian men dressed as women, imitating as well as berating their emotional tendencies, Indian women acted like men, exaggerating toxic masculinity gestures. The performance flipped traditional norms, experimented with modernity and the crossing of cultural and heteronormative and patriarchal boundaries, albeit through the lens of a comedy or magical realism. This scene contrasted the sorrowful poetics of the bachata music, depicting the reality of migration from the Dominican Republic, one in which women take the lead as principal heroines but also traitors. The bachata lyrics, sung mostly by men, depicted cruel abandonment by these migrant women and the men's lamentations of unrequited or betrayed love. I wondered further about different and similar forms of gender schisms created by migration among women from traditional Indian and Latina societies. While in this and most other Asian businesses I have observed, spouses or older sons were often included; in Dominican beauty salons, that was hardly ever the case. When I asked Salome, the Dominican woman who rented the back space from the Indians, if her husband ever worked with her in the salon, both she and her peer, the other hairstylist in the next station, cracked up laughing. "You're crazy! I would not stand for him controlling or meddling in my business!" Salome, married now for a third time, shared how nice her latest husband had turned out, perhaps because he was almost twice her age. Her work peer, a Black Dominican, who unlike Salome's mixed Black and White phenotype, had very dark skin and strong Afro-Caribbean features. She looked at the woman drying her hair under the bonnet head dryer and said, "Ask her [Salome] how old he [her husband] is!" laughing and prodding Salome. Salome looks at me from behind the chair where she is drying another Dominican woman's hair. She hesitates, perhaps because it is my first time at the shop, but then says, while holding her laughter, "¡Ah Dios! ¡Lo mismos años mio, pero al revés—cuarenta y siete, y setenta y cuatro!" (Oh my God! the same age as mine, but in reverse!—forty-seven and seventy-four!) Salome admitted at first rejecting her husband during the courtship: "¡A mi no me gustan los hombres viejos ni negros, pero mi esposo es mas gente que todas nosotras!" (I don't like men too old or too Black, but my husband turned out to be a better person than all of us together).

I remarked how the Indian woman's husband seemed even nicer than the women. Salome and the other women agreed, but then recounted how his sister-in-law was the smart one; although it was through him that Salome learned about the renting of a space for her salon. The business belonged to his sister-in-law. Both she and his wife worked along with three other Indian women at this salon. The sister-in-law heard about a "Dominican" hair salon, as they are known for the "hair business" among Black and Latina customers, in the same mall where they were looking to rent a space for their hair-threading shop. The Dominican salon was closing, pushed by higher rental fees. The Indian woman procured the space and asked her brother-in-law before she signed the contract to approach the Dominican woman and ask if she would be interested in subcontracting a space from them in which to do hair. Salome had been working in the Dominican salon being displaced for only two years. Both she and her boss, another Dominican woman, accepted the offer to rent the back space in the Indian threading salon. After a year of hair and facial hair-threading appointments, I learned that Salome used to rent two chairs each for $200 a week, but later proposed to the Indians to work for the salon based on wages, taking only half of the money paid by her clients. "This arrangement works best," Salome explained to me, "because I no longer pay for rent or supplies. Besides, these people are very business savvy and this is more convenient for them."

I asked Salome if as a small business owner she used to qualify for product discounts or tax credits. She told me that the Indian woman, as a double minority (given her gender and racial status), perhaps qualified. This may be why she and not her brother held the business license and filed the taxes, listing Salome as an employee even though Salome used to pay rent for the use of the backroom. Two months earlier, Salome had decided to sublet the entire basement from the Indian woman. This was because Salome was not a citizen, only a legal resident, and lacked a business license to rent or own a business. So the Indian man rented the space from his sister-in-law and then leased it to Salome, although she appeared as an employee on the tax records. This gave the Indian family not only the tax credits but also the freedom to displace Salome at any time, as no written contract bound the agreement. This arrangement reveals the multiple forms of gender and class vulnerability that immigrants experience in small business firms where most transactions are informal. It also illustrates how the higher cost of rents in gentrifying neighborhoods pushes minority firms out of business and then their clienteles are co-opted by other, more empowered, minorities. It further illustrates how service employers in gentrifying areas hire or co-opt business partners with ambiguous identities, as Salome, whose mixed skin color and phenotype as well as Dominican culture and reputation in the hair industry, functioned to attract new clients, increasingly foreign- and native-born Black and Latino customers.

DEMEANOR AND THE MANAGEMENT OF RACIALIZED IDENTITIES

During the early stages of my field research, I discerned how an Indigenous Mestizo Mexican man passed as an Asian sushi chef in a Japanese restaurant. He dressed, and moved his hands, head, and body, with the same staged gentleness and precision as the Asian workers behind the counter of the sushi bar. The bar's oblong countertop accommodated ten or so people, seated on high stools; this allowed a view of the chef's skilled and artful preparation of sushi orders for clients both at the bar and in the main dining room, which started immediately past the sushi bar and extended to the back of the restaurant. Somewhat discernible was the view of Brown men, all prep cooks, attired in black kimonos. Their Asian appearance, and the ambience of the restaurant—walls covered in natural wood paneling, bamboo tables, lithographs of nature scenes, and Asian and Japanese instrumental music—all marketed the Asian ethnic identity and culture of the place.

Despite the fast pace of their work, the men inspected dishes with simulated tranquility and an affected demeanor, as if engaged in an elaborate and delicate artistic task. Two expediters decided when the food left the kitchen and where it should be served, after checking a computer on the countertop separating the kitchen from the main dining area. About a dozen men dressed in black worked in close proximity, in different rows, in the kitchen. Standing around a large square, metallic table, four men with dark brown skin, akin to people from Malaysia, the Philippines, or somewhere else in Southeast Asia, inspected dishes before placing them on the counter. To my surprise, I later discovered that about half of them were of Latino stock; I was clued in by their Indigenous Mesoamerican phenotypes, body shapes, skin color, and facial gestures, and later by their use of Spanish. They walked faster than the Asian men inside the kitchen space as they cleaned dishes, made sauces, and cooked hot dishes on a large stove. After several visits and intermittent conversations with one of two Mexican head waiters, I concluded that most of the men in the kitchen were Mexicans.

The main dining area was attended by two waiters, a light-skinned Mexican man in his early fifties and a Malaysian man in his mid-twenties who had light skin, a thin physique, and a gentle demeanor. I later learned that he was in graduate school at my institution. As time went on, my husband and I got to know both of the men, and especially the Mexican waiter. We often sat at our favorite spot, a table across from the kitchen, that was in his serving area. "Good evening," he said to greet us one evening. My husband responded, "¿Como está? Gusto verle." (How are you? Good to see you.) The Mexican waiter smiled, looked into my eyes, and then addressed the two of us in English: "You prefer sparkling water, right"? He looked at my husband, who responded, "¡Si, como no!" (Yes, of course!) My husband insisted on speaking in Spanish, despite my intuition that this and other Latino workers in high-end restaurants feel apprehensive and singled out if they are spoken to in Spanish, especially in front of their supervisors or White clients. I reflected on the different power structures and levels of inequalities that shape our engagement, as the waiter was there to serve and please us. I noticed that he never wrote down our food orders, to make us feel special; this is often a practice in high-end restaurants. [19]

We almost always sat at that same table, directly across from the kitchen window, but one evening we chose to sit at the sushi bar. I noted that one of the chefs looked peevishly at me as my husband spoke Spanish to a younger Mexican floor assistant. I tried to ascertain what seemed different about this sushi chef. His demeanor was carefully orchestrated: the way he held the sushi carving knives and arranged the small layers of fish; the way he gently moved his head, bending over, to inspect the sushi order; the way he bowed, then making eye contact, as the other chefs did, to signal to floor waiters that a sushi platter was ready. Looking at the uniforms of the sushi chefs, I noticed tall white, puffed chef's hats and red samurai kimonos with personal names stitched in white embroidery in scripted letters: "Kaito," "Asahi," "Yuro," and "Dan." The latter name, I suspected, was Latino. I waited until he lifted his head with an inquisitive gaze after overhearing my husband's deliberate use of Spanish. I engaged my husband in Spanish to see if the chef would look at us again. He did. This time he shared a knowing smile as a final gesture confirming my suspicion. The manner in which his eyes held my gaze, along with a prolonged smile, suggested something very familiar and yet different about this setting, almost like the deliberate gestures used by silent film actors. Later my husband and I confirmed that he was a Mexican chef when we spoke with the young Malaysian graduate student. My husband then turned his head to speak to the sushi chef again, to place another order of fatty tuna, this time in Spanish: "¿Puedes poner otra orden, por favor?" My husband used his right hand in a bowing gesture and to symbolically convey a "please." Dan smiled at us pensively, and a bit amused, signaling an okay with a thumbs-up but never uttering a word in Spanish.

A by now classic scholarship has argued that gestures convey information about an individual's class, culture, and authority or status in society.[20] Yet, gestures and affect, or the meaning derived from a gesture, differ depending on the context or cultural milieu, as well as the time. Vilem Flusser's treatise on theory building suggests that a gesture has two components: a mechanical part that involves a physiological response, like the one done with "a movement of the body, the blinking of an eye, or parting of the lips to smile, for which movements there exists no causal explanation." Yet, Flusser notes, "the opposite is also true: if someone points to a book with his finger, we could know the possible causes and still not understand the gesture. Gestures have another component that is experiential, which is acquired with socialization in a culture. To understand a gesture, one must know its 'significance, as "Gestures are encoded in symbols that carry many meanings in different contexts and cultures." According to Flusser, our job is to discover their affect.[21] The ambiguous demeanor and ethnoracial identity of this Mexican worker in an Asian restaurant increased my interest in studying how immigrant workers manage their identities in White and non-White workspaces and how they do "racial performance" or learn how to manage their race, and their emotions, at work. These insights led me to further explore how Dominican and Mexican women's use of a certain demeanor helps them manage their ambiguous identities in beauty salons, and how race, gender, and class intersect to mediate their racial acculturation and presentation of self in White and non-White work environments and neighborhoods. Finally, I explore how the hiring of these ethnoracial minorities with ambiguous identities benefits employers as well as contributes to new forms of racial capitalism. I introduce the case of a Mexican woman who works for a Korean nail salon and that of Dominican woman in a Russian barbershop, next.

When Non-White Groups Gentrify the Neighborhood

About 2.5 blocks from the Indian hair-threading salon in Mount Pleasantville was Kim's Nail Spa, which occupied the corner storefront in a small, one-story, commercial building that included a laundromat, a dry cleaner, and a hardware store, all managed or owned by ethnic Whites—Italians and Jews—of working-class stock. Kim was the only non-White and female middle-class business owner. She was also the only one who was foreign born and the one with the highest education, importing an MBA from a university in Seoul, Korea. Her salon opened at 10:00 a.m. six days a week and was the last business in the building to close, around 7:30 p.m.

After parking my car, I entered the salon from the back. It was apparent that Gloria was not in, but I didn't ask for her, as I was worried that the most senior worker, a Korean woman about my mother's age, whom the salon's owner and the workers called "Eonni," felt I preferred only Gloria. I wanted to avoid hurting Eonni's feelings, as she was always pleased when I came in with my daughters. Kim, the owner, a tall, attractive Korean woman in her late fifties with white, porcelain skin, greeted me as always, warmly and with a hug. She uttered my name with endearment, "Normaaaa." We always exchanged news about our children (both my oldest and her oldest were in professions in the health field), and she always told other clients how proud she was of me and my daughters. She also always asked about my husband. When I would ask about hers, she would quickly retort with eyes fixed on her work, "Oh, he is there—working, you know!" then quickly would change the subject to the news, the weather, or the latest nail colors. On this particular day, Kim told me that Eonni (pronounced in Korean as "Onig") wanted me to choose a color. Eonni, the oldest in the crew, hollered from her booth, "Choose a color, Normaaa!" With Kim, there were four women workers: three Koreans and Gloria, a very light, golden-skinned Mexican in her late thirties, the youngest and a single mother. She had a mixed Indigenous and Mestizo phenotype that increased her somatic dissonance, or an Asian-Latina identity ambiguity in this context. Gloria always wore her very long dark hair wrapped in a bun; it was a traditional classic style, except she colored her own hair with discrete auburn streaks.

A light-skinned African American woman in her late forties or early fifties with a large silhouette and a middle-class authoritative demeanor sat fully stretched and relaxed while having a pedicure done in the station next to mine. Eonni called me again, from her booth—"Normaaaa!"—patting the seat, signaling I should sit in her station. "Okay, Eonni," I answered, as I had learned to call her in the proper and endearing way Kim and others addressed her as the older member of the group. Eonni waited for me to choose a color for my feet and hands; she was always quick to suggest one whenever I came alone, because my youngest daughter was usually the one to do this labor of love. She prepared her station with anticipation: running hot water and adding aromatic salts. As the plastic basin filled with water, she pulled over a small working cart with a few see-through drawers containing her tools, looked at my face, and smiled. "Gloria not in," she said, "Ha! Maybe coming later!" I nodded, smiling back.

I have come to this nail salon for a long time. I met Kim and Gloria when they worked in a different Korean salon about five minutes north of Kim's salon. Kim decided to leave that other salon and take Gloria with her. Now she was the owner and Gloria the next-best manicurist and hair waxing expert. Kim talked to me while doing a manicure, as she was the expert on nail tips or extensions; she was also the one to perform cashiering and supervisory duties and sort the walk-in clients, assigning them to the women. Next to Kim, Gloria had imported the highest education: she completed two years at a vocational college training in accounting and business administration while working as a live-in domestic in a town about two hours from Mexico City.

The woman next to me had her phone on loudspeaker, talking to a man who sounded to be younger and a close relative. He did most of the talking and she most of the listening. I avoided turning my head toward her to give her privacy, though our chairs were barely two feet apart. At one point I heard the man say, "I have to be careful how I pay for that." I lost track of what else he was saying. I wondered for the first time how I had not heard other clients using their phones on loudspeaker at Kim's. I wondered if this was a new client and if she thought the Korean workers' limited English and constant speaking of Korean guaranteed her privacy. I also took note of how the majority of Kim's clients were increasingly Black and Latina women of middle-class origins and how Asians and Whites were a small minority.

I noted how the owner and the other three Asian women spoke Korean to each other all day, using English minimally to ask clients whether they wanted a manicure, pedicure, change of color, or wax. The regular clients tried to speak minimally or louder to make themselves understood. Kim had mentioned a few times that she was getting tired and wanted to retire. She had held this business for twenty years. Her children had completed school and were now professionals. She looked for my face, and signaled from her desk near the cashier station that Gloria would be coming soon. She made hand gestures to insinuate that Gloria was delayed because of another problem, winking with her left eye, which signaled trouble. She was the first to let me know when Gloria had changed boyfriends: "You did know, right?" I would always say, "No, I did not know!" I noticed that small entrepreneurs in new immigrant destinations increasingly relied on their Black or Latino staff and clientele to attract other clients, as I was always a client of Gloria's.

Gloria walked in and I noticed something different about her face. She had cut her long hair and now wore it at the nape of her neck in a stylish, rectangular bob. The highlights and Ambrose were gone, and her darker color and blunt haircut made her look more Asian than Latina, especially in her black kimono uniform.

I told Gloria, in Spanish, that I did not know she was coming, making a gesture with my eyes to explain why Eonni was doing my feet. Like the Asian women, Gloria had mastered the art of responding to the women's conversation while staying focused on her work of doing a pedicure on the Black woman seated to my right, who had her phone's loudspeaker on. Gloria kept her eyes downcast. "Don't worry," she tells me, "I still can do your manicure!" I looked at her and asked about her children. She reached for her phone in her pocket and showed me a picture of her youngest. I noticed that he is the handsomest of the three. The picture had him as the smallest in a group of children, mostly girls, standing in front of a birthday cake, with a few pastel color balloons. A paper tablecloth in pink and white read "Happy Birthday." "I remember those days," I told Gloria. I asked her whose birthday it was. She said her daughter's, with a bit of a smirk and disappointment on her face, as I had forgotten that she had invited me to the party a few months earlier. Of her children, her daughter looked the most like Gloria, but with dark brown skin and a nose, facial shape, and hair that were much more Indigenous looking. "¡Ah, here is a picture of my boyfriend!" she said. "¡Remember, I spoke to you about him!" and I took that to mean she had forgiven me. "¡He is so handsome!" I exclaimed. A light-skinned Mestizo, he wore a modern crewcut and held his head very close to her in the picture. She told me that her boyfriend really liked her new look and that, with eyes fixed on my manicure, she had some news to share later. I could tell by her smile that it would be good.

While Gloria took out her tools from a small plastic cart she wheeled next to Eonni's station, Kim, the owner, spoke loudly in Korean, looking in our direction. Familiar with her facial gestures, I gathered she was talking to both Gloria and Eonni, who was halfway through my pedicure. Gloria rushed what she was doing and began soaking my hands. She always spoke very softly, as the Korean workers did with each other while doing their work, never looking at each other or at the clients, or making facial gestures. I asked Gloria how it was that she understood what Kim said. With a complicit smile, and keeping her head down, she gave no answer; instead, she steadily held my hands, filing my index finger's nail with a dexterity that spoke of years of experience. I asked again: "You understand lots of Korean, no?" Gloria's smile this time was much more amused; with eyes downcast, fixed on her task, she said, "They think I don't understand them; the boss thinks I understand a few things, but I understand a lot after fifteen years with them." I replied, "I see that your boss spoke to you and that you imme-diately came to do my nails." Gloria nodded. "She spoke to the two of us; she asked that we do you fast because there are other clients in the queue."

Eonni, who gave me the pedicure, could not speak English well, but her car-ing gestures always seduced me to choose the most expensive pedicure she rec-ommended. I asked her what the difference was between the sixty-five-dollar and the fifty-five-dollar versions. She answered, and I understood that it was the longer massage, as she made emphasis with her hands. She held my feet with motherly care. This gesture always moved my heart, as I grew up with my grand-mother and hold the greatest of reverence for other grandmothers. As her body slouched to touch the water, check my feet, and gather her work tools, I wit-nessed the hard labor this job imposes on the body. Every movement entails a very delicate act, to hold the feet, inspect the smallest imperfections, the texture and color of every painted nail with a slouched body. Eonni washed my feet with a warm cloth, scrubbed them in hot, bubbly water, and dried them, one at a time. She inspected every contour, every rough spot on one foot while the other floated in the bubbly, warm, aromatic water. When I forgot to move either foot, often absorbed with my work, she would look up, smile, and then take over, using both of her hands to guide my feet out of or back into the water.

Eonni's left leg always hurt when she finished a pedicure. She would rise and shake her leg, hit it with her closed fist a few times, and then look into my eyes. I told her she needed to go for physical therapy or rest from work for a few months. But Eonni said, "Home! no, Normaaa! Husband big pain!" We all laughed. I feel very guilty that Eonni does this kind of work; people at this age, especially women, should not have to work this hard. They should be on a collective salary, or retirement, even if they have worked and gotten paid informally. Employers should be forced to pay for their retirement and medical insurance, with govern-ment support. The COVID-19 pandemic has laid bare the vulnerable conditions of immigrants who do essential work, often behind the scenes and without med-ical or salary protection. Service employers and workers like these women con-tribute to the local economy and people's mental health. When I asked Kim if she had retirement insurance for herself, she answered, "Normaaa! That is crazy, I cannot pay insurance for everyone, I would have to close my business. My hus-band and I pay for our own insurance, but we cannot afford to pay for retirement. Besides, some of our workers won't qualify." I know she is referring to Gloria, who has worked as an undocumented immigrant for her for over fifteen years.

Gloria approached me to see if my nails were dry and applied fast-drying pol-ish. She gave me a neck and back message, a free perk for clients with manicure-pedicure packages. She then told me she had a secret to share: "I am four months' pregnant!" She explained she did not want to share the news with her boss yet, and hoped I would not. After I asked her about her health, I also asked if she had obtained her business license, knowing she was trying to pass an exam to qualify for a beauty salon nail and spa license. She told me she had taken the exam and was awaiting the results. She planned to buy the salon from Kim in two or three years. Her boyfriend now had a secure job at a restaurant, and they were planning to get married and open a business. He was a "1.5 generation" immigrant and a naturalized citizen. I remained in my chair, afraid to call too much attention if I hugged Gloria. I squeezed her hands, careful not to mess up my nails, and told her I would keep coming back to check on her. She began to write up my bill when Eonni spoke to her in Korean from her station. Looking at the pad on which she was tallying my bill, Gloria crossed out the ten-dollar manicure price and rewrote it as fifteen dollars, explaining that Eonni had just told her I had chosen a more expensive nail color. "Indeed," I said, still marveling at Gloria's grasp of the Korean language. I ask, "Are you taking lessons?" She answered, "Who knows, maybe soon!"

A Russian Barbershop Co-opts a Dominican Salon: A White Business in a Non-White Neighborhood

Since the mid-1990s, Kika, short for Francisca, has lived near Twelfth Avenue, a five-minute walk from Lincoln Center in Manhattan. From the early 1960s through the 1980s, the area was settled largely by African Americans and Puerto Ricans. Due to the large availability of affordable and public housing, Kika considers her immediate neighborhood to be one of the few areas unchanged by redevelopment and gentrification in New York City.

Kika arrived in New York in the early 1990s, sponsored by her husband, an older Dominican man. During a short summer visit to see her mother, who had already migrated to New York, she met this man in a Cuban restaurant near 181st Street and Broadway in the Washington Heights neighborhood. Two years later they married, after he had traveled a few times to court her in her family's small rural village near Santiago in the Dominican Republic. Her husband died fifteen years later, leaving Kika and her two teenage children. As a sole provider, she first found work as a hairstylist at a salon owned by a Colombian and Dominican couple in Central Harlem. Later she moved to a job at a Russian barbershop much closer to her apartment.

At her previous job Kika assisted the main hairstylist, washed hair, set hair in rollers, did blow dries, and used a hot iron to straighten hair for a mostly working-class clientele of African Americans and Latinos. The hair salon was unisex and included two chairs rented to a Russian barber, Stevin, a recent immigrant in his late thirties. Six years into the business, the Colombian and Dominican couple could not renew their lease. The neighborhood's economy was on the upswing, and it was attracting new residents and investors; the landlord had other plans. The news prompted Stevin to find work at another place, a small barbershop on the Upper West Side. His Ukrainian friend had proposed that the two become partners in the opening of this barbershop on Amsterdam Avenue in what was still a very Latino community. To increase the clientele of his new shop, Stevin called Kika. "He called to ask if I knew of a Latina worker," she told me. "Someone who could cut men's hair and speak Spanish. I said I would call a friend of mine who was excellent at styling men and women." About three months later, Stevin called her again to propose a new business idea. "He asked what I was doing and if I was interested in running a hair salon in his shop!" Kika's daughter was graduating from college and had secured a job in the college's public safety office. She told her mother she would help her procure a loan to equip the small salon.

Kika was a light-skinned Dominican with a hint of an Afro-Caribbean phenotype. The blond highlights in her short wavy hair enhanced her golden skin tone. I was curious to learn how immigrant workers like Kika navigated racial, class, and cultural boundaries in a hybrid barbershop and salon, and how gentrification mediated the hiring of local, ethnic, or racial minorities by new, gentrifying White business owners.

To enter Kika's salon, one had to walk through the Russian barbershop, passing by five black vinyl chairs near the entrance where men awaited their turns for haircuts and beard trims. The owner, who was about fifty years old, stood about five foot ten and had a full shape and a belly. He had tawny skin; thick, wavy dark brown hair streaked with gray; and almond-shaped, deep-seated brown eyes. Dark circles around his eyes gave the impression that he had had a hard life. As I entered the shop he looked at me discerningly, aware that I was a new client. He had watched earlier as I parked my small car, making a few attempts to fit into a parking space on the highly trafficked commercial avenue.

I walked straight to the back and found my cousin, whom I was to meet for lunch after her hair appointment. She introduced me to Kika, who greeted me with a broad and endearing smile as the close relative of an esteemed client. Her Cibaeño accent was reassuring, bringing back memories of my childhood, my grandmother's piquant ways of speaking in double entendres, especially when strangers or men were around. Kika's English was limited, so she spoke to us in Spanish. I noticed that she understood a lot more English than she could speak. A light-skinned Dominican man in his late thirties also spoke to Kika with a Cibaeño accent from the Russian side of the barbershop, saying that he was leaving and wishing everyone a good weekend. Kika answered him in an endearing and playful way: "¡No se vaya, joven!" (Don't leave, young man!) He smiled back, acknowledging my cousin and me and realizing that all the women were looking at him. He continued to talk with another Latino man whose hair was being cut by Mercedes, a Dominican woman whom Kika had recommended to Stevin. She alternated between the Russian barbershop in front and Kika's small hair salon in back. Mercedes had beautiful, rare dark molasses skin accentuated by black hair, which seemed colored to emphasize her non–African American West Indian facial features. Kika was from Samaná, a popular tourist area in the southeastern coastal region of the Dominican Republic, an area initially settled by African slaves, and then by immigrants from the West Indies and also free Blacks from southern states in the United States, who came to work in the sugar mills.

A White man in his seventies awaited his turn at one of the barber chairs. Another White man, in his late fifties and with dark-rimmed spectacles, leisurely read the *New York Times*. A young boy of about ten, with blond wavy hair covering most of his forehead, was busy with a game on his iPhone. Mercedes was cutting the hair of a Brown man. From where I saw him, I couldn't tell if he was Latino or Russian. A Ukrainian woman in her early thirties seemed to be the main barber. She wore her hair in a geometric shape, with the sides shaved, and had a yellow-green Apple Watch on her arm and a Bluetooth device in her left ear. I noticed that Kika also had a Bluetooth device in her ear, and I surmised that the women used the Wi-Fi provided by the Russian barbershop. I wondered if immigrant workers were more susceptible to the harvesting of information about themselves and their online activities due to the use of Wi-Fis controlled by their employers, and decided that it was a topic deserving of further investigation. The young female barber spoke Ukrainian with her client, who was about her age, with a short beard and trimmed mustache. I wondered if Mercedes could understand any of this conversation. Kika's coworker, who was washing the hair of an African American woman in her mid-sixties, said, somewhat in jest, that Mercedes was indeed learning Russian. When I asked if Mercedes's client was Dominican or Russian, Kika answered, "They are all from over there. Even Mercedes is turning Russian! She acts dumb, but I swear that she understands much of their conversations. The other day she understood they were talking about her!" My qualitative insights reveal that close to four of ten Dominican respondents in my study (39 percent) work in hair salons. But only about one-third of these women manage their own businesses, renting booths or spaces for their salons, as the cases of Angela and Kika illustrate. A small fraction work in unisex shops, as Angela did in both salons in Mount Pleasantville. These workers earn higher wages. On average, the salary for a New York City barber in 2014 was $47,296, about $5,000 higher than the national average. This does not include an additional $15,000–$20,000 earned in tips or compensation commensurate with years of experience. Analysis of salaries for women in service occupations suggests that hairstylists, especially women who do coloring, earn higher salaries than others who work in low-wage sectors, including women who work as in-home health care attendants. But these jobs do not include retirement or health benefits, as home attendant and health care jobs do.

My observations in this salon for over a year led me to further understand how gentrification and demographic shifts in the structure and organization of small businesses lead employers to hire or co-opt non-White workers or partners to increase their clienteles in gentrifying neighborhoods in historically

Black and Latino communities. I also observe how the racial capital of Black and light-skinned Dominican service workers increases their selection among White and other ethnic employers, as in the cases of Salome, a Dominican sharing space in an Indian salon; Gloria, a Mexican working at a Korean salon; and Kika, a Black Dominican sharing space at a Russian barbershop. I observe that in businesses where immigrant workers are a minority, their interactions with White and non-White middle-class clients require the crossing of spatial, class, and racial boundaries, as well as the highest degree of managing their emotions, including their racial or ethnic identities, which put additional burdens on their psyche, as demonstrated in the case of Angela in the two salons she worked in Mount Pleasantville and further illustrated below, in the case of Kika.

My cousin returned twice to Kika's salon because of problems with her highlights. She is unhappy because they make her hair brittle and are too light for her taste and skin color, a dark-sugared amber. My cousin has worn her hair in natural, soft Afro curls for thirty years, much before the style was adopted by non-White millennials. When I arrived on a subsequent visit, Kika was fussing, separating strands with the thin, long end of a plastic comb, parting and examining my cousin's thick shoulder-length mane. She checked the hair, one part at a time, carefully trying to divine if the color is good or if my cousin will be pleased, before showing her a mirror for a final view. My cousin used her ethnic and female manner to let Kika know in a friendly, funny, yet serious way that she was not happy with the outcome. I can tell by the way Kika fussed that my cousin was a revered or important client. She lived nearby, came in often, and brought her husband and son to the barber; she also engaged Kika in warm conversations about their shared taste for Dominican food and music and on other female topics, as they were the same age. By virtue of her education, but mostly her European immigrant husband's occupation and high salary, my cousin is a member of the established upper class in this neighborhood. Both she and I were exceptions in Kika's salon, as most of her clients were of low- and middle-class origins. We were also exceptions in the Russian barbershop, where most clients were older, White, and members of an established elite in nearby affluent apartments. While Kika checked her hair, my cousin asked about Kika's granddaughter. Almost instantly Kika produced a picture to show my cousin and me, noticing my curiosity. Her granddaughter was about two years old. "She now attends a nursery school," Kika explained. "The love of my life—the main reason I am alive!" My cousin told me later that Kika's daughter interrupted her college studies because of an unexpected pregnancy: "¡Metió la pata!" (She screwed up!) Kika paid for a nursery so that her daughter could graduate from college.

Kika's coworker was rinsing a new tint from her own hair. Another Latina client sitting at the hair dryer laughed, seemingly amused by several flies buzzing around us. "Kika, why so many flies?" the woman asked. Kika replied, "No one knows where they come from!" Kika's assistant, who was drying my cousin's hair, chuckled, saying, "It is the owner's armpits; they attract flies!" We all laughed. The owner passed by a few seconds later to go to the bathroom. The silence was unnatural. My cousin approved her new highlight color. I was relieved, and so was Kika; there are smiles and a sense of relief.

I visited Kika's salon intermittently to have my hair styled, trimmed, or colored. I came first with my cousin, then alone, and later with my daughters. Kika became very happy when I told her I was bringing the girls. I try to understand the roles that race, gender, and class have in the relationship service workers like Kika build with different clienteles. More on point, I want to examine who benefits most from the fusing of a non-White and a White small business in a neighborhood where gentrification is driven by White people, mostly small business entrepreneurs and developers. What material and symbolic boundaries define the spaces and modes of interaction between Kika and her Russian partner, Stevin? And, will Kika's ties with this new ethnic White immigrant benefit her work mobility, as they seem to have done? How does working with a White partner represent a reversed form of racial commodification or racial capitalism for minority business owners like Kika?

For one thing, Kika gets clients who are mostly African Americans and Dominicans, but infrequently she gets older ethnic Whites, too, including Latinas who live or work in the area as high-end domestics, babysitters, or restaurant workers. The Russian barbershop attracts mostly upper-class residents from the neighborhood, like my cousin and her European husband, but also a handful of people who tend to their needs, like my cousin's live-in babysitter or a few women who babysit children after school or walk dogs, including an eastern European woman in her mid-thirties whom my cousin befriended at a nearby restaurant.

On another visit, Kika did my highlights. Looking at my hair, and combing it to see where she needed to color it, she said, "Mi amor, Usted tiene una melena [alluding to it being fine, non-Black hair]. ¡Ahí si hay pelo! ¿Y, a quien salio tu prima?" (My love, you have such a mane. This is hair! And, who did your cousin take after?) I guessed she had never dared ask my cousin directly, showing the deference she must exercise in front of her VIP clients but also knowing the stigma that exists in the racialization of people from the Caribbean and most of Latin America based on their hair.[22] Both Kika and her peers resented the owner of the barbershop. They regularly found fault in his looks and his low hygiene standards, and they resented his control, including his limiting the use of the microwave, hair supplies, coffee, and cleaning products.

RACIAL CAPITAL IN GENTRIFYING NEIGHBORHOODS

My qualitative insights illustrate that when Dominican and Mexican women work in mainstream small service firms, especially in gentrifying neighborhoods,

they often have light skin or ambiguous ethnoracial identities that I have conceptualized as a form of resource or racial capital. These workers also often have
higher education or better work skills than their coworkers and, at times, their
employers. Despite their gender, class, and racial capital, dark-skinned workers
and undocumented immigrants occupy the least visible "backstage" positions
and often experience the most marginalized work conditions; and they often
receive lower wages. In informal service sectors, the less visibility there is, the
more oppressive the work conditions, as an established scholarship shows has
been the experience of domestics and sex workers.[23] Within small ethnic firms,
immigrant women like Angela tend, irrespective of racial capital, to have less
authority. In larger firms, however, there are more regulations to safeguard against
gender, racial, and class bias, as my earlier research suggests.[24] In small firms it
appears that gender, racial, class, and immigrant vulnerability sometimes combine
to increase the oppression and abuse of workers, such as the case of undocumented
immigrants like Carolina and her Mexican peers.

Since the 1990s, the share of all foreign-born Dominican women working in
manufacturing has declined by over one-third, or from 35.0 percent to 7.8 percent;
for men it declined from 19.0 percent to 8.6 percent. From the 1990s until 2008,
the share of both ethnic groups in service sectors dramatically increased, from
40 percent to 76 percent.[25] More Mexican men than women work in service
jobs. Among Dominicans this pattern is reversed, with women overrepresented
in service jobs, especially in functions with higher interactions with the public.
Yet my qualitative insights suggest that more foreign-born Mexican than Dominican women work in new destination areas outside of New York City, such as
Mount Pleasantville.

Table 6.1 illustrates the initial types of jobs my women respondents found
upon arrival in the United States. While Mexican women initially concentrate in
factories (53 percent) and domestic sectors (20 percent), Dominican women

TABLE 6.1   Migrant Women's First Job Found Upon
             Arrival in NYC

	Dominicans $n = 43$	Mexicans $n = 41$	Sample $N = 84$
Type of work found			
No job	2.2	13	7.1
Domestic	11	20	15
Restaurant	22	2.5	13
Factory	22	53	37
Other services	24	0	13
Self employed	18	13	15

SOURCE: N. Fuentes's Survey Data, New York, 2000–2003.

TABLE 6.2   Distribution of Service Occupations, by Gender

	Women		Men	
	Mexican (%)	Dominican (%)	Mexican (%)	Dominican (%)
Health care support	5	34	0.6	2.9
Food preparation and service	21	12	79	32
Building cleaning and maintenance	51	19	18	51
Personal care and services	23	35	2.4	14

SOURCE: Author's calculations using data from the 2006–8 American Community Survey–U.S.A. downloaded from infoshare.org, February 2011 (http://infoshare.org/main/directip.aspx).

appear more evenly distributed in domestic (11 percent), restaurant (22 percent), and other service (24 percent) jobs. These other services include semiskilled positions such as home attendants, beauticians, and entertainers, which pay higher salaries than most other service jobs. Among middle-class women, or those who import at least one year of a college education or skilled work, Dominicans, more than Mexicans, occupy positions "backstage" as home health attendants, babysitters, and domestics. My fieldwork confirms a general pattern of work and spatial segregation among both groups, despite initial overlaps.

Table 6.2 illustrates the distribution of Dominican and Mexican women in low-skilled service job functions. In a previous publication (Fuentes, 2011) I analyze service jobs in front and backstage, based on different levels of interactions immigrant workers have with employers, coworkers, but mostly with White, mainstream clienteles. As the table reveals, almost eight times as many more Dominican (34 percent) than Mexican (5 percent) women work in health care support jobs, often in positions such as home health care attendants. These jobs require close interactions with the clients, but often "backstage," in homes or nursing facilities. On the other hand, nearly twice as many Mexican women (21 percent) as Dominican women (12 percent) work in food preparation and related services, often with limited direct interaction with clients. The table also shows unexpected patterns: both Dominican men (51 percent) and Mexican women (51 percent) concentrate in building cleaning and maintenance services; yet the two women groups concentrate in low-skilled service and in maintenance jobs. On the other hand, Mexican men are overrepresented (79 percent) in the food preparation and food service sectors, and Dominican women (34 percent) in health care and support services. Dominican men remain mostly in "backstage" building cleaning and maintenance jobs.

Aside from ethnic distinctions, years of residence and an immigration status also affect the types of jobs and functions that the two Latino groups experience. For example, women who have legal immigrant status and some level of educa-

tion (or English proficiency) and have lived in New York for six to ten years seem
to concentrate mainly in other service jobs, such as hair salons, the hospitality
and health care industries, and public-sector jobs, as chapter 5 illustrates.

CHAPTER SUMMARY

This chapter brings new insights into the ecosystem of neighborhoods and service jobs in which Latina immigrants find work. Small service employers in the
beauty industry stratify these workers by race (skin color and phenotype) and
immigrant status. The cases of Carolina, the Mexican woman returning to Mexico for the first time in twenty-five years, and Kika, a Dominican woman in a
Russian barbershop, illustrate how demographic and economic shifts increase
the chances of ethnoracial minorities to improve their work mobility.

Within new immigrant destination areas, where a non-White Latino middle
class emerges and drives the gentrification of White neighborhoods, immigrant
workers with ambiguous identities face greater pressures to adopt gestures and
demeanors and navigate both non-White and White identities, as the cases of
Angela, Carolina, and Gloria illustrate. The higher the education, the more adept
these workers are at managing their racial identities and emotions in the act of
serving their clienteles. Even when service jobs increase the chances of mobility
for these women, they often lack authority. This is the reason Angela decided to
quit her job at the first salon and Carolina left her job after twenty-five years.

Extending Nancy Leong's argument that White employers benefit from
diversity, or the commodification of non-White workers in a process she conceptualizes as "racial capitalism,"[26] I find that in service jobs that require lots of
attention to and interaction with clientele, such as the beauty, hospitality, and
food industries, the commodification of immigrant workers is more complicated, for it requires the stratification of workers by gender, age, skin color, and
immigrant status to match the clientele. It also requires that immigrant workers
learn to manage their racialized identities and adopt the demeanor and gestures
of the larger demographics of the clientele, which is often from the middle class.
Yet racial capitalism also entails the opposite: the White business owners who
settle in mostly minority or non-White neighborhoods adopt and acculturate to
the culture and gestures of the larger community and clientele, as the cases of
the Indian hair-threading salon and the Russian barbershop illustrate.

Yet, unlike Leong's conceptualization, I argue that employers' valuation of
immigrants' racial capital entails different forms and degrees of discrimination
based on skin color, phenotype, and immigrant status. I agree that racial capitalism is valued differently in different contexts. My findings show how this is more
complicated for mixed-race groups, and especially for women who must meet
standards of beauty that are usually stereotypical. More significantly, I find
that White employers opening businesses in inner-city Black and Latino areas

undergoing gentrification benefit from hiring non-White workers, as the case of Kika and her darker-skinned peer in the Russian barbershop illustrates. These Black Latino workers do not face pressures to change their demeanor or personae to impersonate a White or a Russian identity, as it is precisely their non-White racial capital or diversity that is used to attract other non-White, middle-class minorities from the larger neighborhood.

Finally, I observe that gentrification in White neighborhoods where a non-White middle class arrives drives small business owners, especially of foreign stock, to develop new strategies for collaboration with other minorities, as the beauty industry shows in the cases of the Indian and Korean salons.

Beyond these benefits, in small service firms undocumented immigrants face high risks of exploitation and racialization, as my earlier work has illustrated. Yet in larger, bureaucratized organizations, as in the airline industry (in which I conducted years of observations during flights to the Dominican Republic and Mexico, but due to space limitations these observations are not included here), Black and Latina immigrant women experience high labor demand, especially after 9/11. Many are given preeminent roles as proxy "border police." It is unfortunate that it is in this policing industry, as in many other public bureaucracies, that non-White women are given the most authority and visibility, enforcing immigration and punitive sanctions, mostly against people who look just like them.

CONCLUSION

As I write this conclusion, the COVID-19 pandemic continues to unveil the legacy of structural and social inequalities that have ravaged the Black and Latino population in the United States. Most relevant to this book's main focus on the inequalities of Afro-descendant and Indigenous immigrants, the pandemic has revealed the hidden ecology and gendered nature of the essential jobs these ethnic and racial minorities perform, predominantly in an expanding and informal service economy. In fact, nearly 80 percent of the service jobs requiring close contact are done by women. While the pandemic has more gravely affected the health of men, women have experienced the greatest employment shocks.[1] Yet, the factors or mechanisms explaining the higher rates of employment or incremental deaths among Black or Indigenous minorities—especially among the most vulnerable of immigrant households, those with undocumented status—require a more careful examination. Historically, African American women and Latinas in the United States have experienced the highest inequality in the labor market.[2] Yet, as new immigrant cohorts concentrate in informal, low-skilled service sector jobs,[3] at old and new immigrant destinations, they also contribute to the replenishment of Black and Brown populations and to the revival of moribund economies in historically marginalized neighborhoods undergoing fast economic and demographic changes.

THE MIGRATION OF BLACK AND INDIGENOUS LATINAS IN NEW YORK

Longitudinal ethnographies, semistructured interviews, and U.S. Census data help document that contemporary cohorts of Dominican and Mexican women increasingly lead both domestic and international migration to New York. This feminized migration is reversing a pattern of gendered migration, especially for Mexicans, as until recently men had led this historical migration. This book also demonstrates that this emerging pattern of women-led migration originates in new geographies of origin, including urban areas on the peripheries of the capitals Santo Domingo and Mexico City, where traditionally the poor (including

Haitians, in the case of Santo Domingo) and domestic immigrants from rural areas find temporary shelter. It is at these peripheral destinations that immigrant women coming from rural areas or from marginalized groups reinvent themselves through access to higher education that is usually paid for through remittances sent from families living abroad.

Whereas a higher education is known to decrease the odds of male migration, for women it increases the likelihood of migration.[4] This book's findings extend over two decades of a scholarship on gendered migration,[5] with a new focus on the experiences of middle-class Afro-descendant and Indigenous female minorities from the Caribbean and Mesoamerica. It also documents the contributions these ethnoracial migrant minorities make to the sending and receiving communities, which until now have not received much attention by international migration or feminist intersectional scholars.

The findings expand a foundational literature on the odds of migration for women in Latin American nations organized around male or patriarchal institutions.[6] Most important, the findings reveal that in matrifocal cultures, or in nations where women are mainly responsible for the family and the care of children, the odds of migration are higher, as the case of the Dominican Republic has shown. But in nations with patrilocality, or where men mainly control the family unit and economic resources, such as in Mexico, the odds of women migrating decrease with marriage. This book's findings show that, in matrifocal societies, marriage or cohabitation for Afro-descendant and Indigenous middle-class families increases, rather than deters, the odds of migration for women.

As chapter 2 reveals, women who lead their families' migration from Latin America come mostly from nations with the largest shares of Afro-descendant populations. This trend may be explained by the historical legacies of Black women carrying burdens as primary providers, devoid of the support of spouses or fathers, with the government as complicit. The literature documents that in the coastal regions of Central America and the Caribbean, a system of slavery and the migration of men have contributed to a culture of women as heads of households.[7] Historical accounts show that Afro-descendant women in Latin America (Blacks and Mulatas) have had higher labor force participation rates than White women and have acted as primary providers for families.[8] The typology of women's migration defined by race and family structure in chapter 2 illustrates that domestic migration, engagement in paid labor, and access to higher education all increase the odds of migration for women in the Dominican Republic and Mexico. In the case of Mexico, it is interesting to note—though not unexpected—that women migrate from the same states and municipalities from which men have traditionally led the migration to the United States.

Earlier literature has argued that economic and emotional desperation push women to migrate.[9] Abandoned by spouses and the government, and deprived of resources for their children, family women—especially those who are undocumented—are often pushed to migrate under perilous conditions. Many of the women that sociologists Ramona Hernández and Nancy López studied in the Dominican Republic in the 1980s and early 1990s came mostly from rural origins. They embarked sometimes in makeshift *yolas* (open raft boats) or were forced to engage in temporary sex work to finance their migration.[10] This book's findings extend this foundational work with new insights on how intersectional forms of inequality, including the liabilities of racial and class institutional exclusion, exacerbate the migration of women after joining the middle class in the Dominican Republic and Mexico.

While highly educated Indigenous Mexican women often owe their ascendancy to the domestic migration of families, one often led by men, women today increasingly lead the international migration to New York City, as the cases of Gloria and Magdalena in chapter 2 reveal. Even when these women follow spouses, they often expect that migration will increase their economic independence, especially for their daughters. Yet a good number of women head their migration from rural to urban areas and then to New York. Many migrate from their rural areas of origin to seek access to work or a higher education, as Gloria's case illustrates in chapter 2.

The migrant and work experiences of Indigenous women who lead their migration from small towns or municipalities to urban centers in Mexico are depicted in the 2018 film *Roma*. The acclaimed Mexican director Alfonso Cuarón captures the marginalized and oppressive conditions that a Ladina woman (played by actress Yalitza Aparicio) experiences as a domestic worker in an inner-city neighborhood of Mexico City. Ladinas are Indigenous minorities who assimilate to urban Mestizo culture in Latin America, including open sexual mores. The movie's portrayal of 1970s Mexican society shows how both the poor, dark-skinned domestic and her White, European-looking, female employer experience parallel forms of sexual and class oppression, as well as alienation from the men on whom they depend for subsistence. More on point to my analysis, Cuarón's film takes place in the neighborhood of Colonia Roma. It was known as an upper-class enclave until the 1990s, after which it began to decline and subsequently experienced gentrification.[11] The arrival of ethnic and racial minorities, like the Ladina played by Aparicio, is representative of women who migrate from smaller cities, thus increasing the pool of cheap labor available to the comfortable classes. These migrants settle in peripheral areas of the larger metropolis, often amid squalor and overcrowding. Despite the limitations, the access to wage employment or higher education increases these women's opportunities, as well as the odds of international migration.

This book documents that the migration of women from the Dominican Republic and Mexico includes growing shares of Afro-descendants and Indigenous women, as well as Ladinas who, despite their higher educational merits, are forced to migrate. The findings reveal that the higher the education, the higher the odds of migration. In chapters 2 and 5, I argue that despite sustained economic growth in Latin America, Afro-descendants and Indigenous minorities experience systemic class and racial inequality and that race, family structure, and education intersect to increase the odds of migration.

Sociologist Cecilia Menjívar's extensive qualitative research in Central America documents how Indigenous women, increasingly Ladinas, become victims of institutional violence, often with the state's direct or implicit consent.[12] Rising waves of violence and repression in El Salvador, Guatemala, and Honduras have pushed unprecedented numbers of women and unaccompanied youth to migrate, seeking human rights protection in Mexico and the United States.[13] Altagracia's story in chapter 5 illustrates how a similar culture of repression reached its heights during the dictatorship of Rafael Trujillo in the late 1950s and early 1960s in the Dominican Republic, with irrevocable consequences for generations of women who were sexually abused and then abandoned as single mothers. The detailed oral histories in chapter 5 also extend the long-term consequences of a legacy of racialization and sexual oppression endured by Black women, many of whom were forced to share living quarters with their elite masters, as slaves, and later as paid live-in domestics starting with the colonial subjugation by Europeans.[14]

While White or light-skinned Dominicans were often coveted as the sexual pastimes or concubines of rich men, including members of the military, Afro-descendant women have been historically abused and abandoned or used as free possessions since colonial times, as the Spanish crown never legalized their marriage with Iberian or Mestizo men.[15] These findings extend a literature on the contemporary marriage and family structures of women in the Dominican Republic and Mexico and how they contribute to both these women's migration and new forms of inequality. The findings also contribute a new understanding of the social construction of race in Latin America and the United States with the experiences of more highly educated Black and Indigenous Ladinas through the use of a feminist, intersectional lens.[16]

THE NEW FACES AND GEOGRAPHIES OF LATINO NEIGHBORHOODS IN NEW YORK

A key finding of *From Homemakers to Breadwinners to Community Leaders* is a nuanced understanding of the settlement experiences of women who join the middle class in Latin America and then are forced to migrate. It details the strategies of undocumented families to find and hold on to housing through group living arrangements—what Sarah Mahler calls the "encargado system."[17] I argue that several paradoxes emerge about the new spatial integration, distribution, and segregation of Dominican and Mexican immigrants at traditional and new immigrant destinations. One of these paradoxes is how an evolving foreign-born

Black and Brown middle class draws symbolic boundaries to separate from its poorer, historically racialized, coethnics. The economic and demographic restructuring or gentrification of inner-city neighborhoods complicates this process. While urban poverty has been attributed to the exodus of the White middle class and local employers, gentrification has been explained by the arrival of developers and a young, upwardly mobile, professional middle class that is also White.[18] Yet longitudinal ethnographies of neighborhoods in Harlem reveal that academic institutions, municipal government, and the immigration of middle-class non-White residents also contribute to this larger transformation. In addition, small businesses owned mainly by immigrants, long-term residents, and low-wage workers, including the undocumented, play a key role in the economic development, increased diversity, and cultural attractiveness of inner-city neighborhoods experiencing gentrification, as chapter 3 illustrates.

Another key finding of this book is the distinct spatial integration and spatial mobility that Latino immigrants experience in public or subsidized housing compared with those using the encargado system. As chapter 4 reveals, a pattern of group living arrangements increases Mexican families' ability to move out of poor, inner-city areas sooner and find jobs among White ethnics and mainstream employers. Another key finding is that Mexicans, more than Dominicans, tend to rent rooms or apartments from their employers, as the case of Magdalena and her husband illustrates. Despite the higher incidences of work and housing exploitation they experience in this dual living and working arrangement, Mexicans' more scattered networks among ethnic White employers increase coethnic women's chances of finding work and better schooling for their children at new destinations, as chapter 5 also illustrates.[19] Despite Dominican women's higher access to affordable housing units in the city and their importing higher levels of education, Black women and the undocumented, like Berkis, face the worst forms of housing and gender precarity.

The literature on spatial integration and gentrification has associated the arrival of a White, upwardly mobile, professional middle class, and deindustrialization to the increased displacement and poverty of inner-city minorities, mostly Black and Latino individuals, in New York City.[20] My earlier research also finds that employers in these gentrifying minority neighborhoods often import workers from outside the neighborhood, excluding local residents as potential employees.[21] My updated findings reveal how the return of the middle class to inner-city areas includes a Black and Indigenous Latino middle class that equally contributes to local development but also increases the displacement of poorer African Americans and Latinos, as the case of Harlem suggests. Some of this new ethnoracial middle class includes the college-educated children of immigrants, who benefit from their poorer parents or relatives with access to public or affordable housing. They, too, contribute to the cultural and economic revivals of these abandoned and racialized neighborhoods. Yet how the arrival of a new Black and Brown middle class will reduce legacies of class and racial distance that have characterized the relationships and divided native-born Black and White groups requires further research.[22]

THE MANAGEMENT OF EMOTIONS: RACIAL CAPITAL AND RACIAL CAPITALISM IN A SERVICE ECONOMY

Another key contribution of this book is to the theory of racial formation, or the social construction of race, with new insights based on the work mobility experiences of minorities with "in-between" non-Black and non-White racial identities. To understand how people with mixed-race or ambiguous identities are stratified by employers in the service sector, I analyze how racial capital affects the chances of finding work in jobs such as those of the beauty industry but also in skilled public functions in community-based migrant organizations. As explained in the introduction, I conceptualize that *racial capital* (skin color, phenotype, and demeanor, or the performance of a White or non-White racial identity) will vary in White and non-White workplace environments. I also assume that what Nancy Leong has termed "racial capitalism," a process through which White employers' benefit from the material or symbolic commodification of non-White workers,[23] will be different in gentrifying neighborhoods and workplaces at old and new immigrant destinations. A key finding is that the more fluid ecology of small service firms increases workers' ability to interact with clients, and such interactions will more often demand the management of these workers' racialized and gendered identities. I also find that the management of racialized identities entails different forms of emotions and impressions, and that these will vary depending on the demographics of the workplace and the larger community.[24]

With the rise of a "service society" and a Black and Brown service class, emotional labor has become more important for a consumer experience, one that has normalized Whiteness.[25] Yet, with few exceptions, the literature on emotion has not included the experiences of racial minorities, as Arlie Hochschild's foundational research includes mostly White women. In this book, I find that emotional labor in ethnic White, small-scale work environments like beauty salons requires that Brown and light-skinned immigrant women more frequently match perceived notions of what a White racial identity entails, as predicted by Patricia Chong and Kiran Mirchandani.[26] Yet, as far as I know, this is the first study that examines the management of racial identities and emotions among White and non-White Latinas in service jobs in gentrifying neighborhoods. I find that ethnic White employers, many of whom are themselves foreign born, as in the case of the owner of the Eden's Paradise salon in chapter 6, hire immigrants with clearly non-Black or ambiguous phenotypes for "frontstage" functions. These women often import a higher education than what the

White European workers and their employers hold. In older, gentrifying inner-city neighborhoods, however, White ethnic employers usually capitalize on the non-White or Black racial identity of their immigrant workers—as demonstrated by a Dominican woman, Kika, running a salon at the back of a Russian barbershop—to attract a middle-class non-White clientele (see chapter 6). Yet in majority White middle-class or upper-class neighborhoods, Latino workers often occupy "backstage" functions, without much visibility. Occasionally an "exotic" Black hostess or Indigenous-looking busboy may be positioned in front; their interaction with the clientele is mostly symbolic, as they arrange seating, remove dirty dishes at the end of a course, or serve water or bread, thus reinforcing their lower-class and racialized servile positions. In working-class White businesses, or small establishments at new destinations with a growing Black and Latino middle class, the hiring of immigrants with ambiguous identities attracts and caters to both White and growing non-White middle-class clienteles, as the case of Angela at the salon in Mount Pleasantville suggests in chapter 6. Often these workers experience greater pressures to conform to both non-White and White middle-class identities, with the result being possible impact on their mental health.

Mirchandani and other scholars argue that these performances are "scripted" and often involve a gendered dimension. I find that these performances also include a racialized dimension, as workers must impersonate the racial or ethnic identity of the workplace, as the cases of the Mexican sushi chef in a Japanese restaurant and Gloria in the Korean nail salon illustrate in chapter 6. I agree with Mirchandani that the undocumented, or those with less power, are more inclined "to perform scripts."[27] These workers are more pressured to conform as their status depends on being on good terms with their employers; Alma explains this painful reality in chapter 6.

A White identity almost always has guaranteed access to secure jobs and higher wages.[28] The passing of the Civil Rights Act of 1964, the enactment of affirmative action laws, and the recent Black Lives Matter movement have heightened public awareness about the benefits of a diverse labor force, especially in a globalized service economy.[29] Yet emphasis on diversity alone and not on the causes or eradication of inequality has, as a consequence, contributed to a new form of racialization that also involves racial capitalism.[30]

As my ethnographic observations in a handful of service firms reveal, in the sectors where immigrants work, employers value what I have conceptualized as racial capital: a non-Black, non-White, "in-between" identity that functions to attract both White and non-White clients. I also find that the valuation of a White or non-White identity by employers will vary in different contexts, especially in neighborhoods undergoing gentrification. Employers' valuation of a racial identity will be determined by which racial group is driving the gentrification or the demographic change in the neighborhood. For example, in older inner-city neighborhoods gentrified by middle- and upper-class Whites, employers like the Russian barbershop owner in chapter 6 will value more highly the hiring of non-White minorities like Kika to work and attract other middle-class, or economically solvent, non-White clients. These workers do not feel pressured to adopt or perform the workplace's White identity, however. In fact, employers value their ethnoracial differences to attract another stratum of clients and at once legitimize their presence as new business owners in neighborhoods where racial minorities are displaced.

At new destinations, however, the case may be different. Carolina, the light-skinned Mexican receptionist and Angela, the White Dominican, skilled hairstylist, are pressured to conform to the adoption of a White identity. They are often reminded to repress the use of the Spanish language, music, or even the presentation of a Latina or non-White identity self with changes in their hairstyles, colors, or dress. They may even adopt a different demeanor with clients, as the cases of Gloria and the Mexican sushi chef reveal. The management of race and emotions, I argue, will be greater for workers at new destinations, where a new influx of Black and Brown immigrants, most of middle-class origins, is viewed as a threat to the racial homogeneity of their lesser-schooled White employers and neighbors. The findings contribute to a literature, one mostly focused on the valuation of non-White identities involving relations between Black and White workers in the previous industrial period, and to a new discussion about the impact of service jobs and gentrification on the work and life chances, as well as racial acculturation, of workers with "in-between" non-Black, non-White identities.[31]

A new feminist Latina intersectional approach has questioned whether intersectionality frameworks have been appropriated and "whitewashed" by mainstream feminists.[32] Does this analytical schema represent subordinate groups, or does its current use prompt their exclusion or misrepresentation?[33] Nancy López and Vivian Gadsden, and Maxine Baca Zinn and Ruth Zambrana, among others, have called for the revisiting of intersectional frameworks introduced by Chicana feminist scholars like Cherríe Moraga and Gloria Anzaldúa, such as the analysis of "borders" for a new understanding of the overlapping inequalities women of color experience based on race, class, gender, sexuality, and immigrant status.[34] In chapter 2, using border and boundary analysis, I explore the domestic and international migration of women. I document the multiple forms of structural and social inequality that push Dominican and Mexican women to migrate even after they have joined the middle class. I also draw on these feminist intersectional frameworks to illustrate the institutional inequality and praxis that affect the new forms of oppression and exclusion that Afro-descendant and Indigenous women experience in systems dominated by a long and pervasive culture of patriarchy and governmental repression, as the case of Alejandra demonstrates in chapter 2. I also document the price Dominican women pay for their domestic migration and access to an education or professional work. I also describe how Latinas who migrate with an elite education, often one that combines transnational socialization, contribute their imported human and racial capital to the host community of New York City in leadership positions traditionally controlled by coethnic men and mainstream African American and majority White groups.

In chapter 6, I draw on the recommendations of Moraga and Anzaldúa, and Baca Zinn and Zambrana, to explore the intersection of identities in service sector jobs and how gender, race, and class affect the stratification and acculturation of immigrant women in the workplace.[35] I also draw on the cogent methodological and analytical recommendations of López and Gadsden to portray the different forms and levels of inequality that racialized Latinas, like Dominicans, experience before and after migration.[36] My use of ethnographies, participant observations, and U.S. Census data attempts a more nuanced, comparative understanding of the different forms of structural and social inequalities that intersect to affect Dominican and Mexican women's distinct modes of immigration to and integration into New York City. Dominican women face higher levels of isolation and poverty, despite their longer tenure in New York City and access to a viable economic enclave.

ON MIGRATION AND MENTAL HEALTH

Domestic or international migration, and not marriage, appears as a main conduit for women to experience economic and patriarchal independence and to improve educational opportunities for their children. I struggled to hold back tears when, in chapter 2, Alejandra explained why she migrated: so that her sons would never have to work like their father in the rice fields, from dusk to dawn, their backs bared to the sun, and that her only daughter would not be forced into marriage or motherhood at age fifteen (as was the norm in her isolated mountain community). The typology of women's migration and race in chapter 2 illustrates that women who lead their migration experience different forms of oppression and inequality than those who accompany or reunite with spouses or conjugal partners who migrate before them. The price Alejandra must pay to change the futures of her sons and her daughter is to migrate and then to live, undocumented, in the margins of society after her visa expires. This means missing her daughter's graduation from high school and not seeing her children at all for fifteen years—until interactive smartphones closed this communication void in her life.

After settling in New York City, Dominican and Mexican women experience overlapping yet different trajectories. Dominicans—especially the undocumented, and those who are single heads of households—experience greater bouts of poverty. Yet, it is not poverty, immigrant status, or racial discrimination alone that keeps women of color trapped in low-income jobs, substandard housing, or oppressive relations with spouses or conjugal partners but multiple forms of structural and social inequality. Legacies of intersectional forms of inequality led a good share of my respondents to experience mental health declines.

An accumulation of several forms of vulnerability, including the lack of secured employment due to an undocumented status, the dissolution of a marriage of nearly fifteen years, and an inability to keep up with the burden of rent, led Berkis, like other women in my study, to face eviction. Gloria, who shared space with two brothers-in-law in a small basement apartment that her husband's employer rented to them in the Bronx, was able to keep her home even after her husband was deported. But for Berkis, who rented an apartment alone, eviction and the loss of her belongings meant homelessness and the harpooning of her soul, leading to a nervous breakdown and forcing her and her two small children into a shelter.

As sociologist Mathew Desmond has argued, eviction or losing a home takes a debilitating toll on poor Black mothers, with long-term and unimagined consequences for their and their children's mental health.[37] Eviction depletes mothers of the joy and energy they require to nurture and protect their children. Even so, the mental health counseling Berkis received at an immigration center was key to her slow recovery, and the strong support from a social worker at her children's school and a temporary court-appointed legal guardian helped her find housing and hold on to her children. Berkis's therapist told her she needed to learn how to cope with her immigration, the failure of her marriage, her inability to make ends meet despite working three and four part-time jobs, and the stigma and fear of losing control of her life. When we met for a follow-up interview six years later, in 2009, Berkis had resolved her immigration status based on a domestic abuse petition, completed certificate training as a health care attendant, and found work as a bookkeeper in a health care agency. The older of her two sons attended an elite Catholic high school in the city, with a scholarship due to his school merits and the coaching of a highly educated mother. As I complete this book he is attending college.

Intersectionality shapes the marginalized experiences of women of color in the United States. This is the consensus among Chicana and Latina scholars, including those of Afro-Caribbean immigrant groups.[38] They agree that a lack of employment or underemployment, or the lack of access to housing or health care (including mental health care), affects mental health. The findings in this book extend this scholarship to the experience of migrant women of color and its impact on their mental health. The case of Mirna in chapter 5 allows a nuanced and painful depiction of the price undocumented mothers pay for migration. The crossing of the Mexican-U.S. border is risky for women; they risk theft, extortion, trafficking, and sexual abuse.[39] Mirna had to cross the border twice—the first time by herself, and the second time with a cousin and a coyote. Mirna was, thankfully, spared any harm, but many women who cross the border are sexually accosted. One of my Mexican respondents was raped for over a week, until the end of the journey, as a coyote demanded she pay with her body for what he claimed she owed for the second leg of the trek, even though her family had paid him the full fee in advance.

An emerging scholarship on mental health and women of color is now focused on socioecological models that include the experiences that affect mental health in immigrants, and it advocates research focused on mental health and the multiple inequalities women confront in the access to services, forms of stigmatization, and divergent acculturation processes.[40] Equally important is how different forms of isolation or the lack of support networks affects migrants upon arrival. Studies on Central Americans reveal how ethnoracial minorities in Latin America experience new forms of racialization and stigmas associated with their lower status as Indigenous people or rural peasants.[41] I find that Indigenous Mexican women migrants share similar experiences in New York City. My findings also reveal the structural and social forms of isolation that middle-class Afro-descendant and Indigenous Dominican and Mexican women experience before and after migrating. Immigrant women may face a variety of obstacles accessing the social and health care system due to communication, psychological, social, cultural, spiritual, or religious barriers.[42]

Research shows that unprecedented and increasing waves of immigrants, mostly women and children fleeing violence and oppression, experience high rates of psychological distress.[43] Unfortunately, sexual, class, and gender oppression have often been associated with poor immigrants. Yet this book's findings reveal that different forms of intersectional inequality and a legacy of sexual abuse and oppression also characterize the migrant experiences of middle-class Dominican and Mexican women.

Finally, new analysis shows that immigrants with "in-between" racial identities but who are members of racialized U.S. minorities may experience greater mental health distress in their work integration. At new destinations where Latinos have greater contacts with Whites, they are often exposed to racialized ideologies and practices in the workplace, as the case of the Mexican workers at the Eden's Paradise salon in chapter 6 reveals, and the management of emotions and of racialized identities in the workplace is greater for the undocumented.[44] On the contrary, in inner-city neighborhoods, workers are less pressured to manage their racialized Black or Latino identity, for it is precisely their racial capital and difference that are commodified by White employers. At new destinations, the prevailing ideology suggests that Black or Brown residents' arrival will decrease property values.[45] In areas where the majority of the population is White, such as Mount Pleasantville, gentrification is driven by the arrival of a Black and Brown middle class and their businesses. In such places, White and non-White small business owners may have a higher stake in safeguarding their reputation as White, or as nonracialized entities. This may lead them to hire immigrants with lighter skin or an ambivalent ethnoracial identity, like Angela, or Mexicans with ambiguous White-Mestizo identities. Different contexts will pose different pressures on workers to assimilate or conform to a White or a non-White identity or to reject it.

POLICY AND PRACTICE DISCUSSIONS

As the demographic characteristics of Latinos in the United States have changed and will continue to change,[46] new studies should address how race and the workplace environment affect the integration of different Latino groups, including their mental health, especially in view of the decimation and higher inequality the group has and will continue to experience as a result of the COVID-19 pandemic. I say this because immigrants from different class and racial groups, including those with an undocumented immigrant status, may experience different stressors in the migration experience and the adaptation process, including the rejection or acceptance of a White or non-White identity. Therefore, international migration and mental health professionals must think about these heterogeneities when designing immigration policies, especially as women increasingly lead in migration. Policy makers must strive to hire a diverse and culturally sensitive staff to work with the Latino community, one that is sensitive to the intersectional inequality that forces families to leave their nations, and often mothers to leave their children behind, as the case of Alejandra illustrates in chapter 2. Community organizations are key in these efforts.

Since 2013, I have volunteered at a nongovernmental organization in the Bronx that serves the immigrant—increasingly Central American and Mexican—Latino community. With the input of academics, health care providers, consulates, transnational diasporic bureaucracies, and professionals in New York City, Mexico, and other Latin American nations, the agency has implemented telemedicine programs, and especially those that target mental health, for its immigrant clientele. Immigrants are matched with psychologists and professional counselors in their nations of origin who are sensitive to their cultural beliefs and health care models. One direct outcome of this effort has been the training of immigrants, many of whom import higher education, to offer these mental health services to fellow immigrants. This culturally sensitive approach increases immigrants' receptiveness and adherence to treatment, improves utilization rates, and furthers the contributions these migrants can make in the host and sending communities.

Finally, immigration policies should be amended to address gender-specific issues among vulnerable undocumented immigrants, as the prevalent image of the undocumented is often associated with men and manual labor. These policies should make it a priority to help integrate and make productive the imported social and human capital of immigrants, and especially women, as research shows the effect of women's education on their children, especially daughters. Presently the United States benefits from the importation of skilled workers, but it incurs no costs and makes no investment in their education. It takes an average of twenty-two to twenty-five years of schooling, and the investment of families and governments, to produce highly educated individuals, and often an additional five years for them to accumulate professional skills in their nations of origin. International literature on the migration of women documents that small developing nations export more highly educated people.[47] This is especially the case for the Caribbean and Central America, as well as rural areas of Latin America. This literature advocates for research and policies designed to halt human capital loss, or "brain drain," from developing nations, as such loss depletes their resources and contributes to furthering their national inequality. However, a more nascent, conservative approach advocates for the termination of family reunification policies and instead the enactment of employers' use of temporary visas that will target the importation of skilled professionals to the United States.[48] My study contributes to this literature with case studies and a typology of migration and race to increase knowledge on the geographies of origin of an increasingly feminized migration that imports higher human capital. Yet new policies should be in place to help these workers transfer their higher education into gainful employment so they will be able to generate higher taxes for the host society and help their communities of origin through their remittances.

Finally, this book's findings also contribute a new understanding about the social mobility of Afro-descendant and Indigenous minorities and the role of feminized remittances on social mobility. A study by Cinzia Solari on the migration and remittances of Ukrainian women illustrates how deficiencies in nation-states lead to increased migration of the professional class. As Ukraine struggles to become economically independent, it is unable to provide basic services for its citizens; migrant women's remittances often make up for the state's deficiencies. The current war in Ukraine will most likely increase the significance of migrant remittances for years to come. Remittances from migrant women, according to Solaris, help provide services, such as jobs for women as care providers, and allow young families to send their children to daycare centers. In traditional Ukrainian society, patriarchal notions kept women invisible, relegated mostly to the role of family caretakers and not to building the nation-state as remitters of money and a culture of capitalism.[49] In a similarly ambitious study, I try to compare the intersectional, structural forms of inequality that push Dominican and Mexican women to migrate to New York City and their contributions to the educational mobility of daughters and family women left behind. Extending Solari's documentation of the key role played by previously invisible Ukrainian grandmothers, I attempt to document the significant contributions of Afro-descendant and Indigenous women in the Dominican Republic and

Mexico to the sending and receiving communities. I similarly document how intersectional forms of structural and social inequality push Black and Indigenous middle-class women to follow their mothers and migrate, despite the investment of families and of the local government in their education. I mostly document the pernicious history of racialization and gendered exclusion and how a culture of patriarchal oppression and abandonment pushes highly educated women to migrate, leaving their country to mourn the losses of mothers, wives, sisters, and future leaders and builders of their society.

ACKNOWLEDGMENTS

I owe the original idea of comparing the integration of Dominican and Mexican immigrants in New York City to my doctoral sponsor, Herbert J. Gans, and cosponsor, Robert C. Smith. I owe them, and Angela Aidala and Lyn Chancer, a lifetime of gratitude for their dedication and for making the completion of my doctoral thesis their mission.

Gans, who was also my mentor, retired soon after I received my PhD, and I was lucky to know him when I did. Without a dedicated mentor, many scholars—and especially people of color and women—flounder or become statistics among the intermittently employed. I have been fortunate for the senior colleagues who have stepped up to hold my hands, like sea otters do, not letting me drift away. Among these, I am indebted to Lynn Chancer of the City University of New York (CUNY) Graduate Center. I thank her for her long-term support, for reading several drafts of my book's proposal, and for reading most of the chapters. Lynn dedicated a good deal of time to this project, and I owe her gratitude for life. I want to thank Darryl McLeod and the Department of Economics and the Center for International Policy Studies at Fordham University for their support. Darryl took the time to help me gather and analyze census data, helped in the preparation of most of the tables, and read several iterations of the book. Without his input and perseverance, neither this book nor I would be as strong.

I also want to thank my colleague and collaborator Alfredo Cuecuecha, former president of El Colegio de Tlaxcala. I thank him for our collaboration on multiple projects in both Mexico and New York, for all have heightened my understanding of the structural and social conditions that push increasing numbers of women to migrate.

To my junior colleagues, Maria Abascal at New York University, Ernesto Castaneda at American University, Denia Garcia at the University of Wisconsin–Madison, and Yana Kucheva at the City College of New York, I give thanks for your enthusiasm and suggestions. To Maria and Denia I owe immense gratitude for emotional support during the most critical years of my nascent academic career, especially while I visited Princeton University during the early writing stages of this book. I also thank Lisa Moore for coming to the rescue and editing every draft of my proposal and chapters.

I owe gratitude to my colleagues at City College's Department of Sociology. First, to the department chairs, Iris Lopez and Marisa Poros, for protecting and supporting me during these past few years. I wish to thank Leslie Paik for checking on me and offering support during the critical stages of getting a book publisher. I owe James Biles my gratitude for checking on me always and recommending my book proposal to a highly ranked editorial house. Unfortunately, I must thank William Helmreich posthumously for visiting my office at least once a month to check on this book's progress and to ask about my daughters.

I want to thank my colleagues at Princeton University's Center for Migration and Development, where I was a visiting research fellow for two years. I thank my sponsor there, Edward Telles, and especially Patricia Fernandez-Kelly and Alejandro Portes for making the fellowship a reality. I owe gratitude to Marta Tienda for inviting me to coauthor a paper for one of my discipline's most prestigious journals. It was the greatest honor that could be given to a minority scholar in the early stages of a long, lonely, and arduous profession. I wish also to thank Miguel Centeno, with whom I spoke probably only three times during my time at Princeton but who left an indelible mark on my heart, always offering support and treating me like a permanent member of the Department of Sociology.

I owe much to my students at City College, who, besides giving me their love and respect, remind me where I come from as both an immigrant youth and the child of an immigrant. I often tell them that in their presence, in the classroom or in my office, I never feel alone or that I am a minority or a racial "other" but instead a proud member of a rich, diverse, protean, and growing majority. At City College and in their company I do not need to manage my emotions or my ethnoracial identity, as my difference is exactly what connects our history and our future. I particularly want to thank a few students who have worked as my research assistants to make this book a reality: Míriam Aguilar, Gerson Borrero, Yamilex Diaz Bravo, Miledys Guzman, Alejandra Matos, and Manuela Rodriguez. I thank Miledys for bringing me rice and beans, and even coffee, sent by her grandmother in Puerto Rico and for trusting me as a professor, mentor, advocate, and proxy mother in the absence of one. To Yamilex Dias Bravo, thank you for your meticulous work and for being a guardian angel praying for me so that I might finish my book. I also thank Victor Cortés, Matthew Kaufman, and Andrés Portillo for reading and helping with line edits. Andrés dedicated precious time helping with annotated bibliographies and using his writing skills to help make my ideas clearer. I thank these three young men and Dave Spinato for their love for my daughters, their incredible hearts, and their dedication to social justice.

I owe gratitude to my senior colleague, Ramona Hernández, and the CUNY Dominican Studies Institute (DSI), and especially to Sarah Aponte, the DSI's chief librarian, for recommending historical archives to help me document the migration of Dominican women in New York City and the contributions of Black women in the Dominican Republic. My work stands on the shoulders of CUNY's and DSI's legacies. I wish to thank my Mellon Diversity Fellowship mentor, Vanessa Valdéz, and the junior fellows, all women, who read my "housing" chapter and gave me feedback as well as emotional support during a very challenging year. I thank Sheryl Sterling, former director of the Black Studies Program at City College, for encouraging me to apply for the fellowship. Thanks to Jodi-Ann Francis, codirector of the Black Studies Program, for embracing me as a mentor and older sister from the day we met. I thank the many other adjuncts and faculty associated with the Black Studies and Latin American and Latino Studies Programs, especially Iris Lopez, for trusting me as a colleague well before I was invited to join City College.

I would have never finished this book without the emotional support of my family, and especially the love and support of my husband, Henry. Since we met as undergraduates at Columbia University, he has witnessed my long academic trajectories while we raise our daughters. I thank him for his love and enthusiasm for my projects, for spending countless hours helping with bibliographical searches, for line editing and formatting endnotes, and for using his information technology expertise to find ways to optimize my work. I owe to him, but mostly to my daughters, a bunch of motherly time, for time is a precious commodity in the life of a scholar. I hope they have learned the price that women pay for their mobility and motherhood.

I dedicate this book to my unsung heroes: my mother, Caridad Pereyra, and my grandmother, Justina Martinez. Without their courage to migrate from a rural mountain town to Santo Domingo and then to New York, neither I nor my daughters would have ever gotten this far. Thanks go to my aunties, Doris and Felicia; my uncles, Freddy, Manaces, Mario (my proxy father), and Rafael; my beloved maternal siblings, Gisel and Hector in New York City; and paternal siblings, Dalida, Helvia, Jose Luis, Joselyn, Juan Antonio, Luis Jose, and Normita in the Dominican Republic, as well as Hector Bienvenido in Mexico. Thanks also to my other paternal siblings, whom I met only a few years ago. And I thank my daughters, Amalia, Natalie, Oriana, and Victoria, and my twice daughter, Emme, the love of my life, who along with my daughters will continue to honor the legacy of our women-led family in this new land that we call ours!

This book is only possible because of the foresight and dedication of my editors at Rutgers University Press, especially Peter Mickulas, *El Jefe*, who after an arranged meeting at an ASA Conference in Midtown Manhattan agreed to walk with me for about twenty blocks to my next destination, in the heat of a mid-August afternoon, without a sign of distress, while I explained my book proposal. Mostly, I thank him for supporting me all the way to the book's completion despite limitations imposed by my health and work schedule. I am equally indebted to Kristen Bettcher, my production editor, for working during the most critical months of the coronavirus pandemic to ensure this manuscript would be revised, and for teaching me many things in the process—like river otters don't hold hands, only sea otters do. This tells you how meticulous she is. Finally, I owe gratitude to Vince Nordhaus, the production editor, for his unmitigated and genuine support. I must thank without hesitation all the Dominican and Mexican immigrant women who participated in this study, without whose trust and support I could have never written this book.

NOTES

PROLOGUE

1. Georges, 1992; Grasmuck and Pessar, 1991.
2. See images of Flamboyan trees in the Dominican Republic, which are native to the region of my birth. https://search.yahoo.com/search?fr=mcafee&type=E210US105G0&p=dominic an+republic+flamboyan+tress+pictures.

CHAPTER 1   INTRODUCTION

1. In 2017 female migrants outnumbered male migrants in all regions except Africa and Asia; in some Asian nations, male migrants outnumber female migrants by about three to one. In 2017 the percentage of female migrants among all migrants was highest in Europe, at 52.0 percent. Europe is also the sending region with the highest number of all migrants; North America and Oceania follow, at 51.5 percent and 51.0 percent, respectively. The higher proportion of women in these regions is mainly due to the aging of people from earlier migrant cohorts. In addition, women, including female migrants, tend to have longer life expectancies than their male counterparts. United Nations Department of Economic and Social Affairs, 2017.
2. Cuecuecha et al., 2019.
3. Grasmuck and Pessar, 1991; Hernández, 2002.
4. Das Gupta, 2013; Golash-Boza and Hondagneu-Sotelo, 2013; Prieto, 2018; Rivera, 2014.
5. Bean et al., 2014.
6. Bernhardt et al., 2007; Browne, 1999; Duany, 2011; Waldinger, 2001.
7. Baca Zinn and Zambrana, 2019; López and Gadsden, 2016; Moraga and Anzaldúa, 2015.
8. Fuentes-Mayorga, 2011.
9. Gentrification describes neighborhoods that start off predominantly occupied by households of relatively low socioeconomic status and then experience an inflow of households with higher socioeconomic status. Gentrification also describes a range of neighborhood changes, including rising incomes, changing racial composition, commercial activity, and displacement of original residents. Godsil, 2014.
10. Leong, 2013; Omi and Winant, 1994.
11. Desmond, 2016.
12. Golash-Boza and Hondagneu-Sotelo, 2013.
13. The Final Rule on Public Charge Ground of Inadmissibility requires applicants for adjustment of status who are subject to the public charge ground of inadmissibility to report certain information related to public benefits. Form I-944 requires the applicant to report information about whether the alien applied for, was certified or approved to receive, or received certain noncash public benefits on or after October 15, 2019. U.S. Citizenship and Immigration Services, 2021.
14. Lacayo, 2017; Ngai, 2014.
15. Clemetson, 2003.
16. The nine states are Arizona, California, Colorado, Florida, Illinois, New Jersey, New Mexico, New York, and Texas.

17. Rogers and Wilder, 2020.
18. Alba and Foner, 2015; Alba and Nee, 2003.
19. Murray, 2013.
20. Massey et al., 1987.
21. Cordero-Guzmán et al., 2001; Hondagneu-Sotelo, 1994.
22. Cordero-Guzmán et al., 2001; Fuentes-Mayorga, 2005; R. Smith, 2006.
23. Grasmuck and Pessar, 1991; Hernández, 2002; Pessar, 2005.
24. Juarez et al., 2018.
25. Cordero-Guzmán et al., 2001; Kelly and Garcia, 1985; Grasmuck and Pessar, 1991.
26. City University of New York, n.d., Manuscript No. 031; see also Manuscript No. 016 and Manuscript No. 060.
27. R. C. Smith, 1998.
28. Garip, 2019; Ruggles, McCaa, Sobek, and Cleveland, 2015.
29. Flippen, 2014; Lowell and Pederzini, 2012.
30. Garip, 2019; Menjívar et al., 2016.
31. Das Gupta, 2013; Golash-Boza and Hondagneu-Sotelo, 2013; Kaushal, 2019.
32. Fuentes, 2007; Fuentes-Mayorga, 2011.
33. Candelario, 2007.
34. Chin, 2005.
35. Cordero-Guzmán et al., 2001; Fuentes, 2007; Fuentes-Mayorga, 2011.
36. Hondagneu-Sotelo, 1994, p. xi.
37. Ruiz, 2008.
38. Cordero-Guzmán et al., 2001; Fuentes, 2007; Fuentes-Mayorga, 2011.
39. Flores and Telles, 2012; Telles, 2004; Telles and the Project on Ethnicity and Race in Latin America, 2014.
40. Zelizer, 2000.
41. Tienda and Fuentes, 2014.
42. Andersen et al., 2017; Dominguez, 2011; Petrozziello, 2011; Torche, 2015.
43. Hernández and López, 1997; Menjívar, 2009; Menjívar et al., 2016.
44. Petrozziello, 2011; Sana and Massey, 2005.
45. Candelario, 2007; Fuentes, 2007; Grasmuck and Pessar, 1991; Levitt, 2007.
46. Dominican Consulate representative, personal communication, 1997.
47. Dominican Consulate representative, personal communication, 1997; Grasmuck and Pessar, 1991. See also Hernández, 2002.
48. Candelario, 2007.
49. Consulate General of Mexico representative, personal communication, 1997; migrant organization director, personal communication, 2010.
50. Fernández-Kelly, 2008; Gonzalez, 1976; Kelly, 1981; R. Smith, 2006.
51. Ruggles, McCaa, Sobek, and Thomas, 2011.
52. Bernhardt et al., 2007; Browne, 1999; Duany, 2011; Waldinger, 2001.
53. See Telles and the Project on Ethnicity and Race in Latin America, 2014.
54. Bonilla-Silva and Embrick, 2005.
55. Frey, 2012; Lee and Bean, 2010; Tienda and Fuentes, 2014.
56. Baca Zinn and Zambrana, 2019; López and Gadsden, 2016; Moraga and Anzaldúa, 2015.
57. George, 2005; Grasmuck and Pessar, 1991; Hondagneu-Sotelo, 2001; Menjívar, 2000, 2003; Solari, 2017.
58. Donato et al., 2011; Menjívar et al., 2016; R. Smith, 2006.
59. Arriagada, 2001; López-Calva and Lustig, 2010.
60. Candelario, 2007; Telles and the Project on Ethnicity and Race in Latin America, 2014.

61. Cobas et al., 2015; R. C. Smith, 2008; Telles and Ortiz, 2008.

62. Grasmuck and Pessar, 1991; Hernández and López, 1997; Menjívar and Walsh, 2019.

63. Andersen et al., 2017; Dominguez, 2011.

64. Flippen, 2014; George, 2005; Hondagneu-Sotelo and Avila, 1997; Menjívar, 2003; Solari, 2017.

65. Brettell, 2007; Portes and Rumbaut, 2001; R. C. Smith, 2008.

66. Bourdieu, 1986, 1993.

67. Curran and Rivero-Fuentes, 2003; Menjívar, 2000.

68. Fuentes-Mayorga, 2005.

69. Neckerman et al., 1999.

70. Leong, 2013.

71. Chen, 1997; Harris, 1993.

72. Omi and Winant, 1994.

73. Chen, 1997.

74. Robinson, 1983.

75. Ehrenreich and Hochschild, 2003; Hochschild, 1983.

76. Chong, 2009; Fuentes-Mayorga, 2011.

77. Omi and Winant, 1994; Sue, 2013; Telles and Sue, 2009, 2019.

78. Loveman and Muniz, 2007; Roth, 2012; Telles and the Project on Ethnicity and Race in Latin America, 2014; Wade, 1993.

79. Omi and Winant, 1994.

80. Neckerman et al., 1999; Telles and Sue, 2019.

81. Wimmer, 2008, pp. 970–1022.

82. Alba and Nee, 2003.

83. Cobas et al., 2015, pp. 183–199.

84. Telles and Sue, 2019.

85. Crenshaw, 1991, pp. 243–244.

86. Baca Zinn and Zambrana, 2019; López and Gadsden, 2016; Moraga and Anzaldúa, 2015; Segura and Zavella, 2007; Zambrana, 2011.

87. See, for example, Bilge, 2013, p. 1; Baca Zinn and Zambrana, 2019, p. 681; see also López and Gadsden, 2016.

88. Moraga and Anzaldúa, 2015.

89. López and Gadsden, 2016.

90. Baca Zinn and Zambrana, 2019, p. 681.

91. López and Gadsden, 2016.

92. Baca Zinn and Zambrana, 2019, p. 681.

93. Stack, 1975.

94. Ruggles, McCaa, Sobek, and Thomas, 2011; Ruggles, McCaa, Sobek, and Cleveland, 2015. Two senior economists assisted with the analysis of census data: Alfredo Cuecuecha from the Universidad Autónoma Popular del Estado de Puebla and Darryl McLeod of the Department of Economics at Fordham University.

95. Fuentes, 2007.

96. De Souza Briggs, Darden, and Aidala, 1999.

97. Information on the project's director, Audrey Singer, can be found on the website of the Carnegie Endowment for International Peace (https://carnegieendowment.org/experts/30).

98. Aidala et al., 2005.

99. Sue, 2013.

100. Mount Pleasantville is the pseudonym of a city (an ex suburb) in New York where I have conducted longitudinal observations within a handful of small business sites. I use a pseudonym

in order to protect the identities of these businesses, employers, and immigrant workers, many of whom are working with an irregular immigrant status.

101. Goldring, 2003; Sassen-Koob, 1979; R. C. Smith, 1998.

CHAPTER 2 THE MIGRATION OF WOMEN AND RACE

1. Candelario, 2007; Telles and the Project on Ethnicity and Race in Latin America, 2014; Torres-Saillant, 1998; Wade, 1993.

2. Ñopo, 2012; Telles and the Project on Ethnicity and Race in Latin America, 2014.

3. Fernández-Kelly, 2008; Flippen, 2014; Hérnandez, 2002; Menjívar, 2003; Menjívar et al., 2016.

4. Minnesota Population Center, 2017.

5. Cuecuecha and Pederzini, 2012.

6. Menozzi, 2016.

7. For further insights on the share of Black populations in Latin America, see Telles and Bailey, 2013; and Telles and the Project on Ethnicity and Race in Latin America, 2014. For historical accountings about the immigration of women from Jamaica, see Foner, 2009.

8. Montejano, 1987.

9. Fernández-Kelly, 2008; Lowell and Pederzini, 2012.

10. Donato et al., 2011.

11. Fuentes-Mayorga, 2014; see also Fernández-Kelly, 2008.

12. Lowell and Pederzini, 2012.

13. Massey and Constant, 2017.

14. Hernández, 2002; Safa, 1995; Sassen, 1991.

15. Grasmuck and Pessar, 1991.

16. Franco et al., 2011.

17. Goldani, 1999; Nopo, 2012; Telles and the Project on Ethnicity and Race in Latin America, 2014.

18. *CEPAL Review,* 2013; Nopo, 2012.

19. Andersen, 2001; Brahim and McLeod, 2012.

20. CEPALATA, 2010.

21. Ñopo, 2012.

22. Telles and the Project on Ethnicity and Race in Latin America, 2014.

23. Goldani, 1999; Telles and the Project on Ethnicity and Race in Latin America, 2014.

24. Fuentes-Mayorga, 2014; Massey et al., 2006.

25. Brahim and McLeod, 2012; Andersen, 2002.

26. Hernández and López, 1997; Menjívar and Walsh, 2019.

27. Arriagada, 2001; López-Calva and Lustig, 2010.

28. Andersen, 2000.

29. Ruggles et al., 2015.

30. Roth, 2012; Sue, 2012.

31. Telles and the Project on Ethnicity and Race in Latin America, 2014.

32. Guillory et al., 1998.

33. Andersen, 2000.

34. Ruggles, McCaa, Sobek, and Thomas, 2011.

35. Omi and Winant, 1994; Telles and Bailey, 2013.

36. Candelario, 2007; Wade, 1993.

37. Candelario, 2007.

38. On the history of colonization and the formation of racial schemas among Dominicans in the Dominican Republic and in New York City, see Candelario, 2007. For comparative analysis on how migration affects the ethnic and racial schemas adopted by Dominicans in the United States, see Roth, 2012. Finally, see Telles and the Project on Ethnicity and Race in Latin America, 2014, for a more detailed comparison of the history of colonization, how the Casta System instituted by Europeans in Latin America to control colonized race and ethnic minorities affected the stratification of identities and access to resources, and how the ruling elite uses race and ethnicity as political, modernization projects.

39. Telles and Bailey, 2013; Telles and the Project on Ethnicity and Race in Latin America, 2014.

40. Foner, 1994, 2001; Grasmuck and Pessar, 1991; Hernández and López, 1997; Hondagneu-Sotelo, 1994, 2012.

41. The quintale is a unit of weight used in Spain in antiquity. It is equivalent to one hundred Castillian pounds, or forty-six modern kilograms. The measurement is still used in the Dominican Republic and many other Latin American countries.

42. Hernandez, 2002; Safa, 2018.

43. My insights here are based on a number of personal interviews with development and migration Mexican scholar Alfredo Cuecuecha, former president of the Colegio Tecnico de Tlaxcala. They also benefit from informal conversations with members of Cuecuecha's faculty and research team during two conferences held at the college; three visits I made to Puebla and Tlaxcala to conduct fieldwork (focus groups and ethnographic insights) in Santa Ana Chiautempan and two other villages and *municipios*; and visits I made to Ciudad Neza, where some of the women participating in this study reported they lived prior to their migration.

44. McKenzie and Menjívar, 2011.

45. My insights are based on fieldwork and interviews for a project on transnational households and remittances (2008–10) among families living in Mexico and New York City for which I served as field director. Additional historical insights about local development in San Francisco and Santa Ana Chiautempan are derived from informal discussions with Alfredo Cuecuecha. My visits to Mexico (winter 2017, summer 2014, and summer 2015) allowed my gathering of further insights about local development, remittances, and the migration of educated women. I also conducted informal interviews with the owner of a small store in San Francisco, a woman in her late fifties. Her husband and two older sons had immigrated to Texas ten years earlier, and their remittances had allowed her to buy the business, expand her home, and invest in livestock. Additional insights come from informal discussions with a female graduate student at the Colegio Tecnico de Tlaxcala who was also conducting fieldwork for a project on remittances, migration, and access to financial credit. Her insights as well as those from a handful of entrepreneurs, health care providers, and serving staff at small eateries and restaurants in Puebla and Tlaxcala enrich my understanding of local development and its link to the migration of educated women.

46. See Hirsch, 2003.

47. R. Smith, 1998.

48. Ruggles et.al., 2015.

49. Candelario, 2007; Torres-Saillent, 1998.

50. Candelario, 2007.

51. Grasmuck and Pessar, 1991; Levitt, 1991.

52. Candelario, 2007; Telles and the Project on Ethnicity and Race in Latin America, 2014; Torres-Saillant, 1998; Wade, 1995.

53. Ñopo, 2012.

54. Safa, 1995; Sassen, 1991.

55. Mayor, 2016.

56. Lamont, 2002; Telles and Sue, 2009.

57. Bourdieu, 1986.
58. Candelario, 2007; Telles and Bailey, 2013; Torres-Saillant, 1998.
59. Maritza worked in a hair salon in Mount Pleasantville, which I frequented intermittently for about two years, or between 2009 and 2011. Mount Pleasantville, introduced in chapter 1 and mentioned in chapters 3, 5, and 6, is the pseudonym given to a city outside of New York City, a new immigrant destination where I conducted longitudinal ethnographies within a handful of small businesses. These ethnographic insights allowed me to gain a deeper understanding of Maritza's work integration and mobility trajectory, as well as those of other immigrants, in New York and prior to migration.
60. Fuentes-Mayorga, 2011.
61. Most of the family's sustenance was derived from the raising and sale of livestock in their village of origin.
62. "Ciudad Nezahualcóyotl," 2021.
63. https://www.liquisearch.com/neza/the_old_bordo_de_xochiaca_landfill (see also: https://www.worldatlas.com/articles/largest-landfills-waste-sites-and-trash-dumps-in-the-world.html).
64. In 2010, for example, 30 percent of women cited that they had immigrated to the state of Mexico to seek work or a higher education. The author's calculation is based on data from the international microdata (IMPUMS) for Mexico (see Ruggles, McCaa, Sobek, and Thomas, 2011).
65. Author's calculations derived from the international census microdata (IMPUMS) for Mexico (see Ruggles et.al, 2011).
66. Author's calculations derived from the international microdata census (IMPUMS) for the Dominican Republic (see Ruggles et.al. 2011, 2015).
67. Fernández-Kelly, 2008; Lowell and Pederzini, 2012; Menjívar et al., 2016.
68. Conapo, 2010.
69. Conapo, 2010.
70. Hernández and López, 1997.
71. Ñopo, 2012.
72. An emerging literature focused on Muslim nations suggests that increased access to education and a lack of civil rights lead to the migration of women; see, for example, Kenny and O'Donnell, 2016. The findings suggest the need for governments' interventions to avoid the exodus of educated women.
73. Kanaiaupuni, 2000; Lowell and Pederzini, 2012.
74. Lowell and Pederzini, 2012.
75. Fuentes and McLeod, 2011.
76. Hondagneu-Sotelo, 1994. See also similar findings by Massey, Fischer, and Capoferro, 2006.
77. Menjívar, 2003, 2009.

CHAPTER 3   THE NEW SPACES AND FACES OF IMMIGRANT NEIGHBORHOODS IN NEW YORK CITY

1. In 2018, there were about 146,309 people in Central Harlem, with 4.4 percent of the population identified as Asian, 56.1 percent identified as non-Black, 22.9 percent identified as Hispanic, and 13.8 percent identified as White. Median household income in 2018 was $48,500, about 25 percent less than the citywide median household income ($64,850). The poverty rate in Central Harlem was 25.1 percent in 2018 compared with 17.3 percent citywide. Furman Center for Real Estate and Urban Policy, n.d.-a.

2. Data USA, n.d.; Roberts, 2010.

3. I conducted intermittent ethnographic observations for over a year in each of the women's respective homes and over three years of observations in their respective neighborhoods.

4. Furman Center for Real Estate and Urban Policy, n.d.-b.

5. Tienda and Fuentes, 2014.

6. "Manhattanville, Manhattan," 2021.

7. Fuentes, 2007.

8. Gonzales, 1976; Grasmuck and Pessar, 1991.

9. Ramakrishnan and Bloemraad, 2008; Cordero-Guzman, 2005, 2008.

10. Fuentes, 2007.

11. A knowledge economy is based primarily on knowledge-intensive activities. The knowledge economy is also seen as the latest stage of development in global economic restructuring, in the transition from an agricultural to an industrial to a service to a knowledge economy (late 1900s–2000s), largely driven by technological and social innovation that develops from the research and network community (i.e., research and development factors, universities, labs, educational institutes). For more details and leaders in this field, see "Knowledge economy: Evolution," 2021.

12. Hochschild, 1983.

13. Davila, 2012; Hernández et al., 2018a.

14. The djellaba is a long, loose-fitting unisex outer robe with full sleeves that is worn in the Maghreb region of North Africa. In some cultures, the colors of a djellaba indicate marital status. See "Djellaba," 2021.

15. Furman Center for Real Estate and Urban Policy, n.d.-a.

16. Hernández, Marrara, et al., 2018a.

17. "Out-of-pocket" rent is the rent a household pays after any housing subsidies are applied.

18. Hernández, Marrara, et al., 2018b, p. 31.

19. Timberlake and Johns-Wolfe, 2017.

20. Bagli, 2010. See also Massey and Denton, 1993.

21. On gentrification and affordable housing, see Hernández, Kucheva, et al., 2018b; and Hernandez, Sezgin, et al., 2018a.

22. On the housing strategies of Salvadoran immigrants who become *encargados*, or who lease an apartment and then sublet or rent rooms to coethnics as boarders, see Mahler, 1995.

23. Tienda and Fuentes, 2014.

24. Logan, 2002.

25. I use the term *Hispanics* for consistency with U.S. Census categories and the scholarship on spatial integration. See Massey and Constant, 2017; and Massey and Denton, 1993.

26. A growing working-class and middle-class Puerto Rican community lives in Staten Island. Mexican respondents have mentioned this to be the case and that Puerto Ricans' use of the Spanish language has paved the way for work and housing integration for many Mexicans from earlier cohorts.

27. Fuentes-Mayorga, 2011.

28. For a review of the literature on housing displacement in Boston, see Jacob, 2002.

29. Section 8 is a housing voucher that is income-means tested and provided by a local housing administration.

30. Fuentes-Mayorga, 2011; Tienda and Fuentes, 2014.

31. Massey and Denton, 1993; South and Crowder, 2010; Wilson, 1987, 1989.

32. Pais, South, and Crowder, 2009, 2012.

33. Schmalzbauer, 2011.

34. Mahler, 1995.

CHAPTER 4   "UNOS DUERMEN DE NOCHE Y OTROS DE DÍA"

1. I refer to this respondent as "Mrs." to honor the way in which she was introduced to me and the way she referred to herself, given her more traditional Indigenous Mixteca language use and ancestral origin.

2. The Northeast includes nine states: Connecticut, Maine, Massachusetts, New Hampshire, New Jersey, Rhode Island, Pennsylvania, and Vermont.

3. According to the Furman Center for Real Estate and Urban Policy, gentrifying neighborhoods consist of subborough areas (SBAs) that meet two criteria: (1) low-income in 1990, and (2) experienced rent growth above the median SBA rent growth between 1990 and 2014. Nongentrifying neighborhoods also started off as low-income in 1990 but experienced more modest rent growth. Higher-income neighborhoods are the city's remaining SBAs, which had higher incomes in 1990. Using these criteria, fifteen of the city's fifty-five neighborhoods are considered to be gentrifying, seven were nongentrifying, and thirty-three were higher-income. Furman Center Furman Center for Real Estate and Urban Policy, 2015.

4. Desmond, 2016.

5. I made a few phone calls on behalf of Magdalena's family to a Mexican nongovernmental organization where I had participated in a few activities and knew the director. I even asked my mother to ask members of her former Baptist church in Washington Heights and people she knew from that community if they knew of a room or apartment for rent.

6. According to Yana Kucheva, a housing segregation and policy expert and a peer, "most buildings in NYC are rent stabilized but not rent controlled.... Unless someone has been living in the same apartment since the 1960s, that apartment is not rent controlled. So this program is much smaller than the rent stabilization program which replaced it." Yana Kucheva, informal discussions with the author, September 2018.

7. Second-generation millennials, or the children of immigrants (including ethnic Whites), increasingly return to minority neighborhoods undergoing gentrification, able to navigate both mainstream and immigrant spaces. They contribute to the diversity and cultural attractiveness of these historically marginalized urban areas.

8. I had, the previous year, interviewed another Mexican woman who lived on the first floor of Mrs. Uraga's building. By this time I was familiar with a few blocks in the neighborhood and the pattern of room rentals in many of these apartments where poor Latinos and increasing shares of Dominicans and Mexicans, the latest newcomers, had been settling since the 1990s. I also knew families who owned a Dominican restaurant and a Mexican bakery, as well as a local Puerto Rican cuchifrito establishment, where I bought food and used the occasion to talk with people about the neighborhood.

9. Mahler, 1995.

10. See New York City Housing Authority, n.d.

11. See New York City Department of Housing Preservation and Development, 2014.

12. See report by New York City Department of City Planning, 2013.

13. Most Mexican workers at the butcher shop entered the store through the basement, through a street-level side door with a stairway used for the delivery of meat packages or carcasses.

14. Rosenblum, 2009.

15. For research on the benefits of public housing for families, see Dominguez, 2011; and Kucheva, 2013.

16. Kucheva, 2013.

17. Hernandez, Kucheva, et al., 2018.

18. Mahler, 1995.

19. Furman Center for Real Estate and Urban Policy, 2012. For further insights on how deportations affect mostly working-class Brown, Black, Latino, and Muslim men, see Das Gupta, 2013; Golash-Boza and Hondagneu-Sotelo, 2013; and Rivera, 2014.

20. Fear of deportation pushes the undocumented to save more money than the documented save, and to send remittances back home more frequently. This is documented in a transnational survey study I codirected in collaboration with the Center for International Policy Studies at Fordham University and the North American Integration Development Center at the University of California–Los Angeles between 2008 and 2009. See Fuentes and McLeod, 2011.

21. See Baranik de Alarcón, Secor, and Fuentes-Mayorga, 2021; Golash-Boza and Hondagneu-Sotelo, 2013.

22. This in turn led more immigrants to take the risk of the *pasada* without legal documents, as a desperate response to the inevitability of a permanent family separation. Massey et al., 2002; Salcido and Menjívar, 2012. Earlier scholarship has established that the higher risks of apprehension and increased costs of return migration increased the immigration of Mexican women and children starting in the late 1980s. Pedraza-Bailey, 1991; Donato, 1993; Hondagneu-Sotelo, 1994, 1997. As chapters 2 and 3 of this book reveal, more highly educated women from urban areas in the Dominican Republic and Mexico, like Berkis and Gloria, tend to overstay their visas or risk crossing the Mexican-U.S. border alone, respectively. Women with less than nine years of school often follow their spouses or conjugal partners; since 2010, however, this pattern has also been changing.

23. Block, 2018.

24. Fuentes, 2007; Fuentes-Mayorga 2005.

25. Desmond, 2016, pp. 298, 299.

26. Block, 2018.

27. Block, 2018. The Disabled Rent Increase Exemption and the Senior Citizen Rent Increase Exemption are important benefits that freeze rent for tenants in rent-regulated units so that they can stay in their homes without the fear of being displaced by escalating rents. Block, 2018.

28. Hernández, Sezgin, and Marrara, 2018.

29. Block, 2018.

30. Hernández, Kucheva, et al., 2018.

31. Finding a place to live through work was also the case for one woman I met in Bronx Little Italy, where she worked in the kitchen of a small Italian restaurant owned by a family with a legacy in the neighborhood. The original Italian owner sold the premises to an Albanian manager/head waiter who had worked in the restaurant for over ten years. The new owner and his wife decided to fire my respondent, informing her that she had two weeks to move. Her apartment was conveniently located in the second floor of a small building across from the restaurant and was owned by the new restaurant owner's mother-in-law. With the help of his mother-in-law and wife, the new restaurant owner renovated the small, three-story building, brought in a twenty-four-hour guard, and increased the rent. By 2016 the new housing facilities attracted mainly students as tenants, and the restaurant attracted faculty and administrators from the university and hospitals in the area.

32. Hernández, Sezgin, and Marrara, 2018.

33. Kucheva, 2013, p. 8.

CHAPTER 5   AN INTERSECTIONAL VIEW AT SOCIAL MOBILITY, RACE, AND MIGRATION

1. Ehrenreich and Hochschild, 2003; Foner, 2009; Hondagneu-Sotelo, 1994; Sassen 1990.

2. Zelizer, 2000, 2013.

3. Goldring, 2003; Pessar, 2005; Sassen-Koob, 1979; R. Smith, 1995.
4. Baca Zinn and Zambrana, 2019; López and Gadsden, 2016; McCall, 2005.
5. McCall, 2005; López and Gadsden, 2016.
6. Hernández and López, 1997.
7. Menjívar and Walsh, 2019.
8. Office of the United Nations High Commissioner for Refugees, 2015. See also Cuevas, 2021.
9. Torres-Saillant, 1998, p. 139.
10. Telles and the Project on Ethnicity and Race in Latin America, 2014; Torres-Saillant, 1998; Wade, 1993; Whitten and Torres, 1998.
11. Alvarez, 1994.
12. Andersen, 2001.
13. Solari, 2017.
14. Andersen, 2001.
15. Flippen, 2014; Menjívar et al., 2016.
16. Fuentes, 2007; Fuentes-Mayorga, 2011.
17. Grasmuck and Pessar, 1991; Levitt, 2001.
18. Arriagada, 2001; Franco, 2015; Ñopo, 2012; Telles and the Project on Ethnicity and Race in Latin America, 2014.
19. Flores and Telles, 2012; Telles and the Project on Ethnicity and Race in Latin America, 2014.
20. I owe this observation to Dominican sociologist Ramona Hernandez, as she once explained her own ancestry to me, around 2017, at a meeting with two other colleagues affiliated with the Latin American and Latino Studies Program at the City College of New York.
21. I met up with Mirna's daughter at a later date to discuss her plans for work following her graduation from a top MBA program.
22. Section 245 of the Immigration and Nationality Act allows persons to become permanent residents without leaving the United States through a process called adjustment of status. The law was first added in 1994, and the U.S. Congress passed section 245i on January 14, 1998. Shusterman, n.d.
23. Lowell and Pederzini, 2012.
24. Dreby, 2010; Hirsch, 2003.
25. Fuentes, 2007; Fuentes-Mayorga, 2005.
26. Romero and Pérez, 2016. See also Fretto, 2011.
27. Fuentes, 2007; Fuentes-Mayorga, 2005.
28. Romero, 2011.
29. Fuentes, 2007; Fuentes-Mayorga, 2005.
30. See earlier detailed analysis in chapter 2. See also Fuentes-Mayorga, 2005, and Fuentes, 2007, on the different network structures of Mexican and Dominican women in New York City.
31. Cordero-Guzmán et al., 2001; Mollenkopf and Pastor, 2016.
32. Curran and Rivero-Fuentes, 2003; Grasmuck and Pessar, 1991; Menjívar, 2000, 2003; Pedraza-Bailey, 1990.
33. Das Gupta, 2013; Golash-Boza and Hondagneu-Sotelo, 2013.
34. The name of this agency is a pseudonym to protect the identity of this agency and the of the people I interviewed.
35. Portes and Rumbaut, 2001; R. C. Smith, 2008.
36. Hernández and López, 1997.
37. Grasmuck and Pessar, 1991.
38. Kanaiaupuni, 2000; Lowell and Pedersini, 2012.
39. Franco et al., 2011.

40. Fernandez-Kelly, 2008; Lowell and Pederzini, 2012.
41. Foner, 2001, 2009.
42. Fernandez-Kelly and García, 1986; Menjívar, 2000.
43. Foner, 2009; George, 2005; Hondagneu-Sotelo, 1994, 2001; Menjívar, 2003.
44. George, 2005.
45. George, 2005.
46. Baker and Marchevsky, 2019; Das Gupta, 2013; Rivera, 2014.
47. See Wang, Parker, and Taylor, 2013; and Zong and Batalova, 2018.
48. Baca Zinn and Zambrana, 2019; López and Gadsden, 2016.
49. Solari, 2017.

CHAPTER 6 "¡Y ELLOS PENSABAN QUE YO ERA BLANCA!"

1. Hochschild, 1979, 1983, 2015; Chong, 2009.
2. Leong, 2013.
3. Cordero-Guzmán et al., 2001; R. C. Smith, 2008; Telles and Sue, 2019.
4. Hersch 2008, 2011; Telles and Murgia, 1990.
5. Telles and the Project on Ethnicity and Race in Latin America, 2014.
6. Salary ranges for hair colorists like Angela can vary widely nationwide, depending on the worker's education, certifications, and years of experience. As of July 2022, in Manhattan the average hair colorist gross salary is $44,718, or an equivalent hourly rate of $21. This is 17 percent above the national average salary for hair colorists. Economic Research Institute, n.d.
7. For more on the economic impact of salon booth rentals versus commissions, see "Booth rental," 2018.
8. Harris, 1993; Leong, 2013.
9. Leong, 2013.
10. After meeting Angela, and having had her color or cut my hair a few times, I suspected that she might meet my study's criteria, so I asked if she would be willing to be a participant. When I said that I offered a small compensation and that I was working on two research projects, she mentioned she would help in whatever way she could and recommended that I also speak with her college-age daughter and Alma, one of her floor assistants, a Mexican woman in her late thirties. Yet when I explained to Alma that my study was on immigrant women's experiences, her eyes seemed very apprehensive. So I decided not to ask her again or to approach her coethnic peers. I also never mentioned the nature of my study to the owner of the salon or anyone else, so as not to cause Angela or any of her assistants worry about their jobs.
11. Refers to a light-skinned person, often someone with light hair or light eyes, irrespective of phenotype.
12. Gans, 2005, 2019.
13. Sue, 2013; Telles and the Project on Ethnicity and Race in Latin America, 2014.
14. Sue, 2013.
15. Katzew, 2004.
16. Leong, 2013.
17. Bonilla-Silva and Dietrich, 2008.
18. I have explained in earlier chapters that the name "Mount Pleasantville" is a pseudonym used to protect the identities of the migrant women workers and of the small firms that inform my ethnographic insights; therefore, I am unable to provide a citation for the demographic statistics or other factual information.
19. In a *New York Times* op-ed, Edward Frame (2015) describes how people in restaurant jobs are "acting out their roles" as servers while amusing themselves with games on the job—for

instance, trying to decipher clients' identities and social positions. He notes, "You experience a special rush when your job is to project an aura of warmth and hospitality while maintaining an almost clinical emotional distance."

20. Flusser, 2014; Goffman, 2002.

21. Flusser, 2014, pp. 2, 3.

22. See Ginetta Candelario, 2007; Roth, 2012; and other race and Latin American scholars I have discussed in this and other chapters.

23. Ehrenreich & Hochschild, eds., 2003, *Global woman: Nannies, maids, and sex workers in the new economy* (Macmillan).

24. Fuentes-Mayorga, 2011.

25. Author's calculations from the U.S. decennial Census, 1990 and 2000, and calculations by author based on updates from the American Community Survey, 2005 and 2008.

26. Leong, 2013.

CONCLUSION

1. Albanesi, 2020.

2. Browne, 1999.

3. Fuentes-Mayorga, 2011.

4. Kanaiaupuni, 2000; Lowell and Pedersini, 2012.

5. Fernandez-Kelly, 2008; Kelly and Garcia, 1985; Grasmuck and Pessar, 1991; Hondagneu-Sotelo, 1994, 1999; Massey, Fischer, and Capoferro, 2006; Menjívar, 2000; Safa, 1995, 2018.

6. Massey, Fischer, and Capoferro, 2006; Safa, 1995, 2018.

7. Massey, Fischer, and Capoferro, 2006; Safa, 1998.

8. City University of New York Dominican Studies Institute, n.d.; Franco, 2015; Goldani, 1999; Safa, 1998; Torres-Saillant, 1998.

9. Fuentes-Mayorga, 2005; Hernández and López, 1997.

10. Hernández and López, 1997.

11. For more on Colonia Roma, see "Where to stay in Mexico City: Roma Neighborhood Guide," n.d.

12. Menjívar and Walsh2019, 2012.

13. Office of the United Nations High Commissioner for Refugees, 2015.

14. Goldani, 1999; Safa, 1998.

15. City University of New York Dominican Studies Institute, n.d., Manuscript No. 015; Safa, 1995, 1998, 2005; Wade, 1993, 2008.

16. Candelario, 2007; Roth, 2012; Telles and the Project on Ethnicity and Race in Latin America, 2014.

17. Mahler, 1995.

18. As foundational to this debate, see Denton, Massey, and Grigorova, 1993; and Wilson, 1987, 2018.

19. Fuentes, 2007; Fuentes-Mayorga, 2011.

20. Crowder and South, 2008; Denton, Massey and Grigorova, 1993; Wilson, 1987, 2018.

21. Fuentes-Mayorga, 2011.

22. Pais, South, and Crowder 2009, 2012.

23. Leong, 2013.

24. Chong, 2009. See also Wharton, 2009.

25. Chong, 2009; Mirchandani, 2003.

26. Chong, 2009; Mirchandani, 2003.

27. Mirchandani, 2003, p. 8.

28. Roediger, 2010.
29. Garza, 2016; Park and Leonard, 2016.
30. Leong, 2013; Sales, 1978.
31. Baca Zinn and Zambrana, 2019; Garcia, 2017; López and Gadsden, 2016.
32. García, 2017; López and Gadsden, 2016; Moraga and Anzaldúa, 2015.
33. Bilge, 2013; Baca Zinn and Zambrana, 2019.
34. Baca Zinn and Zambrana, 2019; López and Gadsden, 2016; Moraga and Anzaldúa, 2015.
35. Baca Zinn and Zambrana, 2019; Moraga and Anzaldúa, 2015.
36. López and Gadsden, 2016.
37. Desmond, 2016.
38. Baca Zinn and Zambrana, 2019; López and Gadsden, 2016.
39. Bucay-Harari et al., 2020.
40. Delara, 2016; Keller et al., 2017.
41. Menjívar and Abrego, 2012; Menjívar and Walsh, 2019.
42. Delara, 2016.
43. Bucay-Harari et al., 2020; Keller et al., 2017.
44. Mirchandani, 2003.
45. de Souza Briggs, Darden, and Aidala, 1999.
46. Flippen, 2014; Menjívar et al., 2016.
47. Dumont et al., 2007; García, 2017; Landau and Achiume, 2017.
48. Orrenius and Gullo, 2018.
49. Solari, 2018.

REFERENCES

Aidala, A., Jackson, T., Fuentes, N., and Burman, R. (2005). *Research report: Housing, health and wellness study: A collaborative project by Columbia University School of Public Health and Bailey House* (electronic publication no longer available; see https://sociology.columbia .edu/sites/default/files/content/Aidala_CV_acc.pdf).

Alba, R., and Foner, N. (2015). *Strangers no more: Immigration and the challenges of integration in North America and western Europe.* Princeton University Press.

Alba, R. D., and Nee, V. (2003). *Remaking the American mainstream: Assimilation and contemporary immigration.* Harvard University Press.

Albanesi, S. (2020). *Changing business cycles: The role of women's employment* (Working paper 25655). National Bureau of Economic Research.

Alvarez, J. (1994). *In the time of the butterflies.* Algonquin Books.

American Community Survey. (2006–2008). U.S. Census Bureau's American Community Survey Office, 2008.

Andersen, L. (2001). *Social mobility in Latin America: links with adolescent schooling.* Inter-American Development Bank. Latin American Research Network. Research Network (Working paper #R-433).

Andersen, L. E., Verner, D., and Wiebelt, M. (2017). Gender and climate change in Latin America: An analysis of vulnerability, adaptation and resilience based on household surveys. *Journal of International Development,* 29 (7), 857–876. https://doi.org/10.1002/jid .3259

Arriagada, I. (2001). *¿Familias vulnerables o vulnerabilidad de las familias?* United Nations Economic Commission for Latin America and the Caribbean.

Baca Zinn, M., and Zambrana, R. E. (2019). Chicanas/Latinas advance intersectional thought and practice. *Gender and Society,* 33(5), 677–701. https://doi.org/10.1177/0891243219853753

Bagli, C. V. (2010, June 24). Court upholds Columbia campus expansion plan. *New York Times.* https://www.nytimes.com/2010/06/25/nyregion/25columbia.html

Baker, B., and Marchevsky, A. (2019). Gendering deportation, policy violence, and Latino/a family precarity. *Latino Studies,* 17(2), 207–224.

Baranik de Alarcón, S. E., Secor, D. H., and Fuentes-Mayorga, N. (2021). "We are asking why you treat us this way. Is it because we are Negroes?" A reparations-based approach to remedying the Trump administration's cancellation of TPS protections for Haitians. *Michigan Journal of Race and Law,* 26(1), 1–48.

Bean, F. D., Brown, S. K., Bachmeier, J. D., Hook, J. V., and Leach, M. A. (2014). Unauthorized Mexican migration and the socioeconomic integration of Mexican Americans. In J. Logan (Ed.), *Diversity and disparities: America enters a new century,* 341–374. Russell Sage Foundation.

Bernhardt, A. D., McGrath, S., and DeFilippis, J. (2007). *Unregulated work in the global city: Employment and labor law violations in New York City.* Brennan Center for Justice.

Bilge, S. (2013). Intersectionality undone: Saving intersectionality from feminist intersectionality studies. *Du Bois Review: Social Science Research on Race,* 10(2), 405–424.

Block, L. (2018, April 12). *How is affordable housing threatened in your neighborhood?* Association for Neighborhood and Housing Development. https://anhd.org/2018-how-is -affordable-housing-threatened-in-your-neighborhood

Bonilla-Silva, E., and Dietrich, D. R. (2008). The Latin Americanization of racial stratification in the US. In *Racism in the 21st century*, 151–170. Springer.

Bonilla-Silva, E., and Embrick, D. (2005). Black, honorary White, White: The future of race in the United States? In D. Brunsma (Ed.), *Negotiating the color line: Doing race in the color-blind era and implications for racial justice*, 33–49. Lynne Rienner.

Booth rental vs. commission salons: Which structure is right for you? (2018, May 3). StyleSeat. https://blog.styleseat.com/en/blog/booth-rental-vs-commission-salons-which-structure/

Bourdieu, P. (1986). The forms of capital (trans. R. Nice). In J. Richardson (Ed.), *Handbook of theory and research for the sociology of education*, 241–258. Greenwood.

Bourdieu, P. (1993). *Bourdieu: Critical perspectives* (ed. C. J. Calhoun, E. LiPuma, and M. Postone). University of Chicago Press.

Brahim, S. A., and McLeod, D. (2016). Inequality and mobility: Gatsby in the Americas. *Modern Economy*, 7(05), 643–655.

Brettell, C. B. (Ed.) (2007). *Constructing borders / crossing boundaries: Race, ethnicity, and immigration*. Lexington Books.

Browne, I. (1999). *Latinas and African American women at work: Race, gender, and economic inequality*. Russell Sage Foundation.

Bucay-Harari, L., Page, K. R., Krawczyk, N., Robles, Y. P., and Castillo-Salgado, C. (2020). Mental health needs of an emerging Latino community. *Journal of Behavioral Health Services and Research*, 74(3), 388–398.

Candelario, G. E. B. (2007). *Black behind the ears: Dominican racial identity from museums to beauty shops*. Duke University Press.

Chen, J. (1997). Embryonic thoughts on racial identity as new property. *University of Colorado Law Review*, 68, 1123.

Chin, M. M. (2005). *Sewing women: Immigrants and the New York City garment industry*. Columbia University Press.

Chong, P. (2009). *Servitude with a smile: An anti-oppression analysis of emotional labour* (Global Labour University Working Paper No. 7). https://www.econstor.eu/handle/10419/96387

City University of New York Dominican Studies Institute. (n.d.). *First Blacks in the Americas* [Web database]. https://firstblacks.org/en/

Ciudad Nezahualcóyotl. (2021, October 8). In *Wikipedia*. https://en.wikipedia.org/wiki/Ciudad_Nezahualc%C3%B3yotl

Clemetson, L. (2003, January 22). Hispanics now the largest majority, census shows, *New York Times*.

Cobas, J. A., Duany, J., and Feagin, J. R. (2015). *How the United States racializes Latinos: White hegemony and its consequences*. Routledge.

CONAPO (Consejo Nacional de Población) (2012). Índices de intensidad migratoria. México-Estados Unidos 2010, Ciudad de México, enero. ____(2010), "Índices de marginación" [en línea], Ciudad de México http://www.conapo.gob.mx/es/ CONAPO/Indices_de_Marginacion.

CONAPO (Consejo Nacional de Población). *Plan de desarrollo 2011–2017*. Analysis of CONAPO data conducted by author in collaboration with visiting postdoctoral fellow, Dr. Zumaya Ali Brahim, Colegio de Tlaxcala. Tlaxcala, Mexico.

Cordero-Guzmán, H. R., Smith, R. C., and Grosfoguel, R. (2001). *Migration, transnationalization, and race in a changing New York*. Temple University Press.

Crenshaw, K. W. (1991). Mapping the margins: Intersectionality, identity politics and violence against women of color. *Stanford Law Review*, 43, 1241.

Crowder, K., and South, S. J. (2008). Spatial dynamics of white flight: The effects of local and extralocal racial conditions on neighborhood out-migration. *American Sociological Review*, 73(5), 792–812.

Cuecuecha, A., McLeod, D., Fuentes, N., and Balderas, U. (2019). *The decline in Mexican migration to the US: Why is Texas different?* (Mission Foods Texas-Mexico Center Research 5). https://scholar.smu.edu/cgi/viewcontent.cgi?article=1004&context=texasmexico-research

Cuecuecha, A., and Pederzini, C. (Eds.). (2012). *Migration and remittances from Mexico: Trends, impacts, and new challenges.* Lexington Books.

Cuevas, F. (2021, March 26). Niña de 9 años muere al cruzar el Río Grande. Noticias Telemundo. https://www.nbc.com/noticias-telemundo-en-la-noche/video/muere-ahogada-una-nina-mexicana-mientras-intentaba-cruzar-el-rio-grande-con-su-madre-y-su-hermano/4334143

Curran, S. R., and Rivero-Fuentes, E. (2003). Engendering migrant networks: The case of Mexican migration. *Demography*, 40(2), 289–307.

Das Gupta, M. (2013). Don't deport our daddies. *Gender and Society*, 28(1), 83–109. https://doi.org/10.1177/0891243213508840

Data USA. (n.d.). *East Harlem PUMA, NY.* https://datausa.io/profile/geo/east-harlem-puma-ny/

Delara, M. ((2016). Role of ethnography in exploring mental health experiences of female Muslim immigrant youths. *Journal of Mental Disorders and Treatment*, 2(3), 108.

Denton, N. A., Massey, D. S., and Grigorova, A. (1995). *American apartheid.* Descartes & Cie.

Desmond, M. (2016). *Evicted: Poverty and profit in the American city.* Crown.

de Souza Briggs, Darden, and Aidala. (1999). In the wake of desegregation: Early impacts of scattered-site public housing on neighborhoods in Yonkers, New York. *Journal of the American Planning Association*, 65(1), 27–49.

Djellaba. (2021, October 8). In *Wikipedia.* https://en.wikipedia.org/wiki/Djellaba

Dominguez, S. (2011). *Getting ahead: Social mobility, public housing, and immigrant networks.* New York University Press.

Donato, K. M. (1993). Current trends and patterns of female migration: Evidence from Mexico. *International Migration Review*, 27(4), 748–771.

Donato, K. M., Alexander, J. T., Gabaccia, D. R., and Leinonen, J. (2011). Variations in the gender composition of immigrant populations: How they matter. *International Migration Review*, 45(3), 495–526. https://doi.org/10.1111/j.1747-7379.2011.00856.x

Dreby, J. (2010). *Divided by borders: Mexican migrants and their children.* University of California Press.

Duany, J. (2011). *Blurred borders: Transnational migration between the Hispanic Caribbean and the United States.* University of North Carolina Press.

Dumont, J.-C., Martin, J. P., and Spielvogel, G. (2007, July). *Women on the move: The neglected gender dimension of the brain drain* (IZA Discussion Paper Series no. 2920). IZA Institute of Labor Economics.

Economic Research Institute. (n.d.). *Salary Expert* [database]. https://www.salaryexpert.com/salary/job/hair-colorist/united-states

Ehrenreich, B., and Hochschild, A. R. (2003). *Global woman: Nannies, maids, and sex workers in the new economy.* Metropolitan Books.

Fernández-Kelly, P. (2008). Gender and economic change in the United States and Mexico, 1900–2000. *American Behavioral Scientist*, 52, 377–404. https://doi.org/10.1177/0002764208323512

Kelly, M. P. F., & Garcia, A. M. (1985). The making of an underground economy: Hispanic women, home work, and the advanced capitalist state. *Urban Anthropology and Studies of Cultural Systems and World Economic Development*, 59–90.

Flippen, C. A. (2014). Intersectionality at work: Determinants of labor supply among immigrant Latinas. *Gender and Society, 28*(3), 404–434. https://doi.org/10.1177/0891243213504032

Flores, R., and Telles, E. (2012). Social stratification in Mexico. *American Sociological Review, 77*(3), 486–494. https://doi.org/10.1177/0003122412444720

Flusser, V. (2014). *Gestures.* U of Minnesota Press.

Foner, N. (2001). *New immigrants in New York* (completely rev. and updated). Columbia University Press.

Foner, N. (2009). Gender and migration: West Indians in comparative perspective. *International Migration, 47*(1), 3–29.

Foner, N. (2018). Benefits and burdens: Immigrant women and work in New York City. In *Immigrant women,* 1–20. Routledge.

Frame, E. (2015, August 22). Dinner and deception: Serving elaborate meals to the super-rich left me feeling empty. *New York Times.* https://www.nytimes.com/2015/08/23/opinion/sunday/dinner-and-deception.html

Franco, F. J. (2015). *Blacks, mulattos, and the Dominican nation.* Routledge.

Fretto, A. (2011). New York's Domestic Workers' Bill of Rights: Progress toward guaranteeing domestic workers protection from employment abuse. *Georgetown Journal of Gender and the Law, 12,* 691.

Frey, W. H. (2012). *New racial segregation measures for large metropolitan areas: Analysis of the 1990–2010 decennial censuses.* Population Studies Center, University of Michigan.

Frey, W. H., and Myers, D. (2005). Racial segregation in US metropolitan areas and cities, 1990–2000: Patterns, trends, and explanations. *Population Studies Center Research Report, 5,* 573.

Fuentes, N. (2007). The immigrant experiences of Dominican and Mexican women in the 1990s. In C. B. Brettell (Ed.), *Constructing borders / crossing boundaries: Race, ethnicity, and immigration,* 95–119. Lexington Books.

Fuentes, N., and McLeod, D. (2011). Remittances, technology and financial access in three Mexican immigrant corridors. https://gdsnet.org.

Fuentes-Mayorga, N. (2005). *Gender, racialization and the incorporation to work among Dominican and Mexican women in New York City* (Doctoral dissertation). Columbia University, New York.

Fuentes-Mayorga, N. (2011). Sorting Black and Brown Latino service workers in gentrifying New York neighborhoods. *Latino Studies, 9*(1), 106–125. https://doi.org/10.1057/lst.2011.13

Furman Center for Real Estate and Urban Policy. (n.d.-a). *Central Harlem.* https://furmancenter.org/neighborhoods/view/central-harlem

Furman Center for Real Estate and Urban Policy. (n.d.-b). *East Harlem.* https://furmancenter.org/neighborhoods/view/east-harlem

Gans, H. J. (2019). The possibility of a new racial hierarchy in the twenty-first-century United States. In *Social Stratification* (pp. 642–650). Routledge.

Gans, H. J. (2005). Race as class. *Contexts, 4*(4), 17–21.García, S. J. (2017). Racializing "illegality": An intersectional approach to understanding how Mexican-origin women navigate an anti-immigrant climate. *Sociology of Race and Ethnicity, 3*(4), 474–490.

Garip, F. (2019). *On the move: Changing mechanisms of Mexico-U.S. migration.* Princeton University Press.

Garza, A. (2016). A history of the #BlackLivesMatter movement. In Janell Hobson (Ed.), *Are all the women still White? Rethinking race, expanding feminisms,* 25–28. State University of New York Press.

George, S. M. (2005). *When women come first: Gender and class in transnational migration.* University of California Press.

Georges, E. (1992). Gender, class, and migration in the Dominican Republic: Women's experiences in a transnational community. *Annals of the New York Academy of Sciences, 645,* 81–99.

Godsil, R. D. (2014, May). *Transforming gentrification into integration.* NYU Furman Center. https://furmancenter.org/research/iri/essay/transforming-gentrification-into-integration.

Goffman, E. (2002). *The presentation of self in everyday life.* 1959. Garden City, NY, 259.

Golash-Boza, T., and Hondagneu-Sotelo, P. (2013). Latino immigrant men and the deportation crisis: A gendered racial removal program. *Latino Studies, 11*(3), 271–292. https://doi .org/10.1057/lst.2013.14

Goldani, A. M. 1999. Racial inequality in the lives of Brazilian women. In R. Reichmann (Ed.), *Race in contemporary Brazil: From indifference to inequality,* 179–193. Pennsylvania State University Press.

Goldring, L. (2003). Gender, status, and the state in transnational spaces: The gendering of political participation and Mexican hometown associations. In P. Hondagneu-Sotelo (Ed.), *Gender and U.S. immigration: Contemporary trends,* 1–19. University of California Press.

Gonzalez, N. L. (1976). Multiple migratory experiences of Dominican women. *Anthropological Quarterly, 49*(1), 36–44.

Grasmuck, S., and Pessar, P. R. (1991). *Between two islands: Dominican international migration.* University of California Press.

Harris, C. I. (1993). Whiteness as property. *Harvard Law Review, 106*(8), 1707–1791. https:// doi.org/10.2307/1341787

Hersch, J. (2011). The persistence of skin color discrimination for immigrants. *Social Science Research, 40*(5), 1337–1349.

Hersch, J. (2008). Skin color, immigrant wages, and discrimination. In *Racism in the 21st Century* (pp. 77–90). Springer.

Hernández, R. (2002). *The mobility of workers under advanced capitalism: Dominican migration to the United States.* Columbia University Press.

Hernández, R., Kucheva, Y., Marrara, S., and Sezgin, U. (2018). *Restoring housing security and stability in New York City neighborhoods: Recommendations to stop the displacement of Dominicans and other working-class groups in Washington Heights and Inwood.* City University of New York Dominican Studies Institute. http://dominicanlandmarks.com/Restoring-Housing -Security.pdf

Hernández, R., and López, N. (1997). Yola and gender: Dominican women's unregulated migration. In L. Alvarez-López, S. Baver, J. Weisman, R. Hernández, and N. López (Eds.), *Dominican studies: Resources and research questions,* 59–78. City University of New York Dominican Studies Institute.

Hernandez, R., Sezgin, U., and Marrara, S. (2018). *When a neighborhood becomes a revolving door for Dominicans: Rising housing costs in Washington Heights/Inwood and the declining presence of Dominicans.* City University of New York Dominican Studies Institute. https:// academicworks.cuny.edu

Hirsch, J. S. (2003). *A courtship after marriage: Sexuality and love in Mexican transnational families.* University of California Press.

Hochschild, A. R. (2015). Global care chains and emotional surplus value. In *Justice, politics, and the family* (pp. 249–261). Routledge.

Hochschild, A. R. (1979). Emotion work, feeling rules, and social structure. *American Journal of Sociology, 85*(3), 551–575.

Hochschild, A. R. (1983). *The managed heart: Commercialization of human feeling.* University of California Press.

Hondagneu-Sotelo, P. (1994). *Gendered transitions: Mexican experiences of immigration*. University of California Press.

Hondagneu-Sotelo, P. (2001). *Doméstica: Immigrant workers cleaning and caring in the shadows of affluence*. University of California Press.

Hondagneu-Sotelo, P. (2012). Families on the frontier: From braceros in the fields to braceras in the home. In *The New Immigration* (pp. 181–192). Routledge.

Hondagneu-Sotelo, P. (1999). Introduction: Gender and contemporary US immigration. *American Behavioral Scientist, 42*(4), 565–576.

Hondagneu-Sotelo, P., and Avila, E. (1997). "I'm here, but I'm there": The meanings of Latina transnational motherhood. *Gender & Society, 11*(5), 548–571.

Juárez, M., Gómez-Aguiñaga, B., and Bettez, S. (2018). Twenty years after IIRIRA: The rise of immigrant detention and its effects on Latinx communities across the nation. *Journal on Migration and Human Security, 6*(1), 74–96. https://doi.org/10.1177/233150241800600104

Kanaiaupuni, S. M. (2000). "Reframing the migration question: An analysis of men, women, and gender in Mexico." *Social Forces,* 1311–1347.

Katzew, I. (2004). *Casta painting: Images of race in eighteenth-century Mexico*. Yale University Press.

Kaushal, N. (2019). *Blaming immigrants: Nationalism and the economics of global movement*. Columbia University Press.

Keller, A., Joscelyne, A, Granski, M., and Rosenfeld, B. (2017). Pre-migration trauma exposure and mental health functioning among Central American migrants arriving at the US border. *PLoS One, 12*(1), 10–19. doi:https://doi.org/10.1371/journal.pone.0168692

Kelly, M. P. F. (1981). The sexual division of labor, development, and women's status. *Current Anthropology, 22*(4), 414–419.

Kenny, C., and O'Donnell, M. (2016). *Why increasing female migration from gender-unequal countries is a win for everyone*. Center for Global Development. https://www.cgdev.org/publication/why-increasing-female-immigration-flows-gender-unequal-countries-could-have-significant

Knowledge economy: Evolution. (2021, October 19). In *Wikipedia*. https://en.wikipedia.org/wiki/Knowledge_economy#Evolution

Kucheva, Y. A. (2013). Subsidized housing and the concentration of poverty, 1977–2008: A comparison of eight US metropolitan areas. *City & Community, 12*(2), 113–133.

Lacayo, C. O. (2017). Perpetual inferiority: Whites' racial ideology toward Latinos. *Sociology of Race and Ethnicity, 3*(4), 566–579. https://doi.org/10.1177/2332649217698165

Landau, L. B., and Achiume, E. T. (2017). International migration report 2015: Highlights. *Development and Change, 48*(5), 1182–1195.

Lee, J., and Bean, F. D. (2010). *The diversity paradox: Immigration and the color line in twenty-first century America*. Russell Sage Foundation.

Leong, N. (2013). Racial capitalism. *Harvard Law Review, 126,* 2151–2226.

Levitt, P. (2001). *The transnational villagers*. University of California Press.

Levitt, P. (2007). *God needs no passport*. New Press.

Lichter, D. T., Parisi, D., Taquino, M. C., and Grice, S. M. (2010). Residential segregation in new Hispanic destinations: Cities, suburbs, and rural communities compared. *Social Science Research, 39*(2), 215–230.

Lobo, A. P., and Salvo, J. J. (2013). *The newest New Yorkers: Characteristics of the city's foreign-born population*. City of New York, Department of City Planning, Office of Immigrant Affairs.

Logan, J. R. (2002). *Separate and unequal: The neighborhood gap for non-Blacks and Hispanics in metropolitan America*. Lewis Mumford Center for Comparative Urban and Regional Research, University at Albany.

López, N., and Gadsden, V. L. (2016). *Health inequities, social determinants, and intersectionality* (NAM Perspectives discussion paper). https://doi.org/10.31478/201612a

López, N., O'Donnell, M., Pedraza, L., Roybal, C., and Mitchell, J., 2019. Cultivating intersectional communities of practice: A case study of the New Mexico Statewide Race, Gender, Class Data Policy Consortium as a convergence space for co-creating intersectional inquiry, ontologies, data collection, and social justice praxis. In O. Hankivsky and J. S. Jordan Zachery (Eds.), *The Palgrave handbook of intersectionality in public policy*, 215–243. Palgrave Macmillan.

López-Calva, L. F., and Lustig, N. (Eds.). (2010). *Declining inequality in Latin America: A decade of progress?* Brookings Institution Press.

Loveman, M., and Muniz, J. O. (2007). How Puerto Rico became white: Boundary dynamics and inter-census racial reclassification. *American Sociological Review, 72*(6), 915–939.

Lowell, L., and Pederzini, C. (2012). Gender differentials in emigration by level of education: Mexican-born adult migrants in the United States. In A. Cuecuecha and C. Pederzini (Eds.), *Migration and remittances from Mexico: Trends, impacts and new challenges*, 159–184. Lexington Books.

Mahler, S. J. (1995). *American dreaming: Immigrant life on the margins*. Princeton University Press.

Manhattanville, Manhattan. (2021, August 29). In *Wikipedia*. https://en.wikipedia.org/wiki/Manhattanville,_Manhattan

Massey, D. S., and Constant, A. F. (2017). *Latinos in the northeastern United States: Trends and patterns* (Working paper). Princeton University.

Massey, D. S., Durand, J., Alarcón, R., and González, H. (1987). *Return to Aztlan: The social process of international migration from western Mexico*. University of California Press.

Massey, D. S., Durand, J., and Malone, N. J. (2002). *Beyond smoke and mirrors: Mexican immigration in an era of economic integration*. Russell Sage Foundation.

Massey, D. S., Fischer, M. J., and Capoferro, C. (2006). International migration and gender in Latin America: A comparative analysis. *International Migration, 44*(5), 63–91.

Mayor, B. (2016, May 5). *Arrivals surge puts Puerto Plata on Dominican Republic travel map*. Travel Pulse. https://www.travelpulse.com/news/destinations/arrivals surge-puts -puerto-plata-on-dominican-republic-travel-map.html

McCall, L. (2005). The complexity of intersectionality. *Signs: Journal of Women in Culture and Society, 30*(3), 1771–1800.

McKenzie, S., and Menjívar, C. (2011). "The meanings of migration, remittances and gifts: Views of Honduran women who stay." *Global Networks: A Journal of Transnational Affairs, 11*, 63–81. doi: 10.1111/j.1471-0374.2011.00307.x.

Menjívar, C. (2000). *Fragmented ties: Salvadoran immigrant networks in America*. University of California Press.

Menjívar, C. (2003). The intersection of work and gender: Central American immigrant women and employment in California. In P. Hondagneu-Sotelo (Ed.), *Gender and U.S. immigration: Contemporary trends*. University of California Press.

Menjívar, C. (2009). Who belongs and why. *Society, 46*(5), 416–418. https://doi.org/10.1007/s12115-009-9248-z

Menjívar, C., and Abrego, L. (2012). Legal violence: Immigration law and the lives of Central American immigrants. *American Journal of Sociology, 117*(5), 1380–1421.

Menjívar, C., Abrego, L. J., and Schmalzbauer, L. C. (2016). *Immigrant families*. John Wiley and Sons.

Menjívar, C., and Walsh, S. D. (2019). Gender, violence and migration. In K. Mitchell, R. Jones, and J. L. Fluri (Eds.), *Handbook on critical geographies of migration*, 45–57. Edward Elgar.

Menozzi, C. (2016). *International migration report 2015.* United Nations, Department of Economic and Social Affairs. Population Division.

Minnesota Population Center. (2017). *Integrated public use microdata series, international: Version 6.5* [Data set]. University of Minnesota. https://doi.org/10.18128/D020.V6.5

Mirchandani, K. (2003). Challenging racial silences in studies of emotion work: Contributions from anti-racist feminist theory. *Organization Studies,* 24 (5), 721–742.

Mollenkopf, J., and Pastor, M. (Eds.). (2016). *Unsettled Americans: Metropolitan context and civic leadership for immigrant integration.* Cornell University Press.

Montejano, D. (1987). *Anglos and Mexicans in the making of Texas, 1836–1986.* University of Texas Press.

Moraes Dias da Silva, G., and Paixão, M. M. (2014). Mixed and unequal: New perspectives on Brazilian ethnoracial relations. In E. E. Telles and the Project on Ethnicity and Race in Latin America, *Pigmentrocacies: Ethnicity, race, and color in Latin America,* 172–217. University of North Carolina Press.

Moraga, C., and Anzaldúa, G. (Eds.) (2015). *This bridge called my back: Writings by radical women of color* (4th ed.). State University of New York Press.

Murray, C. (2013). *Coming apart: The state of White America, 1960–2010.* Crown Forum.

Neckerman, K. M., Carter, P., and Lee, J. (1999). Segmented assimilation and minority cultures of mobility. *Ethnic and Racial Studies,* 22(6), 945–965.

New York City Department of City Planning. (2013). *The newest New Yorkers: Characteristics of the city's foreign-born population* (2013 ed.).

New York City Department of Housing Preservation and Development. (2014). *The ABCs of housing: Housing rules and regulations for owners and tenants.* https://www1.nyc.gov/portal/apps/311_literatures/HPD/ABCs-housing-singlepg.pdf

New York City Housing Authority. (n.d.). *NYCHA policies & procedures.* https://www1.nyc.gov/site/nycha/about/policies-procedures.page

New York City Mayor's Office of Immigrant Affairs (2018, June 26). *Impact of the travel ban on NYC* [Fact sheet]. https://www1.nyc.gov/assets/immigrants/downloads/pdf/travel-ban/june-travel-ban-fact-sheet-june-27.pdf

Ngai, M. M. (2014). *Impossible subjects: Illegal aliens and the making of modern America* (updated ed.). Princeton University Press.

Ñopo, H., 2012. *New century, old disparities: Gender and ethnic earnings gaps in Latin America and the Caribbean.* World Bank Publications.

Office of the United Nations High Commissioner for Refugees. (2015). *Women on the run: First-hand accounts of refugees fleeing El Salvador, Guatemala, Honduras, and Mexico.* https://www.unhcr.org/en-us/publications/operations/5630f24c6/women-run.html

Omi, M., and Winant, H. (1994). *Racial formation in the United States: From the 1960s to the 1990s.* Routledge.

Orrenius, P. M., and Gullo, S. (2018). The economic and fiscal effects of immigration: Implications for policy. In S. Pozo (Ed.), *The human and economic implications of twenty-first century immigration policy,* 7–32. W. E. Upjohn Institute for Employment Research.

Pais, J. F., South, S. J., and Crowder, K. (2009). White flight revisited: A multiethnic perspective on neighborhood out-migration. *Population Research and Policy Review,* 28(3), 321–346.

Pais, J., South, S. J., and Crowder, K. (2012). Metropolitan heterogeneity and minority neighborhood attainment: Spatial assimilation or place stratification? *Social Problems,* 59(2), 258–281.

Park, S., and Leonard, D. (2016). Toxic or intersectional? Challenges to (White) feminist hegemony online. In J. Hobson (Ed.), *Are all the women still White? Rethinking race, expanding feminisms,* 205–225 State University of New York Press.

Pedraza-Bailey, S. (1990). Immigration research: A conceptual map. *Social Science History*, *14*(1), 43–67.

Pessar, P. R. (2005, November–December). *Women, gender, and international migration across and beyond the Americas: Inequalities and limited empowerment*. Paper presented at the United Nations Expert Group Meeting on International Migration and Development in Latin America and the Caribbean, Mexico City.

Petrozziello, A. J. (2011). Feminized financial flows: How gender affects remittances in Honduran-US transnational families. *Gender and Development*, *19*(1), 53–67. https://doi.org/10.1080/13552074.2011.554022

Portes, A., and Rumbaut, R. G. (2001). *Legacies: The story of the immigrant second generation*. University of California Press / Russell Sage Foundation.

Prieto, G. (2018). *Immigrants under threat: Risk and resistance in deportation nation*. New York University Press.

Rivera, C. (2014). The Brown threat: Post-9/11 conflations of Latina/os and Middle Eastern Muslims in the US American imagination. *Latino Studies*, *12*(1), 44–64. https://doi.org/10.1057/lst.2014.6

Roberts, S. (2010, January 5). No longer majority Black, Harlem is in transition. *New York Times*. https://www.nytimes.com/2010/01/06/nyregion/06harlem.html

Robinson, C. J. (1983). CLR James and the Black Radical Tradition, *Review (Fernand Braudel Center)*, *6*(3), 321–391.

Roediger, D. (2010). Accounting for the wages of Whiteness. *Wages of Whiteness & Racist Symbolic Capital*, *1*, 9.

Rogers, T., and Wilder, K. (2020, June 25). *Shift in working-age population relative to older and younger Americans*. U.S. Census Bureau. https://www.census.gov/library/stories/2020/06/working-age-population-not-keeping-pace-with-growth-in-older-americans.html

Romero, M. (2011). *The maid's daughter*. New York University Press.

Romero, M., and Pérez, N. (2016). Conceptualizing the foundation of inequalities in care work. *American Behavioral Scientist*, *60*(2), 172–188.

Rosenblum, C. (2009, August 20). Grand, wasn't it? *New York Times*. https://www.nytimes.com/2009/08/21/arts/design/21concourse.html

Roth, W. (2012). *Race migrations: Latinos and the cultural transformation of race*. Stanford University Press.

Ruggles, S., Flood, S., Goeken, R., Grover, J., and Meyer, E. (2020). *Jose Pacas and Matthew Sobek* (IPUMS US; Version 10.0) [Data set]. IPUMS.

Ruggles, S., McCaa, R., Sobek, M. L., and Cleveland, L. (2015). The IPUMS collaboration: Integrating and disseminating the world's population microdata. *Journal of Demographic Economics*, *81*(2), 203–216.

Ruggles, S., McCaa, R., Sobek, M. L., and Thomas, W. (2011, August). *IPUMS-International: Free, worldwide microdata access now for censuses of 62 countries—80 by 2015*. Paper presented at the Fifty-Eighth Congress of the International Statistical Institute, Dublin.

Ruiz, V. L. (2008). *From out of the shadows: Mexican women in twentieth-century America*. Oxford University Press.

Safa, H. I. (1995). Economic restructuring and gender subordination. *Latin American Perspectives*, *22*(2), 32–50.

Safa, H. I. (1998). Female-headed households in the Caribbean: Sign of pathology or alternative form of family organization. *Brown Journal of World Affairs*, *5*, 203–214.

Safa, H. (2005). The matrifocal family and patriarchal ideology in Cuba and the Caribbean. *Journal of Latin American Anthropology*, *10*(2), 314–338.

Safa, H. I. (2018). *The myth of the male breadwinner: Women and industrialization in the Caribbean*. Routledge.

Salcido, O., & Menjívar, C. (2012). Gendered paths to legal citizenship: The case of Latin-American immigrants in Phoenix, Arizona. *Law & Society Review, 46*(2), 335–368.

Sales, W., Jr. (1978). Capitalism without racism: Science or fantasy. *Black Scholar, 9*(6), 23–34.

Sana, M., and Massey, D. S. (2005). Household composition, family migration, and community context: Migrant remittances in four countries. *Social Science Quarterly, 86*(2), 509–528. https://doi.org/10.1111/j.0038-4941.2005.00315.x

Sassen, S. (1990). *The mobility of labor and capital: A study in international investment and labor flow*. Cambridge University Press.

Sassen-Koob, S. (1979). Formal and informal associations: Dominicans and Colombians in New York. *International Migration Review, 13*(2), 314–332. https://doi.org/10.2307/2545035

Segura, D. A., and Zavella, P. (2007). *Women and migration in the U.S.-Mexico borderlands: A reader*. Duke University Press.

Series, I. P. U. M. (2003). IPUMS-USA. *Online, Minnesota Population Center, University of Minnesota*.

Shusterman, C. (n.d.). Section 245i: Frequently asked questions. https://shusterman.com /245i-frequently-asked-questions

Smith, R. C. (1995). "Los ausentes siempre presentes." *The imaging, making and politics of a transnational migrant community between Ticuani, Puebla, Mexiko, and New York City*. Columbia University.

Smith, R. (2006). *Mexican New York: Transnational lives of new immigrants*. University of California Press.

Smith, R. (1998). Racialization and Mexicans in New York City. In V. Zúñiga and R. Hernández-León (Eds.), *New destinations: Mexican immigration in the United States*, 220–243. Russell Sage Foundation.

Smith, R. C. (2008). Horatio Alger lives in Brooklyn: Extrafamily support, intrafamily dynamics, and socially neutral operating identities in exceptional mobility among children of Mexican immigrants. *Annals of the American Academy of Political and Social Science, 620*(1), 270–290.

Solari, C. D. 2017. *On the shoulders of grandmothers: Gender, migration, and post-Soviet nation-state building*. Routledge.

Stack, C. B. (1975). *All our kin: Strategies for survival in a black community*. Basic Books.

Sue, C. A. (2013). *Land of the cosmic race: Race mixture, racism, and blackness in Mexico*. Oxford University Press.

Telles, E. E., & Murgia, E. (1990). Phenotypic discrimination and income differences among Mexican-Americans. *Social Science Quarterly, 71*(4), 682–694.

Telles, E. E. (2004). *Racial classification, race in another America: The significance of skin color in Brazil*. Princeton University Press.

Telles, E., and Bailey, S. (2013). Understanding Latin American beliefs about racial inequality. *American Journal of Sociology, 118*(6), 1559–1595. doi: 10.1086/670268.

Telles, E. E., and the Project on Ethnicity and Race in Latin America. (2014). *Pigmentocracies: Ethnicity, race, and color in Latin America*. University of North Carolina Press.

Telles, E., and Sue, C. A. (2019). *Durable ethnicity: Mexican Americans and the ethnic core*. Oxford University Press.

Telles, E. E., & Sue, C. A. (2009). Race mixture: Boundary crossing in comparative perspective. *Annual Review of Sociology*, 129–146.

Tienda, M., and Fuentes, N. (2014). Hispanics in metropolitan America: New realities and old debates. *Annual Review of Sociology, 40*(1), 499–520. https://doi.org/10.1146/annurev -soc-071913-043315

Timberlake, J. M., and Johns-Wolfe, E. (2017). Neighborhood ethnoracial composition and gentrification in Chicago and New York, 1980 to 2010. *Urban Affairs Review, 53*(2), 236–272.

Torche, F. (2015). Intergenerational mobility and gender in Mexico. *Social Forces, 94*(2), 563–587. https://doi.org/10.1093/sf/sov082

Torres-Saillant, S. (1998). The tribulations of blackness: Stages in Dominican racial identity. *Latin American Perspectives, 25*(3), 126–146.

Treisman, R. (2021, September 15). *Key facts about the U.S. Latino population to kick off Hispanic heritage month.* National Public Radio. https://www.wypr.org/2021-09-15/key-facts-about-the-u-s-latino-population-to-kick-off-hispanic-heritage-month

United Nations Department of Economic and Social Affairs, Population Division. (2016). *International migration report 2015: Highlights.* https://www.un.org/en/development/desa/population/migration/publications/migrationreport/docs/MigrationReport2015_Highlights.pdf

United Nations Department of Economic and Social Affairs, Population Division. (2017). *International migration report 2017.* https://www.un.org/en/development/desa/population/migration/publications/migrationreport/docs/MigrationReport2017.pdf

U.S. Citizenship and Immigration Services. (2021, March 19). *I-944, Declaration of Self-Sufficiency.* https://www.uscis.gov/i-944

Wade, P. (1993). *Blackness and race mixture: The dynamics of racial identity in Colombia.* Johns Hopkins University Press.

Wade, P. (2008). Black populations and identity issues in Latin America. *Universitas humanística, 65,* 117–138.

Waldinger, R. (Ed.). (2001). *Strangers at the gates: New immigrants in urban America.* University of California Press.

Wang, W., Parker, K., and Taylor, P. (2013). *Breadwinner moms: Mothers are the sole or primary provider in four-in-ten households with children.* Pew Research Center.

Wharton, A. S. (2009). The sociology of emotional labor. *Annual Review of Sociology, 35,* 147–165.

Where to stay in Mexico City: Roma Neighborhood Guide. (n.d.). Our Next Adventure. https://ournextadventure.co/where-to-stay-mexico-city-roma/

Whitten, N. E., and Torres, A. (1998). *Blackness in Latin America and the Caribbean: Social dynamics and cultural transformations.* Indiana University Press.

Wilson, W. J. (1987). The truly disadvantaged: The inner city. *The Underclass, and Public Policy, 8.*

Wilson, W. J. (2018). The truly disadvantaged. In *Color Class Identity,* 109–122. Routledge.

Wimmer, A. (2008). The making and unmaking of ethnic boundaries: A multilevel process theory. *American Journal of Sociology, 113*(4), 970–1022. https://doi.org/10.1086/522803

Zambrana, R. E. (2011). *Latinos in American society.* Cornell University Press.

Zelizer, V. A. (2000). The purchase of intimacy. *Law and Social Inquiry, 25*(3), 817–848. https://doi.org/10.1111/j.1747-4469.2000.tb00162.x

Zelizer, V. A. (2013). The lives behind economic lives. *Introductory Chapters.* Princeton University Press.

Zong, J., and Batalova, J. (2018). *Dominican immigrants in the United States.* Migration Policy Institute.

INDEX

ABOUT THE AUTHOR

NORMA FUENTES-MAYORGA is an associate professor in the Department of Sociology and the director of the Latin American and Latino Studies Program at the City College of New York. Before joining City College, Fuentes-Mayorga was a visiting fellow at the Center for Migration and Development at Princeton University and an assistant professor of sociology at Fordham University.